CHRISTOLOGY
ANCIENT & MODERN

PROCEEDINGS OF THE
LOS ANGELES THEOLOGY CONFERENCE

This is the first volume in a series that will be published by Zondervan Academic. It is the published proceedings of the inaugural Los Angeles Theology Conference held under the auspices of the Torrey Honors Institute of Biola University with the support of Fuller Theological Seminary, in January 2013. The conference is an attempt to do several things. First, it provides a regional forum in which scholars, students, and clergy can come together to discuss and reflect on central doctrinal claims of the Christian faith. It is also an ecumenical endeavor. Bringing together theologians from a number of different schools and confessions, the LATC seeks to foster serious engagement with Scripture and tradition in a spirit of collegial dialogue (and disagreement), looking to retrieve the best of the Christian past in order to forge theology for the future. Finally, each volume in the series will focus on a central topic in dogmatic theology, beginning with Christology. It is hoped that this endeavor will fructify contemporary systematic theology and foster a greater understanding of the historic Christian faith among the members of its different communions.

CHRISTOLOGY, ANCIENT AND MODERN
EXPLORATIONS IN CONSTRUCTIVE DOGMATICS
Oliver D. Crisp and Fred Sanders, editors

ACKNOWLEDGMENTS

THE EDITORS WOULD LIKE TO THANK the staff and faculty of the Torrey Honors Institute, Dr. David Nystrom, Provost of Biola University, and Dr. Howard Loewen, Dean of the School of Theology, Fuller Theological Seminary, for their assistance and support with the Los Angeles Theology Conference (LATC), out of which these published proceedings grew. Thanks are also due to our editor and colleague, Katya Covrett, for her untiring support and assistance with the conference and the publication of this volume. Without her aid this would never have seen the light of day. For this reason, we dedicated this first volume to her. Thanks too to the "Z Team," those at Zondervan — Jesse Hillman, Jerri Helms, Kari Moore, Josh Kessler, Ron Huizinga, and Verlyn Verbrugge — who have been such a great help in getting the LATC off the ground and in the production of this volume. We would also like to express our thanks to Stan Gundry, who has been a believer in this project since its inception.

Writing books is not all about the scholarship and publication process, however. Our families have supported us, fed us, put up with our grumblings, and encouraged us to persevere with the LATC and with this volume of essays. Without them we would be impoverished individuals as well as less productive theologians.

LIST OF CONTRIBUTORS

Michael Allen—is Kennedy Associate Professor of Theology, Knox Theological Seminary, Fort Lauderdale, Florida. He holds the BA, MA, and PhD degrees from Wheaton College.

Oliver D. Crisp—is professor of systematic theology, Fuller Theological Seminary. He was educated at the University of Aberdeen (BD, MTh) and King's College, London (PhD).

George Hunsinger—is Hazel Thompson McCord Professor of Systematic Theology, Princeton Seminary. He received his PhD degree from Yale University.

Peter J. Leithart—is Senior Fellow of Theology, New Saint Andrews College, Moscow, Idaho. He was educated at Hillsdale College (AB), Westminster Theological Seminary (MAR, ThM), and Cambridge University (PhD).

Jason McMartin—is associate professor of theology, Rosemead School of Psychology and Talbot School of Theology, Biola University. He holds the BA and MA from Biola University and a PhD from Claremont Graduate University.

Katherine Sonderegger—is professor of theology, Virginia Theological Seminary. She received her MDiv and STM degrees from Yale University and a PhD from Brown University.

Scott R. Swain—is associate professor of systematic theology and academic dean, Reformed Theological Seminary, Orlando, Florida. He studied at Trinity Evangelical Divinity School, where he received his PhD.

Alan J. Torrance—is chair of systematic theology, St Mary's College, University of St Andrews. He studied in the universities of Edinburgh (MA), Aberdeen (BD), Cambridge, and Erlangen (DTheol).

Jeremy R. Treat—is a minister at Reality LA, a church in Hollywood, that is part of the Reality church network. He received his PhD from Wheaton College.

LIST OF CONTRIBUTORS

Jordan Wessling—is the Frederick J. Crosson Research Fellow, Center for Philosophy of Religion, University of Notre Dame. He was educated at Biola University, receiving his BA and MA degrees there, and his PhD from the University of Bristol.

Telford C. Work—is associate professor of theology and chair of religious studies, Westmont College. He is a graduate of Yale University (PhD).

ABBREVIATIONS

AB   Anchor Bible
ANF   *Ante-Nicene Fathers*
CBQ   *Catholic Biblical Quarterly*
CD   *Church Dogmatics* (by Karl Barth)
CSR   *Christian Scholar's Review*
EBC   *Expositor's Bible Commentary*
HTR   *Harvard Theological Review*
ICC   International Critical Commentary
IJST   *International Journal of Systematic Theology*
Int   *Interpretation*
JBL   *Journal of Biblical Literature*
JETS   *Journal of the Evangelical Theological Society*
LCC   Library of Christian Classics
LNTS   Library of New Testament Studies
LXX   Septuagint
NIVAC   NIV Application Commentary
NPNF1   *Nicene and Post-Nicene Fathers*, series 1
NPNF2   *Nicene and Post-Nicene Fathers*, series 2
NV   *Nova et Vetera*
ProEccl   *Pro Ecclesia*
RS   *Religious Studies*
SBJT   *Southern Baptist Journal of Theology*
SBLDS   Society of Biblical Literature Dissertation Series
SPSBL   *Seminar Papers of the Society of Biblical Literature*
SJT   *Scottish Journal of Theology*
ST   *Summa theologiae*
TDOT   *Theological Dictionary of the Old Testament* (ed. G. J. Botteweck, H. Ringren, and H.-J. Fabry)

INTRODUCTION

THERE CAN BE NO CHRISTIANITY without Christ. There can be no Christian doctrine without Christology. And there can be no future for a church that does not take seriously the dogmatic task of thinking through the implications of the biblical and ecclesiastical traditions and what they say about the person and work of Christ in order to equip the church for today and tomorrow. This volume of essays is offered to the public on the understanding that doctrinal theology requires serious and patient engagement with the Christian tradition, with retrieval of the ideas of past theologians, councils, and creeds, and with the creative task of forging contemporary constructive restatements of such doctrine for the church and academy today.

Theology that ignores the tradition is a thin, insipid thing. It also runs the risk of repeating mistakes that could be avoided by developing greater familiarity with the missteps of our forebears. If theologians do not attempt to dialogue with the past, retrieving the ideas of past thinkers without asset-stripping them, paying attention to the warp and weft of historic theology and the way in which the past may fructify the present, then we risk cutting off our noses to spite our respective faces. We can learn history from those who have gone before us. But they can also teach us how we ought to think, and furnish us with concepts, notions, and doctrines that will ensure our theologies are much healthier than would otherwise be the case.

Systematic theology is not the same as historical theology, of course. The systematician will want to make normative, not merely descriptive, judgments. But resources for such ends can be furnished by attending to theologians of the past and engaging with them in a collegial manner in order to come to normative conclusions about theology today. Theology that steps back in time only to hide there from the problems to be faced in the present ends up hidebound and moribund. Or, worse, it becomes an empty scholasticism that refuses to attend to the needs of the present, accepting only what has been hallowed by time and use, as if it is sufficient to look backward without looking forward. The constructive theological task is not identical to theological retrieval, however. One must be alive to the differences that inform theology of the past and the cultural, intellectual, and scientific changes that have occurred between *then* and *now*.

The essays collected together in this volume all, in differing ways, and to different degrees, engage with Scripture and the tradition, dialoguing with interlocutors dead and alive, in an attempt to provide constructive resources for contemporary systematic theology. They each endeavor to be Janus-faced (in the best sense of that term), looking back to the past and its theological resources as a means to speaking into the present, but without being hidebound and with an appreciation of the important differences that exist between Christologies of yesterday and today.

TWO IMPORTANT THEMES

As might be expected from a collection that began as contributions to a conference, there are also ways in which the different authors say things that overlap and dovetail with one another. Several themes emerge from these papers, at least two of which warrant some introductory comment.

First, there is a historic distinction that informs the discussion that follows in several places, of which readers should be cognizant. This has to do with two alleged schools of Christology that arose in the fourth- and fifth-century debates about the person and work of Christ. In older textbooks, one sometimes comes across reference to the "Antiochene" and "Alexandrian" Christologies. They are named after the respective cities that are said to have spawned them. Then as now the patronage of certain individuals within the church, and the development of different ecclesiastical and theological factions, led to networks of relationships and allegiances that go along with such preferment and partisanship. Hence, in the emerging christological debates of the first few centuries of the life of the church there were those who sided with Arius in his bid to show that Christ was not of the *same* essence as the Father, but only of *like* essence. Similarly, there were those who regarded the Christology of Apollinaris as an adequate understanding of the humanity assumed by the Son. On this way of thinking, Christ was a human being with a divine mind, not a human with a human mind, possessed by a divine person. The Logos took the place of the rational soul that a mere mortal would have normally enjoyed.

However, in the case of the Antiochene and Alexandrian Christologies, there are not clear "schools," as has sometimes been alleged. The idea that theologians aligned with Alexandrian Christology thought of the constitution of God-man in terms of a *Logos-sarx* (Word-flesh) Christology, or that the Antiochenes enunciated a *Logos-anthropos* (Word-man) Christology, is, at best, a kind of heuristic device by means of which to categorize certain emerging emphases in Christology of the period. Such a distinction should not be pushed too far, if it should be pushed at all. There are several reasons for this.

For one thing, it is not at all clear that a *Logos-sarx* Christology is inconsistent with a *Logos-anthropos* Christology. If the former is just the claim that in becoming incarnate, God the Son unites himself to human flesh, that assertion is nonspecific enough to be commensurate with the Logos-anthropos notion that the Son united himself to a particular human man. But even if these are taken as different christological trajectories, it is not clear that they are helpful as designations. Suppose those who adopt a Logos-sarx Christology entertain the notion that Christ is composed of God the Son and human flesh (as St. Cyril of Alexandria, the doyen of Alexandrian Christologists, believed).[1] That is consistent with orthodoxy, and with unorthodoxy depending on how this Cyrilian doctrine is construed. On the orthodox understanding, the claim that the Son unites himself to human flesh is a kind of synecdoche. That is, it is a trope whereby the part (Christ's human flesh) stands in for the whole (his complete human nature). But this might just as easily be regarded as symptomatic of a Christology according to which Christ comprises the Son, united to a human body *simpliciter*. Then, the Son would occupy that body, taking the place normally occupied by a human soul. But this sounds like Apollinarianism, and that, as we have already noted, is beyond the bounds of orthodoxy.

Compare this with the Antiochene doctrine. Suppose the Antiochene Christologists thought Christ comprised the divine person who assumes a particular concrete human individual. Without further qualification, this also could be understood in an orthodox or in an unorthodox manner. On the orthodox view, the incarnation is just the assumption by the Son of a complete concrete human nature. In this way, the Antiochenes could be thought of as preserving the completeness and reality of Christ's humanity. The Son takes on a whole human, not a partial human (as with Apollinarianism). Whatever is necessary and sufficient for a whole human being, Christ possesses. In much traditional theology, humans are thought

---

1. See Cyril of Alexandria, *On the Unity of Christ* (ed. John Anthony McGuckin; Crestwood, NY: St. Vladimir's Seminary Press, 1997).

to be body-soul composites, or the product of such composition. On this construal of the Antiochene Christology, God the Son assumes a complete human nature, that is, a complete body-soul composite (or the product thereof) rightly configured.

However, there is another way of thinking about the *Logos-anthropos* Christology. This is to say that Christ is composed of the Son and an existing human being. Here we begin to get into deep waters. If the complete human being assumed by the Son exists as a fundamental substance at any moment of its existence, then the worry is that this is a step toward Nestorianism. The Nestorians (though perhaps not Nestorius himself) believed that Christ comprises two numerically distinct persons in one body: the Son and a human. But if the *Logos-anthropos* Christology implies there are two independent and fundamental substances in Christ, then it seems there are two persons in Christ, which is unorthodox. For then Christ is not one divine person who acquires a human nature on becoming incarnate (so to speak). He is a divine person who takes possession of an existing human person.

What this shows is just how plastic the designations "Alexandrian" and "Antiochene" are when applied to Christology, and therefore how practically useless they are in accurately describing particular theological positions. When one sets such considerations alongside the dubious origins of these terms (as if there actually was a recognizable and clearly delineated "Alexandrian" and "Antiochene" school in the fourth- and fifth-century church), the utility of this characterization is greatly diminished. Systematic theologians have picked up the habit of talking in these categories, and so the modern literature on Christology is filled with rough-and-ready contrasts between the "Alexandrian" and the "Antiochene." The contrast does manage to communicate, however impressionistically, a distinction worth observing, and some of the essays in this volume make passing reference to it. But it neither describes the patristic period nor maps the contemporary scene.

We come to the second of our distinctions that make appearances, or are assumed, in a number of the essays that follow. This distinction is not so much tied to the historic development of orthodox Christology as it is a way of characterizing both the manner in which the Christologist works and the results generated by these methods. This is the distinction between "high" and "low" Christology. The problem with this distinction is spelled out in some detail by Crisp and referred to by Hunsinger in their respective essays. For present purposes, a rough-and-ready characterization of these two approaches can be given as follows. High Christology denotes an approach to the study of Christ that concludes he is God

Incarnate. There are many ways to get to such a result. One could begin with the texts of Scripture, or the creeds and confessions. One could start with historical biblical criticism and conclude that Jesus of Nazareth is included in the divine identity (as the Early High Christologists have recently done).[2] However one argues for this conclusion, the central claim is that Christ is more than a mere mortal. He is God enfleshed.

By contrast, low Christology might be thought to include any approach to the christological task that concludes Jesus of Nazareth is not God Incarnate. Often, the term is associated with the more specific claim that Christ was merely a human being, or one among many great religious teachers or sages. This is how classical liberal theologians are often thought to have regarded Christ, although the essay by George Hunsinger in this volume gives the lie to this assumption. But, in any case, a certain sort of theological revisionism is consistent with low Christology, and there are examples of those who have held such views in recent times, like the American theologian Gordon Kaufman, and the British philosopher of religion John Hick. Both of these thinkers conclude Jesus of Nazareth cannot literally be God Incarnate.

One of the contributions made by George Hunsinger in his essay is to problematize this "high-low" Christological distinction by placing some modern Christology in between these two poles. If there is a middle approach to the incarnation as well, then plotting where a particular thinker sits on a sliding scale is a little less straightforward. There may even be things to be learned from such "middling" Christology by those who occupy the pole positions.

Yet there is little (if anything) in this volume that could be construed as low Christology. Although there are different positions taken and clear demarcations between at least some of the contributors, they are united in their broad acceptance of classical, orthodox Christology as set forth in Scripture and ecclesiastical tradition, including the creeds. Those looking for a more revisionist account of the person and work of Christ may still find the essays herein an interesting case study of contemporary engagements with christological themes that presume a higher Christology. But those looking for acquiescence to a theologically revisionist program that yields a low Christology (in the sense understood by Kaufman and Hick, for instance) may be disappointed.

---

2. See, for example, the work of Richard Bauckham and Larry Hurtado on the origins of Christian worship.

OVERVIEW OF THE CHAPTERS

The chapters have been arranged in a rough dogmatic order, corresponding to the way in which the topics they tackle might appear in a systematic account of the person and work of Christ. In some cases, the ordering may be thought moot. But there is at least a good theological reason for organizing them as they now appear, even if other orders might have also been appropriate.

The essays cluster around several related themes. Some are focused on method. This is most notable in the pieces by Oliver Crisp and George Hunsinger, which is why they come first in the lineup. However, there are also important methodological considerations that lie behind aspects of Jordan Wessling's paper in chapter 8, as well as Telford Work's proposal in chapter 9. But the majority of the papers focus on doctrinal aspects of Christology, such as the humility of the Son in becoming incarnate (Sonderegger); the relationship between classical Trinitarian doctrine and the Reformed understanding of the obedience of the Son in taking on human nature (Swain and Allen); Christ's state of humiliation and its relationship to his state of exaltation (Treat); the relationship between a thick theological account of the Christology of the Fourth Gospel, and the typology of the temple (Leithart); the relationship between the image of God in Christ and the indwelling of Christ by the Son (McMartin); whether we should affirm that Christ had two wills with catholic orthodoxy (Wessling); a species of Spirit Christology (Work); and the priesthood of Christ and his continued mediation of grace (Torrance).

We offer these essays to the larger theological world as contributions to contemporary doctrinal theology. They represent the firstfruits of a new theological endeavor in Los Angeles and are signs that here, as in other parts of the world, "theological theology" (as John Webster calls unapologetic dogmatic theology) is alive and well, as is exploring old and new avenues for reflection on the incarnation, one of the central mysteries of the Christian faith.

Ad maiorem dei gloriam.

Oliver D. Crisp and Fred Sanders, February 2013

CHAPTER 1

DESIDERATA FOR MODELS OF THE HYPOSTATIC UNION

OLIVER D. CRISP

> Thus the official record of both substances represent him as both man
> and God: on the one hand born, on the other not born: on the one
> hand fleshly, on the other spiritual: on the one hand weak, on the
> other exceedingly strong: on the one hand dying, on the other living.
> That these two sets of attributes, the divine and the human, are each
> kept distinct from the other, is of course accounted for by the equal
> verity of each nature.
> — *Tertullian*[1]

> These are my principles, and if you don't like them ... well, I have
> others.
> — *Groucho Marx*

ON WHAT BASIS should we construct our Christologies? What method
should we adopt? To what authorities should we appeal? These may seem
like questions that admit of obvious answers, but in the history of modern
theology, they have been given anything but traditional responses. Some
want to develop Christologies on the basis of what can be shown via historical investigation independent of any appeal to traditional theological

---

1. Tertullian, *Treatise on the Incarnation* (trans. Ernest Evans; London: SPCK, 1956), §5, pp. 18–19.

authority, such as the catholic creeds, or the Bible understood as Christian Scripture. Usually, this involves an appeal to a certain cluster of practices and methodological assumptions that are loosely collected together under the name Historical Biblical Criticism (or HBC). Some (though by no means all) practitioners of HBC seem to think that this is the only viable means by which to get at what can be known about the historical Jesus.[2] This often goes hand-in-hand with a rather condescending attitude toward theological accounts of Christ that take, say, the Bible as Scripture or the catholic creeds as data for the generation of theological claims about Christ. A celebrated example of this can be found in the work of Rudolf Bultmann, who writes:

> Also finished by knowledge of the forces and laws of nature is faith in spirits and demons. For us the stars are physical bodies whose motion is regulated by cosmic law; they are not demonic beings who can enslave men and women to serve them.... Likewise, illnesses and their cures have natural causes and do not depend on the work of demons and on exorcising them. Thus, the wonders of the New Testament are also finished as wonders; anyone who seeks to salvage their historicity by recourse to nervous disorders, hypnotic influences, suggestion, and the like only confirms this.... We cannot use electric lights and radios and, in the event of illness, avail ourselves of modern medical and clinical means and at the same time believe in the spirit and wonder world of the New Testament.[3]

Accounts of the person of Christ that begin with history and progress to theological claims about Christology are usually termed "Christologies from below." Those that begin with certain theological givens, data that are thought to be divine revelation or approved and authoritative theological statements that depend on divine revelation like the creeds, are usually called "Christologies from above." Neither term is helpful as a description of what the particular theological trajectories involve. Christologies from below often make tacit assumptions about who Christ is at the outset, just as Christologies from above make judgments about how to treat differing reports about Christological texts in the canonical Gospels. And, for the most part, sophisticated Christology involves both textual work (includ-

---

2. There has been some discussion of the methods of HBC amongst Christian philosophers, especially Alvin Plantinga, Peter van Inwagen, and Eleonore Stump. For a recent (and critical) response to Plantinga and Stump from a practitioner of HBC, see C. L. Brinks, "On Nails, Scissors, and Toothbrushes: Responding to the Philosophers' Critiques of Historical Biblical Criticism," *RS* 48/1 (2013): 1–20.

3. Rudolf Bultmann, "New Testament Mythology," reprinted in *New Testament and Mythology and Other Basic Writings* (ed. and trans. Schubert M. Ogden; Minneapolis: Fortress, 1984), 4.

ing the sort of work familiar to practitioners of HBC) as well as appeals to what we might call ecclesiastical tradition, broadly construed.

Nor is it true that approaches to Christology that privilege a method "from below" will inevitably yield "lower" Christologies than those that adopt a "from above" approach. (Here "lower" and "higher" refer to where one pegs Christ metaphysically. If a particular Christology assumes that he is more than merely human, it is a "higher" Christology than one in which he is assumed to be merely human.) This may often be the case, but it need not be. There is certainly nothing like an entailment between, say, Christology "from below" and low Christology, or, for that matter, between Christology "from above" and high Christology. We can point to historic examples that buck this trend, the supreme instance of which is the disciples of Jesus that became the apostles of the early church. Their knowledge of Christ was largely (though not exclusively) "from below," so to speak. But they came to think of Christ in the most exalted terms, as the Son of God. As Richard Bauckham puts it, the "earliest Christology was already the highest Christology." He goes on to say that this

> was not a mere stage on the way to the patristic development of ontologi-
> cal Christology in the context of a Trinitarian theology. It is already a
> fully divine Christology, maintaining that Jesus Christ is intrinsic to the
> unique and eternal identity of God. The Fathers did not develop it so
> much as transpose it into a conceptual framework more concerned with
> the Greek philosophical categories of essence and nature.[4]

There are also historic examples of those whose Christology empha-
sizes a "from above" approach, but whose conclusions are not as high as classical Chalcedonian Christology. Arianism might be thought of as a candidate here, where certain metaphysical assumptions about the unique and undivided nature of God and of how to fit Christ into the divine identity, led to a doctrine of the person of Christ according to which Christ is only of *like* substance to the Father (i.e., *homoiousios*).

Rather than wade into this debate, something I have attempted elsewhere,[5] I will simply stipulate that responsible Christology ought to pay attention to the biblical and postbiblical traditions in formulating

---

4. Richard Bauckham, *Jesus and the God of Israel: God Crucified and Other Studies on the New Testa-*
ment's Christology of Divine Identity (Grand Rapids: Eerdmans, 2008), x.

5. Oliver D. Crisp, *God Incarnate: Explorations in Christology* (London: T&T Clark/Continuum, 2009), ch. 1. See also idem, *Divinity and Humanity: The Incarnation Reconsidered* (Cambridge: Cambridge University Press, 2007). This essay presumes much of the argument of both these earlier works.

arguments for substantive conclusions about the person and work of Christ. This is not to deny that discrimination and judgment will have to be exercised in appeals to different sorts of theological authority. Allowing that Christology should attend to biblical and extrabiblical sources, including canonical and confessional documents, is one thing. The weighting of these different sources in forming Christological judgments is another, and I will not go into that in detail here.[6] Instead, I will assume with the great majority of Christian theologians down through the ages that Scripture is the norming norm in theology this side of the grave. Other theological norms, such as the canons of ecumenical councils or the confessions of particular ecclesial communities, or even the arguments of theologians, are to be understood in light of Scripture and as ancillary to Scripture.

To my mind there is also considerable merit in approaching the theological task in general, and the Christological one in particular, with what Thomas Oden has recently called "consensual Christianity" in mind.[7] That is, paying attention to the consensus about a wide range of theological matters especially matters pertaining to what is central and defining within the Christian tradition. Marginal voices often do help us to see things in a different light and can lead to reevaluations of the canonical consensus. But in formulating Christian doctrine, especially Christological doctrine, more weight should be given to the consensus than to those at the margins. Part of the reason for this is that the consensus view on matters Christological was reached via a complex process of debate, discussion, and reflection in the first five centuries of the life of the church during which the language of Christology was forged. Pains were taken to ensure the church had certain Christological parameters in place, and certain dogmatic markers that indicated the bounds of orthodoxy in this matter.

This is not true of every theological topic. For instance, there is no real consensus view on the atonement, though this is hardly a marginal topic in Christian theology. On the face of it, this seems rather odd. However, the early church debates about Christology were generated because the church was trying to get clear *who* and *what* Christ was. Surely he is more than a mere human. But how is he different from other mere humans? Is he a sort of superman, an angelic being, or a divine entity who merely appears to be human? Or is he both divine and human, not a hybrid of these two things

---

6. I do go into this in *God Incarnate*, ch. 1.

7. Thomas Oden, *Classic Christianity: A Systematic Theology* (San Francisco: HarperOne, 2009 1992.), xvi–xxi. He echoes the claim of Vincent of Lérins that the catholic faith is "that which is believed everywhere, always, and by all" in this respect.

but God and man both together in one person? And if he is both God and man, is he fully God and fully man? How can these things be predicated of one individual when it appears that such a view yields contradictions of the sort that imply one person is both omnipotent and impotent, both omniscient and yet limited in knowledge, both omnipresent and yet circumscribed by a human nature, and so on?

The fact is the same attention was not paid to the doctrine of atonement as was paid to the incarnation, which is why the church today continues to wrangle over how we should understand the nature and scope of this aspect of the work of Christ. But two things must be borne in mind here. The first is that the early Christians all believed Christ was the Savior of the world and that salvation was obtained through his work. This much was not in dispute. The second thing is that many of the theologians of the early church did not think of the atonement as a separable constituent of the work of Christ that could be hived off and analyzed independent of other aspects of his work, or, more importantly, from his person. They believed that the incarnation and atonement were two aspects of one organic whole. Both were parts or phases of the one seamless work of Christ.[8]

The idea was not merely that the incarnation is a necessary prerequisite to the atonement (though this is true). It was that the incarnation is part of the work of Christ that culminates in the atonement and resurrection. This makes a considerable difference, not only to how we view the person and work of Christ, but also to how we think of their relative places in Christian dogmatics. We might put it like this. The mechanism of atonement and its scope (i.e., the extent of Christ's salvific work in its accomplishment and application) were not matters that were so controverted that they required dogmatic definition. The question of who and what Christ was, that is, what it means to say he is the Savior of the world, and how it is that he can be such a Savior—these were matters that were pressing problems for the church, as she sought to establish what the faithful should believe about Jesus of Nazareth.

It is often said that the Christological settlement at which the church arrived after much vituperation was as much a political as a theological resolution; some might say, a *merely* political resolution. It is undeniable that the Christological controversies were hard and often bitterly fought, that some theologians were misunderstood or even misrepresented, and that politics played a significant role in the outcome. However, this fact alone says nothing

---

8. A particularly clear example of this can be found in St. Athanasius, *On the Incarnation*. Kathryn Tanner has reaffirmed this patristic view in her recent work, *Christ the Key* (Cambridge: Cambridge University Press, 2010), which also owes much to the Christology of Thomas Torrance.

one way or another about the truth value of the outcome. A decision can be reached for complex religious and political reasons and still be the right result. I suggest that God would not permit the church to come to a substantially mistaken account of the person of Christ and to encode this in a canonical decision in an ecumenical council, for what we think about the person of Christ touches the heart of Christian doctrine, and therefore the heart of the gospel. It is an impoverished doctrine of providence that claims otherwise.

Before turning to consider the Christology bequeathed to Christian theology by Chalcedon and the dogmatic desiderata its canons provided, one other preliminary matter requires comment. In some recent theology there is a concern to approach the theological task "without metaphysics" or in a "postmetaphysical" manner. In the hands of some theologians, this claim has to do with addressing a particular philosophical project, usually the project associated with the continental tradition, especially Martin Heidegger and his interlocutors.[9] Other theologians seem to think that one can (even, ought to) approach the theological task absent metaphysics per se. But without further explanation this claim is liable to misunderstanding. For it is not that such theologians eschew the project of presenting theological arguments that are ontological in nature. What they reject is the idea that one can make ontological claims on the basis of the most general, metaphysical categories and notions. Instead, it is said, the theologian should begin with the specific and concrete and work from this to general ontological claims. Bruce McCormack articulates a specifically Christological version of this "postmetaphysical" method. He says:

> The word "metaphysical" has often been taken as synonymous with "ontological." It is not so used here.... "Metaphysics" is a way of speaking about transcendent (supramundane) realities, which begins with general concepts rather than concrete particulars. A move is made from a general concept (often a totality that has been abstracted from the individuals of which it is composed) such as "world" or "humanity." The problem is that a totality is only an idea; it is not given to us directly to know. We do not encounter it anywhere. It is simply postulated in order to introduce and explain the unity of a group of items. As such, it lacks reality.[10]

McCormack goes on to relate this specifically to Christology: "It is also possible to construct an ontology ... on the basis of an individual as a

---

9. See Kevin Hector, *Theology without Metaphysics: God, Language, and the Spirit of Recognition* (Cambridge: Cambridge University Press, 2011).

10. Bruce L. McCormack, "The Person of Christ," in Kelly M. Kapic and Bruce L. McCormack, eds., *Mapping Modern Theology: A Thematic and Historical Introduction* (Grand Rapids: Baker Academic, 2012), 168 n. 54.

possibility made necessary by the belief that Jesus Christ is God incarnate. In him, that which 'deity' is and that which 'humanity' is are 'universals' made concretely real in an individual."[11] This Christological method is not "metaphysical," he says, "since it does not draw inferences from general concepts." But because it does result in an account of what a divine and human being is, it counts as "ontological." It is a postmetaphysical method because it was only recognized "after the failings of both classical and modern metaphysics had become clear."[12]

There is certainly something to be said for the claim that Christian theology should be shaped in fundamental respects by the doctrine of the incarnation, or by Christological concerns more broadly construed. But that is not the same as a method that proceeds on the assumption that ontological claims must begin with the concrete moving from there to the abstract. What is more, we have just seen that on McCormack's reckoning abstract metaphysical notions are ideas that lack reality independent of the concrete things from which they are abstracted. Yet they are also universals made concretely real in an individual. Whatever one makes of these claims about universals, concrete particulars, and kind terms like "humanity" or "deity," they are nothing if not metaphysical in nature. We might think of McCormack's comments as the recommendation for a particular sort of metaphysical method. On this reading of his remarks, he begins with the presumption that concrete particulars are the most fundamental ontological things, and that any conceptual apparatus that may be devised on the basis of these concrete things is a kind of purely mental construction, which does not carve nature at the joints. But this is not novel and it is not postmetaphysical in the sense of being nonmetaphysical or beyond metaphysics or even ametaphysical in nature. It is representative of the sort of approach to metaphysics advocated by those who are nominalists about predicates and concepts. Rather than exchanging metaphysics for ontology, McCormack appears to be rejecting one way of conceiving metaphysics (a way often associated in traditional theology with realism about universals and abstract objects) for another.

But I can see no reason why a Christian theologian might not adopt McCormack's general proviso that theology ought to be framed by means of Christological concerns (e.g., that Christology be the "lens" through which we view a particular theological locus, such as the church or Scripture)

11. Ibid.
12. Ibid.

without commitment to the sort of nominalism he seems to think necessary for the successful execution of such a project. To put it another way, McCormack's approval of a Christologically focused theology is appealing (at least to this reader). But for those who are nonplussed about his claim that classical and modern metaphysics have failed, there are other options available. In fact, systematic metaphysics is back in vogue among Anglo-American philosophers, including neo-Aristotelian metaphysics, which is willing to countenance much that would be recognizable to our medieval and patristic forebears. Far from "failing" or heading toward extinction, such "classical" metaphysics is alive and well, and, if anything, flourishing once more.

A Note on the Chalcedonian "Consensus"

With these methodological considerations in mind, we can turn to the question of desiderata. Since I am approaching this question from the perspective of consensus Christianity, and since there is a classical consensus of sorts encapsulated in the Christology of the ecumenical Council of Chalcedon of AD 451, it is its so-called "definition" of the person of Christ that is our point of departure. I do not deny that there are other ways of thinking about the person of Christ, some of which have been historically important. It is just that we will be concerned to think about Christology within this dogmatic frame of reference, the frame of reference that has been accepted by the vast majority of Christians in history as a trustworthy summary statement about the person of Christ, which encapsulates important theological notions found in Scripture.

The Chalcedonian definition is not without its problems, however. For one thing, it does not give us anything like a complete account of the person of Christ or of the natures he possesses. As several recent treatments of the matter have reminded us, it is ambiguous with respect to certain claims that can be made about the hypostatic union. Thus, Richard Sturch observes, "It has long been recognized that the main purpose of most of the early Councils was not so much to lay down an orthodox line as to rule out lines which were *not* orthodox. Provided that these were unambiguously repudiated, language could be, and was, used which allowed other ambiguity, or at least a certain latitude of interpretation."[13]

---

13. Richard Sturch, *The Word and the Christ: An Essay in Analytic Christology* (Oxford: Oxford University Press, 1991), 214. He goes on to say that Chalcedonian Christology is sufficiently open-textured as to permit the believer to conceive of Christ in "scriptural, patristic, medieval or modern terms" (ibid.).

So, for instance, we are told that Christ is one person subsisting in two distinct, unconfused natures (human and divine). But we are not told what a nature is, or what a person is in this instance. Nor are we told how one person can be said to have two natures, nor even how someone who is fully human can be consubstantial with the Godhead.[14] What we have in the Chalcedonian definition is, I suggest, a group of theological statements that constitute a sort of *dogmatic minimalism*, which we see elsewhere in the historic affirmations of the Christian faith. It is minimalistic because the definition says as little as doctrinally possible about the hypostatic union, while making clear that certain ways of thinking about the person of Christ are off-limits, or unorthodox. We might say that the Chalcedonian definition draws a veil over the hypostatic union, so that what we know about substantive questions regarding the union of Christ's human to his divine nature is severely limited. Nevertheless, it does make clear that certain views about the person of Christ are to be avoided, and this in turn gives us certain (minimal) dogmatic claims with which we can construct theological desiderata for the purposes of contemporary systematic theology.

Suppose this claim about dogmatic minimalism is granted. There is a further question in the neighborhood that has to do with the relationship between dogmatic minimalism and the metaphysics of the incarnation. We could frame it thus: Does assent to Chalcedon commit the theologian not only to a particular theological framework for understanding the incarnation, but also a particular metaphysics?

This is an important question, and much turns on it. I have already laid down that Scripture is the norming norm for all theological judgments, and that creeds, including the Chalcedonian definition, are subordinate norms that depend on Scripture as the norming norm. But we might think of Scripture as a sort of data source from which are drawn certain doctrinal theories, like the creeds. These, in turn, form the basis for particular theological models, which provide conceptual structures by means of which the theologian postulates certain ways of understanding

---

14. Sarah Coakley makes the same point when she says, "the relatively undefined character of the key terms 'nature' (*physis*) and 'person' (*hypostasis*) in the so-called Definition ... draws attention to the open-endedness of the document, its unclarity about the precise meaning of key terms. If anything is 'defined' in the 'Definition' it is not these crucial concepts. To be sure, these terms had a pre-history, but it was an ambiguous one and the 'Definition' does not clear up the ambiguity." Coakley, "What Does Chalcedon Solve and What Does It Not? Some Reflections on the Status and Meaning of the Chalcedonian Definition," in *The Incarnation* (ed. Stephen T. Davis, Daniel Kendall, and Gerald O'Collins; Oxford: Oxford University Press, 2002), 148.

the content of the creeds that is metaphysical in nature.[15] The advantage of thinking of matters in this way is that it does not require the contemporary theologian to ensure that her metaphysics are the same as those of the church fathers of the fifth century. But it does take seriously the need to engage with the theological tradition in formulating metaphysical models of the incarnation. Both the Chalcedonian fathers and the modern theologians wishing to stand in the Chalcedonian tradition speak of "one person subsisting in two natures." Both mean by this that Christ is a divine person with a human nature. But their theological accounts of "person" or "nature," respectively, may depend on somewhat different metaphysical views of "persons" or "natures."

I have labored the point about the dogmatic minimalism of Chalcedon (as I see it) because I think theologians are sometimes too quick to say what the hypostatic union does or does not entail, or what it is that they find confusing, befuddling, or downright incoherent about the Chalcedonian account (often as a prelude to some departure from it). As Sarah Coakley has pointed out, the definition is not merely a means by which to regulate our language about the incarnation (though it does include this). Nor is its language purely metaphorical, offering us a picture of how we might think about Christ. And it certainly does not give us a set of necessary and sufficient conditions by means of which we can analyze the incarnation.[16] However, if we bear in mind that the dogmatic hardcore of classical Christology is rather thin, and deliberately so, it should help us to see that there may be many different Christologies that are consistent with the canons of Chalcedon. It may not be too strong to say that the Chalcedonian definition is commensurate with a number of distinct models of the hypostatic union. Hence, a certain intellectual humility is called for in our reflections on this topic.

What, then, are the dogmatic desiderata for models of the hypostatic union consistent with Chalcedon?

DESIDERATA OUTLINED

According to Chalcedon Christ is one person with two natures, one human and the other divine. He is fully divine. He is fully human. His two natures subsist in a personal (hypostatic) union, without being mixed

---

15. A similar account of the relationship between Scripture (as data), creeds (as theories), and metaphysical models of the incarnation (as a second tier of theory) derived from the work of Peter van Inwagen is discussed by Robin Le Poidevin in "Incarnation: Metaphysical Issues," *Philosophy Compass* 4/4 (2009): 703–14, especially 706.

16. See Coakley, "What Does Chalcedon Solve and What Does It Not?"

together into some sort of hybrid thing and without either nature losing its essential integrity. Yet there are not two persons subsisting in Christ. Rather, he is fundamentally a divine person who may be said (in some manner) to acquire a human nature in addition to the divine nature he already possessed prior to the first moment of incarnation.

So, minimally, any Chalcedonian Christology will include the following tenets:

1. Christ is one person.
2. Christ has two natures, one divine and one human.
3. The two natures of Christ retain their integrity and are distinct; they are not mixed together or confused, nor are they amalgamated into a hybrid of divine and human attributes (like a demigod).
4. The natures of Christ are really united in the person of Christ; that is, they are two natures possessed by one person.

Taken together, these four claims comprise what is usually called the two-natures doctrine. But matters are complicated by the decisions reached by two further ecumenical councils, Constantinople II in AD 553 and Constantinople III in AD 681. For our purposes, the relevant decisions reached by Constantinople II were (a) the reaffirmation that the person of Christ and the second person of the Trinity are one and the same, and (b) the notion that the human nature assumed by God the Son at the incarnation was not "personal," that is, that it was not a person or the human nature of a person independent of, or prior to, its assumption by the Son. This latter claim is often summed up in a distinction that has since gained wide currency, although the fathers of the council did not utilize it. The first part of this distinction is that the human nature assumed by the Son is *anhypostatic*, that is, it is not a person independent of the Son. The second part is the claim that the human nature of Christ is *enhypostatic*, that is, it is made personal, or is personalized, in the very act of incarnation by means of which the human nature in question becomes (as it were) the human nature of the Son. Let us call the conjunction of these claims the an-enhypostatic distinction.[17]

As is probably apparent from the characterization just given, this

---

17. I have dealt with the an-enhypostatic distinction in more detail in *Divinity and Humanity*, ch. 3. For a useful discussion of the distinction and its importance in the development of Chalcedonian Christology in the context of the seven ecumenical councils, see Fred Sanders, "Introduction to Christology: Chalcedonian Categories for the Gospel Narrative," in *Jesus in Trinitarian Perspective: An Introductory Christology* (ed. Fred Sanders and Klaus Issler; Nashville: Broadman & Holman Academic, 2007), 1–41. For a summary of the anathemas of Constantinople II, see John H. Leith, *Creeds of the Churches: A Reader in Christian Doctrine from the Bible to the Present* (3rd ed.; Louisville: John Knox, 1982), 45–50.

an-enhypostatic distinction is puzzling at least in part because it is not clear from what was just said exactly what a nature is, or what it would mean for a nature to be "personalized." We will return to this matter presently, when considering the concepts of persons and natures in the context of clarifying the desiderata.

Constantinople III is particularly remembered in the Christological literature for its canonization of dyothelitism, the claim that Christ has two wills. Under the influence of St. Maximus the Confessor in particular, it was argued that if Christ is truly and fully human as well as truly and fully divine (as Chalcedon had claimed), then he must have a human will as well as a divine will. To deny this is to deny his full humanity, or so the argument went. The concern was to rebut the Monothelites, who claimed that one person = one will. If Christ is one divine person who acquires a human nature in the incarnation, then he must have one will. For, they reasoned, how can one person have two wills without being fundamentally dysfunctional or fractured? Once again, much depends on what is meant by a person and a nature in this debate, as well as what is meant by a human will and a divine will.

I have already noted that in modern theology there is disagreement about whether Chalcedonian Christology is coherent, or whether it should be the point of departure for contemporary reconstructions of the doctrine. But there is also disagreement about the additions to Chalcedonian Christology made by the fathers of Constantinople II and III. In explicating what he calls the "impasse" of the two-natures Christology of Chalcedon, Jürgen Moltmann writes this about the an-enhypostatic distinction that encapsulates an important theme of Constantinople II:

> If the eternal Logos assumed a non-personal human nature, he cannot then be viewed as a historical person, and we cannot talk about "Jesus of Nazareth." The human nature that was assumed would then seem to be like the human garment of the eternal Son — something which he put on when he walked on earth. It becomes difficult to find an identity here between this human nature and our own. Or has the eternal Son of God taken on "human nature without personhood" in the modern sense, so that he has assumed the human being who is really a "non-person"?... Or is the "true" human nature itself anhypostatically enhypostasized in the divine person?... But then "real," actual human personhood would in itself already have to be termed the sin of egocentrism.[18]

---

18. Jürgen Moltmann, *The Way of Jesus Christ: Christology in Messianic Dimension* (trans. Margaret Kohl; London: SCM, 1990), 51.

And in a well-known passage in *The Christian Faith*, Friedrich Schleiermacher writes this of dyothelitism, which was canonized at Constantinople III:

> The utter fruitlessness of this way of presenting the matter becomes particularly clear in the treatment of the question whether Christ as one person formed out of two natures had also two wills according to the number of the natures, or only one according to the number of the person. For if Christ had only one will, then the divine nature is incomplete if this is a human will; and the human nature, if it is a divine will. But if Christ has two wills, then the unity of the person is no more than apparent, even if we try to conserve it by saying that the two wills always will the same thing. For what this results in is only agreement, not unity; and in fact the answer to the problem thus is the return to the division of Christ. And one or the other will is always simply a superfluous accompaniment of the other, whether it be the divine will that accompanies the human or vice versa.[19]

Much in these debates turns on two matters. On the one hand, there is the formal question of whether Chalcedonian Christology is still serviceable and, if it is, whether it is incumbent on modern theologians to take into consideration the judgments of Constantinople II and III in addition to the canons of Chalcedon as dogmatic pronouncements that offer the appropriate way to construe what Chalcedon leaves ambiguous (regarding the an-enhypostatic distinction and dyothelitism, respectively). On the other hand, there is the more material consideration of whether the terms of reference that Chalcedon bequeathed to the Christian tradition are helpful, and if they are, how we should construe them. Let us consider these two matters in reverse order, beginning with the key theological terminology of Chalcedon.

One Person, Two Natures

How are we to understand the claim that Christ is one person with two natures? To begin with, let us invoke an axiom implied by the four tenets of Chalcedonian Christology, outlined above. Call it the *Chalcedonian Axiom* (CA). It is this:

---

19. Friedrich Schleiermacher, *The Christian Faith* (trans. H. R. Mackintosh and J. S. Stewart; Edinburgh: T&T Clark, 1999 1830.), §96, 394. This same worry is echoed in more recent theology. See, e.g., Gordon D. Kaufman, *Systematic Theology: A Historicist Perspective* (New York: Charles Scribner's Sons, 1968), 188, who harks back to Schleiermacher's discussion, and John Macquarrie, *Jesus Christ in Modern Thought* (London: SCM, 1990), 167, who speaks of dyothelitism as "a pathological condition" that should not be affirmed of Christ.

(CA) Christ has one of whatever goes with the person and two of whatever goes with natures.[20]

This much is implied by the dogmatic minimalism of Chalcedon. But a moment's reflection on what this means quickly takes us beyond the letter of Chalcedon, as it took the fathers of the church in the post-Chalcedonian Christological controversies that culminated in the canonical decisions of Constantinople II and III. Hence, there is one person in Christ. So there is one subject of predication, one fundamental entity to which we refer when we speak of Christ. But this person has two complete, unconfused natures. So (presumably) there must be two wills, one belonging to his human nature, one to his divine nature; two centers or ranges of consciousness, one belonging to his human nature, one to his divine nature; two sets of predicates that apply to the respective natures; and so on. But given that at least some of these alleged implications of Chalcedon are disputed, we need to say something about persons and natures before going any further.

Much ink has been spilled in trying to make sense of these two terms. It may not be too much to say that the Christological controversy from the fifth and sixth centuries on depends on what we take these terms to mean. Let us begin with the term "person."

It is often said in discussions of the hypostatic union, or of the Trinity, that the term "person" as understood in the patristic Christological debates should not be conflated with modern psychologically influenced notions of persons. Brian Daley makes the point well. He is adamant that, "when Greek theologians in the early church speak of the 'hypostasis' of Christ, or of the three 'hypostases' of the Trinity, it is clear that they are not referring to what we moderns might call a 'person': an independent subject, constituted by a unique and unrepeatable focus of self-consciousness, practical autonomy, and some measure of psychological freedom."[21] Instead, he observes that the church fathers "developed their notion of hypostasis [i.e., person] to meet the needs of clarifying the apostolic faith, with the aid of contemporary philosophy but not necessarily determined by its conclusions."[22] Note, in this connection, his affirmation of the ancillary

---

20. I owe this to Garrett J. DeWeese's essay, "One Person, Two Natures: Two Metaphysical Models of the Incarnation" in *Jesus in Trinitarian Perspective*, 115.

21. Brian Daley, "Nature and the 'Mode of Union': Late Patristic Models for the Personal Unity of Christ" in *The Incarnation* (ed. S. Davis, D. Kendall, and G. O'Collins), 193–94. Daley analyzes the Christologies of Leontius of Byzantium, Maximus the Confessor, and John of Damascus—three key figures in the consolidation of the Chalcedonian doctrine.

22. Ibid.

role philosophical notions played in the theological task. The dogma was fundamental; the philosophy, a means to clarifying what was believed.

What was the concept of "person" or hypostasis in play, then? Daley maintains that a hypostasis "was essentially a particular individual within a universal species, identifiable as such or such a thing by the qualities it (or he or she) shared with similar individuals, yet marked off as unique by a set of characteristics all its own. It was the kind of thing so unique and unrepeatable you could call it by name—not just 'horse,' but 'Silver'; not just 'man,' but Peter or Paul or John, or even Jesus."[23] But beyond this, the fathers did not stray. Their account stopped once the job of clarifying the apostolic faith had been achieved. In this sense, their position was dogmatically minimalist. Suppose Daley is right about this. Then a person is a particular sort of entity, one that may belong to a species, but which is unique, distinguished from others of its kind by the characteristics that make it the concrete particular to which we give the name "Peter" or "Paul" or "John."

As is well known, Boethius's definition of a person as an individual substance of a rational nature was widely discussed in the West, and it is the definition that St. Thomas Aquinas appeals to in *Summa Theologiae* 1a, Q. 29.[24] It was important for much medieval work on the metaphysics of the hypostatic union and seems, on the face of it, to be consistent with Daley's conclusions about representative Greek Christologies. Borrowing from Aristotelian metaphysics, the medieval school theologians thought of fundamental substances or supposits as the subjects of predication. Such entities have natures, such as human nature. These are called secondary substances, or (perhaps more helpfully) substance-kinds. A particular fundamental substance has a particular substance-kind that it instantiates. So, we might say that the particular person Fred instantiates the particular substance-kind human. Fred is made human, so to speak, by instantiating the substance-kind humanity.

It should be clear from this that the substance-kind a particular person instantiates is essential to that person; it cannot obtain without it. Thus, it is essential to Fred that he be human, not horse. The connection between the fundamental substance and the substance-kind it instantiates is necessary *de re*. Such fundamental substances also have accidents or properties

---

23. Ibid.
24. Boethius defines a person in his *Liber de persona et duabus naturis*, ch. III. He writes, "Persona est naturae rationalis individuis substantia. Sed nos hac definitione eam quam Graeci ὑπόστασιν dicunt terminavimus." "A person is an individual substance of a rational nature. But our definition of this is what the Greeks termed 'a hypostasis.'"

that are predicated of them, such as shape, color, size, mass, and so on. So, we might say, Fred is a human. That is essential to his being Fred. But he can change his shape as he grows, have a different size, augment or reduce his mass, and so on. Accidents are not essential to Fred in the same way as is his substance-kind. For Fred can change his size and shape (to some extent) but he cannot cease to be a member of the kind human. Thus, on this way of thinking, we have the following understanding of persons in relation to their natures: persons are fundamental substances of a rational nature. They are concrete things. Natures are substance-kinds that are predicable of certain sorts of things like humanity is predicable of Fred. Accidents are predicates or attributes of a particular entity that are nonessential, that refer to the fundamental substance as the bearer of properties.[25]

However, without some finessing this way of construing the metaphysics of the incarnation poses a problem for the Boethian definition. It proves too much. For if a person is an independent substance of a rational nature, then the human Christ looks like a candidate for being a person. But we do not want to affirm that, on pain of Nestorianism. One way of avoiding this consequence is to add to the Boethian definition the proviso that in addition to being an independent substance of a rational nature, a person cannot be composed with another substance.[26] On the Aristotle-inspired metaphysics just outlined, this would mean that the human nature of Christ fails to be a person, though an individual with a complete human nature would normally form a fundamental substance that does not compose part of another fundamental substance, thereby forming a person.

In contemporary discussion of the topic, some philosophical theologians have opted for something like this Aristotle-inspired medieval account. Others have developed different ways of construing the metaphysics of the incarnation, whilst affirming the same Chalcedonian two-

---

25. For two clear presentations of the Aristotelian metaphysics underlying much medieval school discussion of the incarnation, see C. J. F. Williams, "A Programme for Christology," RS 3/2 (1968): 513–24, and Marilyn McCord Adams, *Christ and Horrors* (Cambridge: Cambridge University Press, 2006), ch. 5. Also of use in this regard is Richard Swinburne, *The Christian God* (Oxford: Oxford University Press, 1994), ch. 9. The previous paragraph is indebted to these accounts.

26. A point made by Richard Cross in *The Metaphysics of the Incarnation: Thomas Aquinas to Duns Scotus* (Oxford: Oxford University Press, 2002), 240. But this goes back at least to Peter Lombard. In *The Sentences*, Bk. III, Dist. V, ch. 3 (16), he tackles the objection that a person was united to a person in the incarnation, citing Boethius's definition as the source of this problem (for if a person is a "rational substance of an individual nature," then it looks like Christ's human nature is a person independent of its union with the divine Word). He replies, "But this does not follow, because the soul is not a person when it is united personally to another thing, but when it exists by itself." Peter Lombard, *The Sentences Book 3: On the Incarnation of the Word* (trans. Giulio Silano; Toronto: Pontifical Institute of Medieval Studies), 23.

natures doctrine.[27] The debate seems to turn on whether one thinks that the human nature of Christ is fundamentally a concrete particular, that is, a substance or substance-like thing, or, whether one thinks of it as fundamentally an abstract object, such as a property or trope. But several things are nonnegotiable, dogmatically speaking, whichever way one construes the metaphysics. The first of these is that whatever we say of the person of Christ, we must be able to affirm that this he is the second person of the Trinity. In other words, our doctrine of the incarnation must fit with our doctrine of the Trinity. It would be a grave theological mistake to affirm that Christ is a person of one sort whereas the divine persons of the Trinity were persons of a different sort. Second, the person of Christ is the subject or fundamental substance to whom a human nature is joined. Third, the natures exist "in" Christ; they are possessed or instantiated by him. His divine nature is essential to him because he is a divine person. But his human nature is contingently related to him, as the nature he voluntarily assumes.

Beyond these minimal dogmatic affirmations Chalcedonian Christologists are divided, depending on what is meant by "nature" in relation to the person of Christ. It is not my task today to adjudicate which way of construing the metaphysics of persons and natures best represents Chalcedonian Christology. I am only interested in outlining the desiderata for such Christology, consistent with the dogmatic minimalism of the Chalcedonian definition.

Personalizing the Natures, Distinguishing the Wills

We come to the question of rightly interpreting the Chalcedonian legacy in the canons of Constantinople II and III.

Recall that Constantinople II defends the Chalcedonian settlement, including the claim that Christ is a divine person with a human nature (and therefore a member of the Trinity), and the claim that his human nature is "personalized" in the life of the second person of the Trinity, so to speak. It has no existence independent of that second person. This latter claim is encapsulated in the an-enhypostatic distinction. Now, depending on what one makes of the terms "person" and "nature," one will have a slightly different account of the an-enhypostatic distinction and the personhood of Christ.

---

27. I discuss this in detail in *Divinity and Humanity*, ch. 2.

This brings us to Moltmann's objection, cited earlier. In truth, there are several aspects to it. First, he worries that the an-enhypostatic distinction implies that Christ's humanity is somehow unreal, that it would be "like the human garment of the eternal Son"—something he puts on and can take off again. Second, he thinks this tells against Christ being a truly historical person. For what sort of concrete, real person has a nonpersonal human nature? Finally, he worries that this an-enhypostatic distinction means "the eternal Son of God" has "taken on 'human nature without personhood'" and that this has implications for how we should think of human personhood since Christ does not need to be a human person to be fully human.

Let us examine this more carefully. Does the an-enhypostatic distinction imply Christ's humanity is unreal, that it is merely a garment worn by the Son, or even that is not really connected to him? Nothing could be further from the truth. The anathemas of Constantinople II make it clear that God the Son unites himself to a complete human nature. However, it is true that (in one respect) this is only contingently related to God the Son. For the Chalcedonian doctrine reiterated by Constantinople II is that in the incarnation we are dealing with a divine person. So he is a person who has the divine nature essentially. He does not have the same relation to his human nature precisely because he voluntarily assumes that human nature as part of his work as the Mediator of salvation. He takes it up and (in theory at least) he could lay it down, though in point of fact he will not do so. For, to press the logic of this view, he is eternally God Incarnate. He eternally deigns to take on this role and therefore to unite himself to human nature, something that he will not revoke.

This brings us to Moltmann's worry about Christ's humanity being nonhistorical if it is nonpersonal. Once again, this misses the point of the Chalcedonian Christology elaborated upon by Constantinople II. The whole point of the two-natures doctrine is to preserve the claim that there is only one hypostasis, or one person "in" Christ, as it were. This is God the Son, the divine person who takes on a human nature. The human nature he assumes cannot be a person independent of the Son, on pain of Nestorianism. But this does not mean his humanity is "nonpersonal," at least not in any theologically damaging way. Nor does it mean there is something lacking in Christ's humanity that is present in our humanity. That is to conflate being human, that is, belonging to the kind humanity, with the particular human to which we are referring, namely, Christ the God-man. If humanity is a substance-kind, as many school theologians taught, then Moltmann's concern is wide of the mark. If human nature is a property of God the Son from the incarnation on, then it is odd to think that this means there is something lacking in Christ, for he possesses the property in common with all other humans. For, on this way of understanding the matter, humanity just is a kind-essence or property had by God the Son and by every other human being. The difference between Christ and the rest of humanity lies not in the property of human nature he acquires but in the relation he has to his human nature. So, whether we understand the humanity of Christ as fundamentally an abstract-nature (that is, a property or property-like thing) or as a concrete-nature (that is, as a substance, or a substance-like thing), Moltmann's concerns are avoided.

Let us turn to Schleiermacher's rejection of dyothelitism, the doctrine canonized at Constantinople III. His objection is subtler than Moltmann's and therefore more difficult to rebut. Recall our Chalcedonian Axiom stated earlier that *Christ has one of whatever goes with the person and two of whatever goes with natures.* Schleiermacher embraces this consequence of Constantinople III and reasons that this means one of two things. Either there are not enough wills in Christ for him to be fully human and fully divine (because either he is a divine person with a human nature and so lacks a human will, or is a human person with a divine nature, and so lacks a divine will). Or, he has two wills, one human and one divine. But then, he says, "the unity of the person is no more than apparent" for what results is "agreement, not unity," which is to divide Christ rather than unite him. If, in other words, the wills go with the person, there can only be one and we end up with monothelitism. One person, one will is the logic of the claim being made here. Alternatively, if the wills go with the natures there must be two of them, but then we end up dividing Christ. No dyothelite wants that.

Notice the care with which Schleiermacher puts this latter objection. He does not say that if the two wills go with the two natures, then Nestorianism results. That does not necessarily follow because dyothelitism does not imply two persons. One would have to show that possession of two wills in two distinct natures requires there to be two persons "in" Christ. But no dyothelite will concede that. Instead, Schleiermacher says that the problem is that this way of carving up the wills would divide Christ. In other words, it tells against the unity of the person. For if one person has two distinct wills that belong to two distinct natures, "then the unity of the person is not more than apparent." Christ might be like someone with multiple personality disorder. Or, as some Christologists have speculated, he might be like the subject of a neurological commissurotomy, where the corpus callosum connecting the two hemispheres of the brain is severed in order to reduce the electrical activity between them that is so damaging to patients suffering from grand mal epilepsy. Such patients suffer significant disruption in their mental lives, rather as Schleiermacher seems to imagine obtains with the dyothelite Christ.

It seems to me that Constantinople III makes it plain that the wills of Christ go with the natures. He has two wills or two theaters of operation in which he acts as a human being and as a divine person, respectively. If Christ's human nature is a property, or a property-like thing (i.e., an abstract nature), then in acquiring human nature the Son acquires the properties necessary and sufficient to will as a human. His human way of willing is just the Son willing certain things as a human, and he is able to do this because he is a human in virtue of acquiring the property human-ity. By contrast, if Christ's human nature is concrete, that is, a substance or a substance-like thing, matters are a little more complicated. Normally, human substances are fundamental substances, that is, persons, capable of willing as humans. Christ is not fundamentally a human substance though he has a human substance, on this view. But if it is possible for God the Son to assume a human substance such that it does not form an entity independent of the Son, and therefore does not become a fundamental substance independent of the Son, then maybe he can will as a human by means of that substance. This concrete-nature view, or something very like it, is how at least some of the school theologians understood the metaphysics of the incarnation in line with Chalcedon and Constantinople III. It may be somewhat awkward and unwieldy. But it is not clear (to me, at least) that it dissolves the personal union of the Son with his humanity. Indeed, if the Son is a divine person and therefore a metaphysically simple entity, there may be good reason for opting for some version of a concrete-nature view, since then Christ is a composite in which God the Son is a metaphysically simple component.[28]

Recently, several evangelical philosophical theologians have argued in favor of monothelite accounts of the hypostatic union. Garrett DeWeese maintains that evangelicals need not balk at this because monothelite

---

28. I have argued this in "Compositional Christology without Nestorianism," in *The Metaphysics of the Incarnation* (ed. Anna Marmadoro and Jonathan Hill; Oxford: Oxford University Press, 2011). See also Brian Leftow, "A Timeless God Incarnate," in *The Incarnation*, 273–99, and idem, "The Humanity of God," in *The Metaphysics of the Incarnation*, 20–44.

Christology follows the Cyrillian tenor of Chalcedonian Christology in virtue of its emphasis on the unity of the person of Christ. He also argues that evangelicals are not bound by conciliar decisions if they turn out to be problematic.[29] He gives two examples of such potentially mistaken creedal statements. These are: the decision of the seventh (and last) ecumenical council, Nicaea II, to endorse iconography in churches, and the Nicene-Constantinopolitan creedal statement that "we believe in one baptism for the remission of sins." Neither of these claims forms a part of what evangelicals take to be biblical religion, so evangelicals should not feel bound by them. In a similar way, perhaps the decision of Constantinople III to endorse dyothelitism is a step away from biblical religion.

The principle that Protestants should not be bound by the ecumenical creeds if they can be shown to conflict with Scripture is a venerable one. It is enshrined in confessions like the Thirty Nine Articles.[30] But the Thirty Nine Articles also says, "The Three Creeds, Nicene Creed, Athanasius's Creed, and that which is commonly called the Apostles' Creed, ought thoroughly to be received and believed: for they may be proved by most certain warrants of Holy Scripture." Even if ecumenical councils may err and have erred, few Protestants would want to withhold confession of the Nicene Creed. Nicaea II is a different matter. Where confessional Protestants are concerned to uphold the Nicene-Constantinopolitan symbol, few are worried about the iconoclastic controversy. Indeed, many will be unsympathetic to iconography.

But I think that is regrettable. To my mind, Protestants should take the decisions of *all* seven ecumenical councils seriously indeed, Nicaea II included. It is not at all clear to me that the decision of Nicaea II regarding the right use of icons is contrary to Scripture.[31] What is more (and returning to the matter in hand), dyothelitism was understood by the fathers of Constantinople III and by the vast majority of Christians ever since as the right way to understand the two-natures doctrine of Chalcedon. They reasoned that if Christ has a complete human nature, he must have a

---

29. DeWeese, "One Person, Two Natures," 148.

30. Article XXI states, "General Councils may not be gathered together without the commandment and will of Princes. And when they be gathered together, (forasmuch as they be an assembly of men, whereof all be not governed with the Spirit and Word of God), they may err, and sometimes have erred, even in things pertaining unto God. Wherefore things ordained by them as necessary to salvation have neither strength nor authority, unless it may be declared that they be taken out of holy Scripture." Compare the *Westminster Confession*, ch. 31. IV, which says, "All synods or councils since the apostles' times, whether general or particular, may err, and many have erred; therefore they are not to be made the rule of faith or practice, but to be used as a help in both."

31. See, for example, St. John of Damascus, *Three Treatises on the Divine Images* (trans. Andrew Louth; Crestwood, NY: St. Vladimir's Seminary Press, 2003).

human will. Whether one thinks of the natures as abstract or concrete, as a property or property-like thing, or as a substance or substance-like thing, sense can be made of this claim. But (obviously) how one construes it will be different, depending on the metaphysics one adopts. Dyothelitism is part of the catholic faith. It is a deliverance of an ecumenical council. It is not contrary to Scripture, and it has been held by the vast majority of Christians down through the ages who affirm Constantinople III as the legitimate extrapolation of Chalcedonian Christology over against mono-physitism and monothelitism. I think this is good reason to retain the doctrine as one of the desiderata for contemporary models of the hypo-static union.

SUMMARY

Let us take stock. Chalcedon provides us with the following dogmatically minimal claims requisite to orthodox Christology:

1. Christ is one person.
2. Christ has two natures, one divine and one human.
3. The two natures of Christ retain their integrity and are distinct; they are not mixed together or confused, nor are they amal-gamated into a hybrid of divine and human attributes (like a demigod).
4. The natures of Christ are really united in the person of Christ; that is, they are two natures possessed by one person.

This yields the following Chalcedonian Axiom:

(CA) Christ has one of whatever goes with the person and two of whatever goes with natures.

Following Boethius, I have reasoned that a person is a fundamental substance of a rational nature. If one adopts the view of at least some of the medieval school theologians, the natures of Christ are to be understood as fundamentally concrete substance-like things, not as fundamentally rich properties, though natures may include properties or predicates. This is the view I favor. However, I do not think that this particular account of the metaphysics of the divine person of Christ or his two natures is the only permissible way of understanding these matters. Other ways of constru-ing both the "person" and the "natures" in the two natures doctrine are consistent with orthodoxy and have found advocates in the church. The main alternative family of views depends on the claim that Christ's human nature is fundamentally an abstract thing, like a property or trope. This difference over the metaphysics of the incarnation is permissible given the dogmatic minimalism of Chalcedon, which does not prescribe the ontology that underpins its theological affirmations.

I have also argued that there is a significant dissimilarity between the two natures in Christ, and failure to attend to these differences can lead to theological mistakes. The nature of God the Son is divine, and the divine nature is something that we have much less grip on than human natures, since the divine essence or nature is in a number of important respects mysterious. Nevertheless, I have affirmed that there is good theological reason for holding to the Christological additions or appendices to Chalcedonian Christology provided by Constantinople II and III. We should affirm that Christ's human nature is an–enhypostatic; and we should affirm that Christ has two wills, though this is not without difficulties. I submit that these are the desiderata for Christology as understood by consensus Christianity. Far from eliminating the need for further theological discussion and debate, it seems to me that a right understanding of the dogmatic parameters for Christology provides a basis on which fruitful work can be done on this central and defining doctrine of the Christian faith.

CHAPTER 2

SALVATOR MUNDI
Three Types of Christology

George Hunsinger

IN A SEMINAL PASSAGE from his book *The Christian Faith*,[1] Friedrich Schleiermacher, the great nineteenth-century theologian and father of modern liberal theology, introduces an interesting set of distinctions. His own Christology, he suggests, can be differentiated from two other approaches, which he labels as the *empirical* and the *magical*. After an initial hesitation, he designates his own view by the term *mystical*.

The mystical view, he says, stands midway between the other two. They are all distinguished, in part, by how they see the natural in relation to the supernatural. The empirical view is said to be entirely naturalistic while the magical view is entirely supernaturalistic. The mystical view is then brought forward to mediate between these two positions. Here Schleiermacher introduces his famous thesis that although God's activity in history is certainly supernatural in origin, it "becomes natural as soon as it emerges into manifestation" (*CF* 430). In a move that would become seminal for modern liberal theology, Schleiermacher wants to naturalize the supernatural without eliminating it completely.

---

1. Friedrich Schleiermacher, *The Christian Faith* (Edinburgh: T&T Clark, 1928). Hereafter pages numbers are cited in the text after the abbreviation CF.

DESCRIBING SCHLEIERMACHER'S TYPOLOGY

The three views he describes can be sketched as follows.

THE EMPIRICAL VIEW

The empirical view, Schleiermacher says, is essentially individualistic. Empirical Christology affirms Christ's "redeeming influence" (an important category for Schleiermacher), but sees it as operating directly on the individual. The written word is sometimes regarded as mediating this influence, while at other times even that is dispensed with. For Schleiermacher, the empirical view is defective at this point, because it fails to grasp how Christ is related to the church. It overlooks his founding of a community to mediate his redeeming influence (*CF* 430).

In favor of empirical Christology, according to Schleiermacher, it can be said that it relieves us of the anxiety of feeling that we must offer God "substitutes" for the perfection that we lack in his sight. This anxiety is seen as a pervasive phenomenon in religion. But then, Schleiermacher continues, we already knew by "our natural intelligence" that the attempt to satisfy God through the offering of sacrifices (as, for example, a spotless lamb) is futile. The contribution of the empirical view is therefore negligible at this point (*CF* 431). Schleiermacher agrees with the empirical view in rejecting substitutionary atonement. In line with much modern theology, he thinks it makes no rational sense.

Schleiermacher emphasizes that empirical Christology is ethical in orientation. In this view, "the relation between teacher and pupil, like that between pattern and imitation, must always remain an external one." Schleiermacher is saying that a merely ethical Christology establishes a merely external relation to Christ. According to him, when those who advocate an ethical Christology are asked whether they have known "a real experience of vital fellowship with Christ," they tend to recoil, feeling that they are being pushed toward "the objectionable magic view" (*CF* 438). It is telling that an ethical Christology is content to separate "the teachings of Christ" from "teachings *about* Christ," as if his person were of secondary importance (*CF* 438, italics original). Schleiermacher, who thinks that the person of Christ is of primary importance, clearly wants to expand the range of options at this point beyond just the empirical and the magical.

For an ethical or empirical Christology, as Schleiermacher presents it, nothing more is needed to understand Christ than "some improvements upon natural ethics and natural theology," and these improvements are "represented as if human reason must have found them out by itself" (*CF* 445). Schleiermacher concludes that the empirical view "is chiefly to blame for the claim of philosophy to set itself above faith and to treat faith as merely a transitional stage" (*CF* 431). While Schleiermacher is certainly willing to criticize the magical Christology from a rational standpoint, he does not want reason to dominate faith as much as he thinks it does in empirical Christology.

Although he would have had more than one opponent in mind, Schleiermacher seems to associate the empirical view largely with Immanuel Kant. By extension, Schleiermacher's critical observations would apply more generally to what we sometimes think of today as exemplarist Christologies.

THE MAGICAL VIEW

At the other extreme is the magical view, which Schleiermacher finds equally dubious, if not more so. Whereas empirical Christology was rationalistic and naturalistic, the magical view, Schleiermacher says, is essentially individualistic. Magical Christology affirms Christ's "redeeming influence" (an important category for Schleiermacher), but sees it as operating directly upon the individual. The written word is sometimes regarded as mediating this influence, while at other times even that is dispensed with. For Schleiermacher the magical view is defective at this point, because it fails to grasp how Christ is related to the church (*CF* 430)."

According to magical Christology, the meaning of Christ's saving significance can be defined without referring to our "vital fellowship with him" (*CF* 435). Redemption is seen as an objective transaction between God and Christ that occurred when he died for our sins. "This means," Schleiermacher explains, "that the forgiveness of sins is made to depend upon the punishment which Christ suffered." Redemption "is presented as a reward which God offers to Christ for the suffering of that punishment" (*CF* 435). An objective efficacy is ascribed to the cross, so that vital fellowship with Christ becomes merely secondary and derivative. For Schleiermacher, union with Christ is experiential, and experiential religion defines what is central to Christology.

Although Schleiermacher does not find this Christology to be wrong in every respect, he argues that blessedness and forgiveness become magical when they are not seen as "mediated through vital fellowship with Christ" (*CF* 435). Apart from this fellowship, God's "rewarding of Christ" is "nothing but divine arbitrariness" (*CF* 435). If salvation were truly accomplished apart from us (*extra nos*), "without any inner basis" within us (*in nobis*), then salvation would lack its decisive component. It would be worked out apart from our spiritual experience of it. The "source of blessedness" would be established objectively rather than within us. Salvation as objectively accomplished could only be "infused" into each individual from without (*CF* 435).

For Schleiermacher, the objective aspect of salvation is important only insofar as it serves as the source of the subjective aspect. Whatever takes place in Christ apart from us (his spiritual blessedness) is only the prologue to that which takes place within us (our spiritual formation through experience of his blessedness). The subjective aspect is central while the objective aspect merely facilitates it.

Forgiveness of sins is also magically conceived if thought to occur apart from our experience of it. When forgiveness is established objectively, the dynamics of salvation become implausible. "The consciousness of deserving punishment is supposed to cease," observes Schleiermacher, "because the punishment has been borne by another" (*CF* 435). Schleiermacher wants sin-consciousness to cease, but not for that reason, which he regards as far-fetched. For him, as for modern liberal theology more generally, all ideas of objective atonement must be rejected as magical. Reconciliation either happens within us or it does not happen at all.

Magical Christology is also wrong to suppose that the decisive experience of "vital fellowship with Christ" would not be possible if Christ had not suffered and died for us (*CF* 436). It sees Christ's saving death as that which makes possible our fellowship with him. It regards the "real sum-total of Christ's redemptive activity," Schleiermacher suggests, as his "giving up of himself to suffering for suffering's sake" (*CF* 436).

For Schleiermacher, what magical Christology fails to grasp is that Christ's inward spiritual blessedness is independent of his passion and death. Whereas for the "magical caricature," his passion and death serve to constitute his saving significance, in fact, according to Schleiermacher, they only confirm it (*CF* 436). Christ's passion and death are merely tests of his spiritual blessedness, not factors that constitute it. For Schleiermacher, the cross is an ordeal, not a satisfaction for sin.

Finally, the magical view mistakenly holds "that Christ's obedience is our righteousness, or that his righteousness is imputed to us" (*CF* 455). These ideas again wrongly posit that Christ's saving significance rests on what he accomplished externally to us, whereas in fact it rests on his influence within us. The fundamental mistake is to think that "the punishment of sin" is taken away "through the suffering of Christ" (*CF* 459).

If in his passion and death the Redeemer had borne the punishment for sin that would otherwise have befallen the world, "then," Schleiermacher concludes, "it is scarcely possible to avoid the supplementary assumption that the divine nature in him also shared in the suffering" (*CF* 460). But according to established tradition, Schleiermacher argues, the idea that God suffers is absurd. It seems that Schleiermacher's Christology tends toward Nestorianism by separating "the divine nature in Christ" from his human suffering.[2]

Furthermore, the magical view, according to Schleiermacher, rests on a crude idea of divine wrath. Only by positing that God must punish sin by his wrath can the magical view teach that sin's punishment was transferred from us to Christ (*CF* 460). It fails to see that if sin is to be decisively overcome, it can only be overcome within us, not outside of us.

In rejecting the magical view Schleiermacher's key opponent seems to be Anselm, or at least some version of Anselm. As a matter of fact, although the medieval theologian had taught that punishment and satisfaction were mutually exclusive, he was commonly misunderstood in Post-Reformation Protestant theology.[3] He was taken to mean that the divine wrath was satisfied through Christ's being punished in our stead. In *Cur Deus Homo*, however, Anselm had seen the sacrifice on the cross as compensating God for the injury done to his honor by sin. The idea of Christ's dying in our place played no role in his argument.[4] Nevertheless, it was not uncommon for later Protestant theologians to read the idea of substitution into Anselm.[5] The magical Christology described and rejected by Schleiermacher would have been broadly Anselmian in that sense. What Anselm and the later Protestant view of satisfaction had in common was a more objectivist understanding of Christ's saving death.

THE MYSTICAL VIEW

Although we will return to Schleiermacher's views in a moment, a preliminary sketch of his Christological alternative can be offered here. He sees his mystical view of salvation as neither ethical nor magical, because it centers on the spirituality of inwardness. It is the spirituality of

---

2. For the substantive issues, see Paul L. Gavrilyuk, *The Suffering of the Impassible God: The Dialectics of Patristic Thought* (Oxford: Oxford University Press, 2006), esp. 135–71.

3. See Robert B. Strimple, "St. Anselm's *Cur Deus Homo* and John Calvin's Doctrine of the Atonement," in *Anselm, Aosta, Bec and Canterbury* (ed. D. E. Luscombe and G. R. Evans; Sheffield: Sheffield Academic Press, 1996), 348–60.

4. For a solid account of Anselm, see David Brown, "Anselm on Atonement," in *The Cambridge Companion to Anselm* (ed. Brian Davies and Brian Leftow; Cambridge: Cambridge University Press, 2005), 279–302.

5. It should be noted that Schleiermacher himself does not seem to have been guilty of this mistake.

Christ, which Schleiermacher calls his blessedness, that carries his saving significance.

The Redeemer's blessedness is the source of all true spiritual formation. It creates a spiritual community, and through this community his blessedness is mediated to each believer. His blessedness is the objective aspect that then becomes subjective in us.

In a state of spiritual blessedness, the believer experiences salvation in Christ. The power of sin is broken, God-consciousness replaces God-forgetfulness, and fellowship with Christ's blessedness is enjoyed. A central ethical imperative is to promote this blessedness in oneself and in others. For Schleiermacher, ethics, though not unimportant, is secondary to spirituality.

Moreover, what takes place within us (*in nobis*) depends in some sense on what has taken place apart from us (*extra nos*), and to that extent the magical view is not wrong. However, what took place apart from us is not satisfaction, but the spirituality of Jesus. His blessedness becomes available to us through the Word received, preserved, and transmitted by his community. This Word contains "the picture ... of his being and influence" through which "his spiritual presence" is mediated (*CF* 467). As we enter into fellowship with his presence or blessedness, we undergo the spiritual renewal that constitutes the meaning of redemption. Redemption takes place as the blessedness of Jesus himself is communicated to those who enjoy fellowship with him by faith.

LOW, MIDDLE, AND HIGH: REVISING SCHLEIERMACHER'S TYPOLOGY

Schleiermacher's typology contains both analytical and evaluative elements. It will be useful to place the evaluative elements to one side while expanding on those that are analytical. The terms *empirical*, *mystical*, and *magical*, after all, are largely uninformative and tendentious. I propose to replace them with the more neutral terms of *low*, *middle*, and *high*.

An immediate advantage of this move is to broaden the field of discernment. As Schleiermacher saw in his own way, by introducing the category of middle Christology, it becomes possible to avoid the pitfall that all Christologies must be either low or high. A recent article on Schleiermacher, for example, proposes quite implausibly that he represents a high Christology.[6]

---

6. Kevin Hector, "Actualism and Incarnation: The High Christology of Friedrich Schleiermacher," *IJST* 8 (2006): 307–22.

"High" in this proposal effectively means "not low," apparently because there are no other known options. While it is correct that Schleiermacher's Christology is not low in any exemplarist sense, it is not high either in any reasonable sense of the term. It is rather a middle Christology, as his own typology helps to make clear. His typology also helps us to see that a rather large and diverse group of modern Christologies exists whose representatives are neither low nor high. Despite the diversity within this group, its members display the lineaments of a middle Christology.

Let me begin with some general remarks about my typological proposal.

1. The first thing to see about the low, middle, and high types is that they are not like points on a line. They are not like little dots that one either occupies or fails to occupy. They are rather more like regions within which one can take up residence. The regions will embrace a certain degree of diversity. Nevertheless, family resemblances will exist within one region that will not be found in another. A citizen of France might live near Belgium or the Netherlands while still being a citizen of France.

2. The second thing to see is that the types are not linear in their relation to one another. If one imagines two bricks sitting side-by-side, with a third brick sitting on top at the midpoint, one can form a better idea of how the types are related when taken as regions. Views that reside near the contiguous borders may sometimes have more in common with views across the border than those removed to the far corners. In the regions of France near Belgium or the Netherlands, the French language might not be spoken as purely as it would be in Paris. Whether that is an advantage or a disadvantage would depend on the circumstances.

3. The third thing to see about the types is that they are not necessarily mutually exclusive at every point. A low Christology removed to a far corner might not include any middle or high elements, but one closer to the contiguous borders might still be low while also being a little mixed. A middle Christology that excluded all ethical elements would not be as compelling as one that took ethics on board. Much the same would be true for high Christologies. A high Christology that allowed ample scope to spirituality and ethics would be stronger than one that lacked those elements.

4. The fourth thing to see is that this proposed typology allows us to think about each type in its strongest terms. It is not uncommon for those who develop a Christology within one region to reject a more defective Christology from another region and then to suppose that the whole region has been effectively dealt with. Schleiermacher's treatment of "magical" Christology is

arguably a case in point. The magical view that he rejects does not necessarily represent high Christology at its best. Although he would probably have rejected any high Christology, the discussion would be improved if he had made an effort to avoid caricaturing his opponents. Schleiermacher does not seem to have noticed any high Christologies in a stronger form. Otherwise he might not have dismissed them so facilely with his term *magical*.

5. Finally, and this cannot be stressed strongly enough, any actually existing Christology may not belong perfectly to any one of these "regions" alone. The terms *low*, *middle*, and *high* represent ideal types, not necessarily actual positions. Some Christologies may travel back and forth across the borders, depending on the question. My types are meant to be used analytically, not predictively or rigidly. They are categories of discernment, not useful pots to put things in. It does not matter if a particular Christology fails to fit perfectly into one of them. What matters is that the ideal types can help us to see why not. The typology can also help us to discern whether anomalies may happen to exist in certain mixed Christologies. Mixed Christologies are not always internally coherent. Furthermore, as mentioned, this typology can help us to sort out stronger versions from weaker versions within one of the Christological "regions."

SOME FORMAL ISSUES AND THEIR DEVELOPMENT

Some formal issues will now be outlined that any Christology must address. How the three types tend to deal with these issues will also be sketched. With that as background, we will turn our attention to some actually existing Christologies from each ideal type.

THE PERSON AND WORK OF CHRIST

The first formal issue pertains to Christ's person and his saving work. How are these terms defined, and how are they thought to be related? The issue can be stated in algebraic form.

Let "p" stand for Christ's person, and "w" for his saving work. For any Christology we can posit the following: If "p," then "w." And if "w," then "p." These formulas assume that the Christology is internally coherent, which is not always the case. As a general rule, however, it is true that a certain sort of saving work requires a certain view of Christ's person. The reverse is also true. A certain view of Christ's person points to a particular understanding of his saving significance.

This simple observation already places us in a position to see something important. Only a high view of Christ's saving work requires a high view of the incarnation or a Chalcedonian view of his person. Low and middle views of his work can dispense with Chalcedon, and often do, although there are notable exceptions. They can dispense with it because of how they understand Christ's saving significance. Only a high view of the atonement requires a Chalcedonian view of Christ's person.

For low Christologies, as Schleiermacher pointed out, Christ has saving significance primarily as a religious teacher and a moral example. His life and teaching put forward an elevated religious and ethical content. Christ teaches us about God's love and forgiveness, and his teaching is exemplified by his life. He saves us from our ignorance, and at least in some low Christologies his Spirit assists us in our weakness. Salvation takes place through our imitation of Christ, which requires our repentance as we strive to emulate his way of life.

If this kind of teaching and example constitute Christ's saving work ("w"), he does not need to be God incarnate ("p"). He does not need to be fully God and fully human in one person. He merely needs to be fully human. Examples of Christology are not unknown, however, in which a high view of Christ's person is somehow combined with an essentially low view of his work. This is the kind of anomaly that the typology can help us to pick out. Some Latin American liberation theologians, for example, such as Gustavo Gutiérrez or Jon Sobrino, seem to combine a high view of Christ's person with a low or ethical (liberationist) view of his saving work.

Other low Christologies have suggested that we might look on Jesus as the "parable of God." However well-intentioned, such proposals are Arian in tendency, offering a low view of Christ's person whereby he is defined as less than fully God, no matter how much he may be "like" God. As a matter of fact, for a typical low Christology, Jesus does not need to be anything more than a gifted and exemplary human being. He can do his saving ethical or religious work without being fully God. All he needs to be is fully human. Schleiermacher is right that low Christologies place Christ and his followers in an essentially external relation.

For middle Christologies, the saving significance of Christ is defined by his spirituality. For those that use traditional categories, the important thing about Jesus Christ is the Holy Spirit. An example would be Hendrikus Berkhof.[7] In other modern Christologies, we encounter essen-

---

7. Hendrikus Berkhof, *The Doctrine of the Holy Spirit* (Atlanta: John Knox, 1976). In this book Berkhof's Christology displays Nestorian tendencies while his understanding of the Trinity tends toward modalism. The combination of Nestorianism and modalism is not uncommon in modern Christologies. Nestorius and Theodore, by contrast, espoused a Nicene doctrine of the Trinity.

tially the same idea in different, more flashy terms. The important thing about Jesus might be his "God consciousness" with Schleiermacher, or the "New Being" with Tillich, or simply "faith" with Bultmann, or "loyalty" to God with H. Richard Niebuhr. Whereas for Berkhof Jesus is the bearer and the sender of the Spirit, for these others he is the bearer and sender of God-consciousness, the New Being, or some other form of life-giving spirituality. In all cases Jesus is the source of some saving benefit other than himself (unless his person is just absorbed into his spirituality, as happens with Schleiermacher). Jesus is the source and the means to a redemptive spirituality, which is thought to be liberating, empowering, or transforming, mostly at the level of inwardness. No matter how hard a middle Christology may try, justification always blurs into sanctification.

If the important thing about Jesus is his spirituality, he does not need to be fully God. He merely needs to be a fully realized spiritual human being. He merely needs to be, as with Schleiermacher, the second Adam who overcomes the disastrous consequences of the first Adam, whose fall dragged us all into sin and death. Christ's saving work consists in his restoring a spiritual relation to God, first in his own case and then through his influence in others after him. While weak versions of middle Christology might tend to be quietist and pietistic, stronger versions will incorporate a more robust ethical element. Middle Christologies, however, tend to be indifferent or hostile toward Nicaea and Chalcedon. Why shouldn't they be, if the whole point of Christ is merely a matter of spirituality?

Only a high Christology requires a high view of Christ's person, because only a high Christology takes a high view of his saving work. Generally speaking, there are two broad reasons for affirming the full deity of Jesus Christ. The first is hermeneutical while the other is soteriological. The hermeneutical reason is that the New Testament documents bear witness to Jesus Christ as God. He is not only described as God, but he is also depicted as God. We see him not only designated with the term *theos*, but also doing things that only God can do, such as forgiving sins and raising the dead.[8] The doctrinal reason, which is essentially threefold, overlaps with the hermeneutical reason. Doctrinally, the focus falls on

---

8. See, for example, Nils Alstrup Dahl, *Jesus the Christ: The Historical Origins of Christological Doctrine* (Minneapolis: Augsburg Fortress, 1991); Murray J. Harris, *Jesus as God: The New Testament Use of* Theos *in Reference to Jesus* (Grand Rapids: Baker, 1992); Martin Hengel, *Studies in Early Christology* (London: T&T Clark, 1995); Larry W. Hurtado, *Lord Jesus Christ: Devotion to Jesus in Earliest Christianity* (Grand Rapids: Eerdmans, 2005); Simon J. Gathercole, *The Pre-existent Son: Recovering the Christologies of Matthew, Mark, and Luke* (Grand Rapids: Eerdmans, 2006).

worship, revelation, and reconciliation, a point that is well brought out in Question 33 of the new Presbyterian Study Catechism:

> Question 33. What is the significance of affirming that Jesus is truly God?
>
> Answer. Only God can properly deserve worship. Only God can reveal to us who God is. And only God can save us from our sins. Being truly God, Jesus meets these conditions. He is the proper object of our worship, the self-revelation of God, and the Savior of the world.[9]

Low and middle Christologies usually dispense with presenting Jesus as the proper object of worship and prayer. From a high Christological standpoint, neither a low Christology, such as we find in someone like John Locke (or in an emaciated version in someone like Marcus Borg), nor a middle Christology, such as we find in the likes of Schleiermacher, Tillich, Bultmann, or H. R. Niebuhr, is satisfactory on this score. None has any real place for Jesus as the object of worship. High Christologies such as we find in Florovsky, Balthasar, and Barth, to mention only three of the most distinguished, affirm Jesus as the object of worship—and I do mean Jesus—precisely because they affirm Jesus as Lord. In this sense, high Christologies are truly ecclesial Christologies in a way that low and middle Christologies are not.

For high Christologies, it is not that Jesus is important because of the Holy Spirit, but the Holy Spirit who is important because of Jesus. It is the Holy Spirit who bears witness to Jesus and his unique saving work, not the reverse. The Spirit does not become incarnate and die for our sins. The Spirit rather attests Jesus for who he is as the mystery of Christmas, which is the mystery of God with us in human flesh. Through Word and Sacrament, the Spirit brings Christ to us and us to Christ that he might give us his very self as the One who died that we might live.[10]

A strong version of high Christology would incorporate a significant element of spirituality and ethics. Here much work remains to be done.

---

9. See "The Study Catechism: Full Version," in *Book of Catechisms: Reference Edition* (Louisville: Geneva, 2001). Available online: www.pcusa.org/resource/study-catechism-full-version-biblical-references/. I was the principal author of this document. (I should add that it was drafted by a committee.)

10. High Christologies, of course, will affirm that Jesus is truly human as well as truly divine. Again, we can see this point being made in the Presbyterian Study Catechism:

Question 34. What is the significance of affirming that Jesus is also truly a human being?

Answer: Being truly human, Jesus entered fully into our fallen situation and overcame it from within. By his pure obedience, he lived a life of unbroken unity with God, even to the point of accepting a violent death. As sinners at war with grace, this is precisely the kind of life we fail to live. When we accept him by faith, he removes our disobedience and clothes us with his perfect righteousness.

While Barth is strong on reconciliation and revelation as well as on ethics, including progressive politics and Christian mission, he is less so on worship, especially eucharistic worship, and even less so on matters of spirituality, to which he had an allergic reaction. A momentous task would be to combine Barth with the best of Jonathan Edwards and Alexander Schmemann with a strong dose of Gustavo Gutiérrez thrown in. Florovsky and Balthasar are strong on Christology, spirituality, and worship, but much less so on mission and ethics.

Nevertheless, for high Christologies, Christ is not just the source of some saving benefits other than himself, whether they be "ethical" or "spiritual" or both. As Thomas F. Torrance has especially made clear, Christ's person is inseparable from his saving work as well as from his saving benefits. His person, his work, and his benefits are indivisibly one, so that none can be had without the others. Only a person of Christ who is fully God and fully human can have this high saving significance. Only he can be the object of worship, the self-revelation of God, and the Savior of the world. If "w," then "p"; and if "p," then "w."[11]

SALVATION HAS THREE TENSES

Low, middle, and high Christologies differ on how they understand the three tenses of salvation. Asking about them is always a good diagnostic tool. How are the three tenses defined in any given Christology, and how are they thought to be related? Which aspects of salvation are thought to take place in the past tense, the present tense, and the future tense? Which tense, if any, provides the decisive locus of salvation?[12]

Low and middle Christologies are strongly oriented toward the present tense. The present tense, for them, is the decisive locus of salvation. The past is prologue, and the future is determined by what happens in the present. Salvation either takes place in the present tense or it does not take place at all.

For low Christologies, the salvation event is the ethical event, even when the ethical event is religiously motivated. These Christologies do not usually have a strong view of human bondage to sin. They tend to be relatively optimistic about unaided human capabilities. The future tense of

---

11. The terms "Christology from below" and "Christology from above" are not analytically perspicuous. A high Christology, at least, can do without them.

12. Asking about salvation's three tenses is generally a more fruitful line of analysis than asking about whether a particular view of salvation is "objective" or "subjective." It enables us to see that any reasonably developed doctrine of salvation—whether low, middle, or high—will involve both "objective" and "subjective" elements in its own distinctive way.

salvation, often conceived in terms of immortality, is thought to depend on a person's ethical performance in the present. Salvation is an ethical process that tends to be conceived in mildly or blatantly Pelagian terms.[13] Low Christologies, with their strong emphasis on the necessity of human effort, are not always sympathetic to the idea of universal salvation. John Locke, Albrecht Ritschl, and Juan Luis Segundo would be examples, each in his own way. Locke leaned toward annihilationism,[14] Ritschl remained open to the possibility of eternal damnation for the recalcitrant,[15] and Segundo regarded hell as a limit-concept (a pole, not a place), indicating the sad fate of human action if it does not take into account the life of the neighbor.[16]

For middle Christologies the present tense is again the privileged tense of salvation. The spirituality of Jesus, however it may be conceived, was forged in the past so that it can be communicated and become effectual in the present. The sanctification experienced through our receiving Christ's spirituality in order to be transformed by it is what determines the quality of salvation's future tense. Sin is seen mainly as an enslaving power rather than as violating the moral law (the low view) or as rebellion against God (the high view). Sin's influence is broken in the present as one appropriates Christ's potent spirituality.

Schleiermacher relies on a doctrine of predestination to argue that universal salvation may be probable, but he is perplexed about how or even whether it will occur. Will it be the result of a gradual process, or will it occur suddenly with the return of Christ? How might all persons come to receive a share in the spiritual blessedness of Christ, since for any given person its appropriation is what sways the future?[17]

Tillich teaches the idea of "universal essentialization," according to which all creatures, whether human or nonhuman, are potentially

---

13. Pelagius was a strong defender of the doctrine of eternal punishment for the wicked and a forceful critic of Origen. See Augustine, "On the Proceedings of Pelagius," in *Saint Augustine: Anti-Pelagian Writings* (ed. Philip Schaff; Grand Rapids: Eerdmans, 1971), 5:186–88.

14. See D. P. Walker, *The Decline of Hell: Seventeenth-Century Discussions of Eternal Torment* (London: Routledge & Kegan Paul, 1964), 93–95, 169.

15. Albrecht Ritschl, *The Christian Doctrine of Justification and Reconciliation* (Edinburgh: T&T Clark, 1900/Clifton, NJ : Reference Book Publishers, 1966), 383.

16. Juan Luis Segundo, *El infierno: un diálogo con Karl Rahner* (Montevideo, Uruguay: Ediciones Trilce, 1998). Segundo represents a mixed type, combining a high view of the incarnation with a relatively low view of Christ's saving work (along ethical, liberationist, and exemplarist lines). See also *Segundo, O inferno como absoluto menos [Hell as an absolute minus]* (São Paulo: Paulinas, 1998), 217–53. A rough translation exists online: http://ciberteologia.paulinas.org.br/ciberteologiaen/wp-content/uploads/2009/08/TheAbsoluteLess.pdf. In this material, hell as an "absolute minus" is perhaps more than just a limited concept.

17. See Daniel Pedersen, "Eternal Life in Schleiermacher's *The Christian Faith*," IJST 13 (2011): 340–57; Matthias Gockel, *Barth and Schleiermacher on the Doctrine of Election* (Oxford: Oxford University Press, 2006), 210.

included in final salvation. Estrangement from God, as opposed to enmity against God, dominates his doctrine of sin. The power of the New Being in Jesus as the Christ conquers estrangement in the midst of our universal brokenness. It does so first in the case of Jesus himself and then for all who receive this power in the present (as mediated by the picture of Jesus as the Christ). How the possibility of universal salvation is supposed to relate to those who do not receive this power through him remains unclear.[18] It would seem logically possible—and perhaps more internally consistent—for middle Christologies to deny final salvation for those who are not transformed by Jesus' spirituality in this life.

High Christologies may or may not teach universal salvation, but in recent times they have tended to leave the question open in hope. Metropolitan Kallistos Ware among the Eastern Orthodox,[19] Hans Urs von Balthasar among the Roman Catholics,[20] and T. F. Torrance among the Reformed[21] have all refused to teach definitively that some (or perhaps many) will not be saved. They hold out a hope that in the end grace will find a way to triumph over sin even in the most hopeless of cases.

In varying ways, such high Christologies differ from low and middle Christologies by placing more emphasis on Christ's finished work on the cross. The cross itself constitutes the decisive locus of salvation. Jesus Christ himself, crucified and risen, is then mediated into the present by the power of the Holy Spirit, especially through preaching and the Eucharist. Salvation as it occurs here and now is a secondary and dependent form of the one salvation accomplished on Calvary there and then. By the same token, the present-tense form of salvation anticipates what salvation will mean in the future, in its final and unsurpassable form. The Eucharist as experienced here and now, for example, may be seen as provisionally anticipating the Marriage Feast of the Lamb in the age to come.

Broadly speaking, we may say that for high Christologies, what took place on the cross, as the culmination of Christ's vicarious obedience, is definitive and constitutive. What takes place here and now through Word and Sacrament celebrates with thanksgiving the gift of the past while also anticipating what is yet to come. Finally, the promised future will bring one and the same salvation, as accomplished by the Lord Jesus Christ for the sake of the world, in its final, glorious, and unsurpassable form.

---

18. See Paul Tillich, *Systematic Theology* (Chicago: University of Chicago Press, 1963), 3:358–59.

19. Timothy (Kallistos) Ware, *The Orthodox Church* (new ed.; London: Penguin, 1997), 262.

20. Hans Urs von Balthasar, *Dare We Hope "That All Men Be Saved?"* (San Francisco: Ignatius, 1988), 187.

21. Thomas F. Torrance, "Universalism or Election?" in *SJT* 2 (1949): 313–14 (310–18).

HOW DOES SALVATION TAKE PLACE?

In summary, we may say that salvation takes place for a low Christology by imitation, for a middle Christology by repetition, and for a high Christology by expiation.

Low Christology is an exemplarist Christology, whereby salvation takes place through the imitation of Christ. All strong Christologies will need to incorporate this ethical element, but for a low Christology *imitatio Christi* is not only imperative but sufficient. As Schleiermacher rightly observed, this Christology sets up an essentially external relationship between Christ and his followers.[22]

Middle Christology is a Christology of spirituality whereby salvation takes place by repetition. The spirituality achieved by Jesus needs to be repeated in those who receive him, which means in those who enter into union with him, or who receive his saving power by faith. The basic movement is from possibility to actuality. What middle Christology preaches is new possibilities. It preaches that the spirituality of Jesus can be repeated in us. That is why Jesus serves as the prologue to salvation as it occurs in the present. Unless the spirituality that was in him is repeated in us, salvation does not take place.[23]

---

22. Low Christologies, or a least Christologies that include a robust low element, are the source for current debates about violence in the atonement. The accusation that high views of the atonement are inherently abusive is essentially moralistic. It is sometimes even suggested that all occupants in the region of high Christology are barbarians, or at least that they hold barbaric beliefs. This suggestion arguably tells us more about the accusers than the accused. If Jesus were a mere human being, as low and middle Christologies tend to assume, then the moralistic objection would be easier to sustain than if he is the incarnate Son who consents to give his life for the sake of the world. All Christologies need to work within their premises to prevent abusive misuse. The rule, however, is *abusus non tollit usum*. The antidote to misuse is not disuse but proper use. The case has not been made that high Christologies are inherently abusive. That is only how matters might seem from a rather parochial, moralistic viewpoint. See, e.g., Denny Weaver, *The Nonviolent Atonement* (2nd ed.; Grand Rapids: Eerdmans, 2011); Stephen Finlan, *Problems with Atonement* (Collegeville: Liturgical, 2005). For a rebuttal see George Hunsinger, "Nicene Christianity, the Eucharist, and Peace," ch. 8, in *The Eucharist and Ecumenism: Let Us Keep the Feast* (Cambridge: Cambridge University Press, 2008), 279–312.

23. Both middle and high Christologies can operate with a concept of "participation," but the object in which we are thought to participate would be different in each case. For middle Christologies we are thought to participate in Jesus' spirituality, whereas for high Christologies we would participate in Christ himself. Even when a middle Christology such as Schleiermacher's uses the rhetoric of vital fellowship with the Redeemer, the object of the believer's participation remains ambiguous at best, because it is not clear whether for Schleiermacher Christ's presence as the living Lord is thought to be directly "supernatural" or whether it is not rather a "naturalized" version of his God-consciousness, whose origin was "supernatural" but whose historical transmission occurs in essentially naturalistic terms through the community. For a theologian like Tillich, grace may "strike" us when we least expect it. "It happens; or it does not happen" (Tillich, "You Are Accepted," in *The Shaking of the Foundations* [New York: Charles Scribner's Sons, 1955], 161). Whether this mysterious happening is natural or supernatural is a moot point. In any case, for middle Christologies there is no real mutual indwelling of Christ in us and of us in Christ, as there would be in high Christologies. For the latter, *participatio Christi* means being incorporated into the mystical body of the risen Christ as the living Lord.

While a high Christology would not need to reject this idea entirely, it could not make it central. A high Christology regards salvation as a perfect, finished, and unrepeatable event. It is a finished work that took place on Calvary apart from us. It does not need to be repeated, nor could it possibly be repeated. It comes to us as a pure gift. It needs be acknowledged, received, partaken of, and confessed, but the one thing it cannot be is repeated. To try to repeat the unrepeatable would be the height of folly. Because grace is new each morning, salvation in Christ makes itself present in ever new forms while always remaining essentially the same.

The expiation of sin on the cross and the accompanying defeat of death by death are Christ's gift of himself to us. He takes our sin and death to himself and gives us his righteousness and life. He breaks the power of sin, because he has done something that we most needed but that only he himself could do. He has borne the terrible consequences of our guilt before God, and in his person he has borne them away. Having made himself one with us in his death, he now makes us one with himself in new life.

A high Christology preaches actualities and not mere possibilities. It moves from the indicative to the imperative. It shows us how much God has loved us in Christ by pointing us to the cross (the indicative), and on that basis calls us to repent and believe (the imperative). High Christologies therefore represent a break not only with the cruelty of moralism, but also with the tragic delusion of salvation by spirituality. For a high Christology, what salvation in Christ means, if it is to take place at all, is the justification of the godless and the resurrection of the dead.

WHAT IS THE STATUS OF JESUS CHRIST?

For a low Christology, Jesus is exemplary but not unique. For a middle Christology, he is unique but not exclusively unique. And finally, for a high Christology, he is not just unique but exclusively unique, because he is unique in kind.

We can elucidate these points by asking two more questions: Is Jesus Christ materially decisive for salvation? And is he logically indispensable to it?[24]

Generally speaking, for a low Christology, Jesus is neither materially decisive nor logically indispensable. What is materially decisive are his religious and moral teachings. He may be a supreme example of them, but

---

24. For these analytical questions I am indebted to Bruce Marshall, *Christology in Conflict: The Identity of a Savior in Rahner and Barth* (Oxford: Blackwell, 1987).

he is not logically indispensable because the teachings and their enactment could exist without him. That is what Schleiermacher had in mind when he remarked that low Christologies tend to give us little more than natural ethics and natural theology as derived from reason alone. As suggested by Kant, Jesus functions in these Christologies mainly as a moral symbol.

For a middle Christology, Jesus is materially decisive but not logically indispensable. He is materially decisive because the spirituality he communicates to others needed first to be achieved in his own life. But he is not logically indispensable, because there is no good reason why this same sort of spirituality might not be achieved and transmitted by another. Schleiermacher is the great exception here, because he made Jesus logically indispensable by grounding his identity as the second Adam in the virgin birth. Modern liberal theology almost never followed him in this move, however. One of Tillich's most sympathetic interpreters, for example, wrote an essay wondering whether for Tillich Jesus was necessary for Christology, by which it was meant whether he was necessary for salvation as grounded in the spirituality of the New Being.[25] The answer was a hesitant no. If Jesus is merely the means to the end of spirituality, then spirituality is more important than Jesus, and spirituality is where you find it.[26]

For a high Christology, Jesus is both materially decisive and logically indispensable. Since no one else will ever be God incarnate, he is logically indispensable; and since no one else will ever die for the sins of the world, he is materially decisive. For high Christologies, Jesus is an exclusively unique person who accomplished an exclusively unique work.

HOW IS THE CROSS UNDERSTOOD?

The last formal issue to be mentioned is the saving significance of the cross. This is another diagnostic question of great illuminating power. Low, middle, and high Christologies differentiate themselves by the significance they ascribe to the cross.

For a low Christology, the cross is exemplary in status. It shows that Jesus was both extremely noble and self-consistent, because he was willing

---

25. John Powell Clayton, "Is Jesus Necessary for Christology? An Antinomy in Tillich's Theological Method," in *Christ, Faith and History: Cambridge Studies in Christology* (ed. S. W. Sykes and J. P. Clayton; Cambridge: Cambridge University Press, 1972), 147–63.

26. It seems that for a theologian like Tillich, spirituality (the New Being) is an intrinsic good while Jesus the Christ is an instrumental good (i.e., the picture of Jesus as the Christ). To claim the "finality" of Jesus the Christ is to claim that as a means to the highest good he is "unsurpassable." He could in principle be equaled, however, by some other means to the highest good. He himself is not "final and universal"; only that to which he witnesses is final and universal. See Tillich, *Systematic Theology*, 1:15–16, 132–35.

to die for his ideals. Low Christologies are therefore sometimes developed as martyr Christologies.

For a middle Christology, the cross is understood as an ordeal. It shows that even in extremis Jesus maintained his spiritual connection with God. As Tillich put it, he remained transparent to the Ground of his Being. For Tillich, he sacrificed himself as Jesus, as a mere particular person, to himself as the Christ, to his spiritual office as the Bearer of the New Being. For Schleiermacher, by contrast, as we have seen, the cross is not really necessary to Jesus' saving significance. His God-consciousness was severely tested by it, but it was already everything that it needed to be without it. The idea of the cross as a spiritual ordeal has ancient roots in Theodore of Mopsuestia and the Antiochene school of Christology.

Finally, for a high Christology, Jesus did something for us by his death that his life could not have accomplished without it. As we have seen, for this view, the cross is the site of the world's reconciliation with God. "God was in Christ reconciling the world to himself" (2 Cor. 5:19). "He made him to be sin who knew no sin so that in him we might become the righteousness of God" (2 Cor. 5:21). I do not know how to understand these New Testament verses, and those like them, apart from the ideas of expiation, substitution, participation, and exchange. Expiation, because he bore our sin and bore it away. Substitution, because he died in our place that we might live. Participation, because it is only in union with him by grace through faith that we are made to be righteous in God's sight. And finally, exchange, because he took our desperate plight to himself and gave us his righteousness and life.

Only a high Christology can make these biblical affirmations, because only a high Christology sees Jesus as fully God and fully human in one and the same person, without separation or division, and without confusion or change. Any different view of his person, as modern theologies amply attest, will give us a very different view of his saving work. The high mystery of our salvation from sin and death depends entirely on the high mystery of Christ.

CHAPTER 3

THE HUMILITY OF THE SON OF GOD

KATHERINE SONDEREGGER

JESUS CHRIST IS the Way, the Truth, and the Life. The aim of this paper, indeed of the Christian life as a whole, is to explicate, unfold, and praise this matchless truth. Such truth is worthy of a whole life—an intellectual life, certainly, for it forms the highest and most mysterious, saving reality of Truth itself. But this truth is worthy of a practical human life, too, of every human life, because it—more properly, Jesus Christ as Truth—is the Truth that ennobles human life, guides it in paths of righteousness, and raises it, even now, even in this darkness, to Eternal light, the Radiance of God's glory. The Truth and Life that is Jesus Christ is also a Way, the Way: his is the path of humility and lowliness, the King manifested in great meekness. Such humility veils—and in just this way, manifests—the Deity of our Lord, who comes in this mode and manner, this Way of Being, which is Truth in the state of humility, the pilgrim's way in this poor exile of ours. Jesus Christ, the Incarnate Truth, is the world's Savior. He it is who comes for this, and this alone: to give his life as a ransom for the many. No other life does he lead but this, to be perfect and whole Redeemer, and his knowledge is just this, perfect and saving Truth.

Looking on the heart, Jesus Christ is Judge, the True Judge. His is the human life fit for this work; his is the majesty that comes from union with Eternal Truth. His is the Deity, perfect and whole, that comes—descends—with the Spirit of Blessing, from the Father of Lights, the Word of Truth and of Life. Never apart from his Spirit, One with this Spirit of Life, yet distinct, matchless, inimitable, the Truth that is Jesus Christ incarnates into a life that will break apart the kingdom of death, break into the stronghold of the Father of lies. Jesus Christ comes into this world, its Savior, as a pilgrim enters into the City of David, lowly, abreast a donkey, the peasant's ride; he makes an entrance fit for a Child borne on a manger's straw; yet triumphant, borne too on the praises of Israel, a *victorious* entering into the rejection and torment and cruelty and death that is our lot. In his Passion, Jesus Christ is the obedient Son, active even in his humility, True even in the darkening falsehood of the world, Life even in our insatiable lust for death. He is *for us* in just this way, our Pioneer and Perfecter, our Ransom and Final Adam. Life and Truth enter into death, and from it, like a seed that breaks forth into a great harvest, a Kingdom is established, the Kingdom of the lowly Prince of Peace, the Ruler of the City of the River of Life. This is the Truth of Jesus Christ—this, the glorious and saving and hidden Truth of the whole world.

That Jesus Christ is the Way, the Truth, and the Life is a revelation given and confessed in Holy Scripture. The verse belongs to the Gospel of John, to that dense section of teaching material scholars have termed the Farewell or Supper Discourses, the solemn gateway in the Fourth Gospel to the betrayal and suffering of Christ. Characteristic of John is the Jesus depicted in this night of fellowship and of treachery, a Jesus filled with consolation, instruction, and commandment, teaching, even in the midst of a danger that presses down on him, the truths about the work he was given to do, and the One who sent him into the world for just this hour, to suffer and to do. The Supper Discourses unfold in a stately measure; time seems to open out leisurely while the Teacher leads the disciples through the mysteries of the Father's working and abiding in the Son. "Let not your hearts be troubled," Jesus counsels in these chapters, and indeed the entire atmosphere kindled about this Speaker during this last meal takes on an air of unhurried solemnity and command. Jesus speaks as One whose sight is fixed on another horizon, a distant shore, while his disciples grasp after his freighted terms and directions only indistinctly and with deep confusion. In this darkened room, the shadows lengthening, Jesus appears in this Gospel remarkably alone, the sole Light, the sole center of Peace, while his disciples are in chaos and covered by the night. He is here himself the stranger, the alien wayfarer "not of this world"; only after their Easter commissioning will his disciples conform to their Master in this way, too, strangers in a hostile world, a world lying under falsehood.

An inclusio brackets the Supper Discourse: Judas Iscariot, the betrayer, brings about the night where no one can work, he alone grasping what hour has come, while the other disciples can give voice only to growing confusion and bewilderment. And at the end of this discourse, Judas, not Iscariot, speaks for the whole when he still cannot understand the Way and Truth Jesus conveys: "What can have happened," Judas asks, "that you mean to disclose yourself to us alone and not to the world?" Jesus stands at an oblique angle to every question raised this night. To Judas he replies, "Anyone who loves me will heed what I say." A response, surely, but hardly an answer. This oblique angle characterizes the whole: Jesus sublime, majestic, sovereign; his disciples querulous, anxious, confused. Christ's Peace is not the world's; his Truth not recognized, either by these alarmed disciples or by the silken worldliness of Pilate; his Way not discerned or followed or even glimpsed in the chaos that swirls around this Passover room, so near the Kidron Valley and its garden there. Two planes intersect and divide. Barth wrote of Christ in the early Romans commentary,[1] and we may say the same of Christ in the Supper Discourses. The danger menaces just outside these walls, the clubs and swords. Satan has entered into the closest circle, and the chaos that is his work, the unmaking of creation that is *his* hour, penetrates into even this dwelling place, the Teacher with his small band, a Master with the towel and the stooping down of a slave, the Life that can only love to the end, the bitter end.

Into the center of this conflict belongs the verse that anchors the whole: "I am the Way, the Truth, and the Life." Drawing to himself the great announcement to Israel of God's own Reality—"I AM has sent me to you"—Jesus reveals at the hour of death his own Reality, Truth: I AM the Truth. His is the Truth that leads into Life, a Life that can emerge only along a Way, a manner and mode and road, that ascends to the Father but only by descending first to Paschal slaughter and burial in another's tomb, a downward Way that can only mark the humility of the Lamb of God, the crucified King who has overcome the world.

Now, in these stately verses from John we have received a teaching of Christ's Person and work that mirrors many of the forms and dogmatic themes theologians have discovered in the great kenotic hymn of Philippians 2 and the stark, austere, and compressed Passion narratives of Matthew and Mark, saturated as they are by desertion, deep silence, and desolation.

---

1. Karl Barth *The Epistle to the Romans* (trans. E. Hoskyns; Oxford: Oxford University Press, 1975), 29: "In this name [Jesus Christ our Lord] two worlds meet and go apart, two planes intersect, the one known and the other unknown."

Very powerful Christologies have been built from these other sources; the great names of Calvin, Luther, and Barth are associated with this work. But we have reason in our day to consider reaching beyond the Synoptic Gospels to St. John for a Christology of authority and sublimity and very deep humility.

We cannot ignore the Synoptic Gospels, of course! Our own summary of Christology given above echoes events and teachings integral to the Gospels of Matthew, Mark, and Luke. But these themes are taken up in a new form in the Gospel of John—a fresh commentary is offered on these events, and they are bathed by a Light that descends from another realm. (As you can see, I have accepted an ordering of the Gospels that carries broad scholarly support: the Synoptic Gospels as the earlier works, the Fourth Gospel as an elaboration and commentary on them.) In the Fourth Gospel we are shown a Christology of Divine Truth come to earth, a Radiant and Glorious Truth that penetrates into a darkened world, our world that knows only timid truths, fragmented polemics and posturings, a truth only for our kind. It may be that in our day John's Christology speaks a fresh word about Truth as universal, a common blessing for the whole of creation, joining earth to heaven, philosophy to theology, the light of reason to the Light of the Gospel. But heaven is also joined to earth: John's Gospel points us to a Christology of Truth, God's Truth, that also truly *descends*, incarnates, and veils itself deep in the earth and makes its home here. Truth manifests itself; it shines. It illumines, irradiates, ennobles every eye. This Light is content to bathe the entire world, suffusing all creation beyond every Church, every nation and partisan and sect, the One Truth—Augustine says so well—by which we see all truths.[2] The Christology of the Fourth Gospel may teach us, in our day, how the boldness of final and universal Truth takes the form of humility and hiddenness, a Truth that does not coerce but rather frees, does not sit at the table commanding, but bends down to serve. "Christ plays in a thousand faces, beautiful in limbs not his," Gerard Manley Hopkins says; John's Gospel shows us how.

We begin with the claim, fresh from the Supper Discourse, that the Deity of Jesus Christ is Truth. Reading with the eyes of the Church, we take the great I AM statements of the Fourth Gospel to be about God— they are proclamations, manifestations, of Divine Reality. In John 14:6, Jesus teaches a threefold character of the Divine Nature Incarnate: that it

---

2. A favorite theme of Augustine's. For an early example, see his *Soliloquies*, Book 2, esp. ch. 15.

has a mode or direction—the Greek is *hodos*—an incommunicable existence as Truth—*aletheia*—and power and effective reality, Life—*zoe*. We are not far here from the exceeding mystery of Trinity, the threefold Reality of the One God. But the Triune mystery being unveiled in this passage is its Incarnate form, the Truth that lives among us, full of grace, and the source of Eternal Life. Thus are joined the two great dogmas of the Church, Trinity and Incarnation, and we must keep both mysteries in view as we meditate further on Christ's teaching in John.

Principally we confess here that the Second Person of the Trinity, the Word that will become flesh, is Truth. To make that confession is to speak in Augustinian and scholastic fashion; it is to knit together Scriptural idiom with the great Hellenistic fabric of the ancient world. In this great ancient tongue, Truth is not simply a property of certain propositions— that the whole, say, is greater than a part—nor simply a state of affairs for which sufficient evidence can be marshalled—that Abraham Lincoln was President of the United States in 1862. Truth, to speak in this ancient way, is more substantial, more exalted and transcendent, than that reached even by the scholastic "correspondence theory of truth." This time-honored definition of truth is an epistemic category—the "adequation of concept to reality," to cite Thomas Aquinas's celebrated treatment of knowledge in the *Summa Theologica*.[3] Truth as transcendent and substantial also supersedes truth as "fact," the events and laws that hold good in our world, and in a practical and commonsense way, are true. The substantial Form of Truth radiates far beyond human knowledge as "justified true belief," to borrow one classic philosophical definition—far beyond the evidence of our senses or the deliverances of our reason. Truth, the ancients would say, simply is: Truth in the end is Reality, Being Itself, lit up from within by its own surpassing Rationality.

Now to speak in this way is so foreign to us moderns, so odd really, that we must feel something like time-travellers when we depict Truth with this kind of metaphysical heft. We seem to be able to label it only with an ironic grammatical expression: Truth with a "capital T." Because it is so alien to us, we reach for historical tags for this teaching: it is, we say now, the "Platonic doctrine of truth," and in just this way give it an honorific—or if our tastes run in this style—a condemnatory place on the shelf of old ideas. We consider it under the prevailing historicism of our day: it is the way some intellectuals of another day and time spoke

---

3. Thomas Aquinas, *Summa Theologica* Prima Pars, Q 16, a. 1, where Thomas comments on Augustine's substantial definition of truth in Soliloquies 2, ch. 5.

and thought and ordered reality. So familiar is this kind of historicism that we turn a blind eye to its presence in our current theological judgments. "Hellenism," we say, was the "philosophical thought-form" of the ancient Doctors of the Church; or, more polemically, the "religion of the ancient Mediterranean," as Robert Jenson would put this complaint;[4] or the "construction of reality" favored by Roman rhetoricians, and free to be replaced by constructions more persuasive or morally useful than theirs.

Now I should be quick to say here that I do not reject historical judgments nor deny the implacable truth that cultures vary, as do their language and concepts of everything that matters. Surely we would have little regard for the creation and peoples the Lord God has made were we to blind ourselves to the many and varied ways peoples of old have spoken of reality itself. Yet we have not entered far into the School of Truth if we have not faced what ancient thinkers have faced, not as "thought-form" nor "social construct," nor less as "ideology," but rather as truth-claim we must acknowledge or reject. Ancient theology is not in fact a "model" to be traded in or up, but rather a confession and argument about Reality Itself. Of these arguments about Reality, Augustine's claims about Truth—his so-called "Platonism"—should have deepest hold, I say, on our intellectual respect and be seriously considered as the strongest candidate for our theological assent. In his early reckoning with historicism and the Bible, Karl Barth exhorted us in his celebrated Preface to *The Epistle to the Romans* to practice the highest "loyalty" with authors of the past, to look not at them or beyond, but *with* them, wrestling alongside them for the truth they set out to find.[5] I propose that we take the substantial doctrine of Truth to be such a confession, a profound wrestling with the Johannine Christ and his Divine-Human Life as Truth. We begin with the essential attributes of the metaphysical Doctrine of Truth.

Truth possesses reality all its own; it is "substantial"—something like a thing, a "substance," to borrow the complex idiom of Aristotle; yet far

---

4. Robert Jenson, *Systematic Theology* (New York: Oxford University Press, 1997), 1:7. "The 'natural' knowledge encompassed in it [classic theology] was thought to be a body of knowledge about God and his intentions not intrinsically dependent on historically particular divine dispositions, and therefore properly the common property of humanity. In fact, however, this body of theology was as historically particular as any other set of theological proposals: it comprised a part of the theology that Greek religious thinkers, pondering the revelations claimed for Homer and Parmenides, had provided for the cultus of Mediterranean antiquity as it became religiously homogeneous, the part that the church's fathers also found themselves able to affirm."

5. Karl Barth, *The Epistle to the Romans*, preface to the 3rd ed. 17: "The question is whether or not he [the commentator] is to place himself in a relation to his author of utter loyalty.... Anything short of utter loyalty means a commentary *on* Paul's Epistle to the Romans, not a commentary so far as is possible *with* him—even to his last word."

beyond it too. It is in the world; it inheres in and animates all our earthly truths; yet it is not exhausted by them, nor is it simply a collection of them. Truth is that ineffable, sublime Light by which we see and judge anything else to be true, the means and measure by which any earthly reality is granted status as true. For that reason we best speak of Truth as Eternal or Timeless, though it participates in a world of change and becoming, it most properly lies beyond them, transcends them, and in just this way, inhabits Eternity. Eternal Truth "stands behind" our historical, cognitive, and empirical truths; it is not the *Object* of our knowledge—we do not see it directly—but is rather the *Subject*, the Transcendent Agent by which all things are shown and manifested and made true. Truth is that haunting good, that treasure and pearl, that lies buried in every earthly fact, that shimmers at the very boundary of every ordinary discovery, and calls every seeker to look further, to lift up one's eyes, to move beyond this truth and that, to the Source, the Fullness, the Immeasurable from which each thing draws breath. In famous eloquence, Augustine speaks of his encounter with the created world, its beauty and harmony: these things say to him, he reports in his *Confessions*, we are not God; but God made me.[6] Just so this tradition teaches us to say about Truth: our little truths are not God; but Truth Eternal made me.

Now just this is what we mean when we say God. Truth just is God in this sense. It is eternal, permanent, unchanging; It does not depend on the creaturely events, laws, and judgments that are true but rather is their Source and Measure; It is not itself material, yet It orders and ennobles matter and bodies; It is not exhausted by the truths that characterize earthly life, yet It can be expressed in them. Truth Itself is not known whole and entire in this life and by our finite minds, yet in every discovery we encounter it, in every insight and deep reflection we rely upon It, in every act of contrition and renewal we call upon It, and embrace It as our end. As God himself, Truth is Sublime. It is not an Object, neither inert nor lifeless, yet It is Objective, Real without measure, constraint, or contingency. It is Omnipresent, a genuine Universal in a world of becoming, confusion, change, and error. Truth is Omniscience: It is what is known and the Means by which it is known, Perfect, Whole, Entire. The Form of Truth, Truth Itself, exhibits the essential properties of the Divine Nature: It is the Being of God as Inexhaustible Rationality and Wisdom and Light.

---

6. Augustine, *Confessions* (trans. R. S. Pine-Coffin; Baltimore: Penguin, 1961), book 10.6. p. 212. "I spoke to all the things that are about me, all that can be admitted by the door of the senses, and I said, 'Since you are not my God, tell me about him. Tell me something of my God.' Clear and loud they answered, 'God is he who made us.'"

Truth, however, although wholly and completely God, remains One Form of God's existence; there are Others. Truth is not the Form of the Good, though It to be sure is an Ineffable Good. Nor is Substantial Truth Oneness, even though Truth as Ultimate, Transcendent, and Eternal can only be One. (In saying this I show myself persuaded by Duns Scotus's doctrine of the Formal Distinction: Divine Perfections differ from one another not just in our minds but in God's Reality, though God remains utterly Simple, One, Complete.) Moreover, Truth, to speak in the language of the ancient dogmas, is a *Divine Person*; It is an "Incommunicable Existence of the Divine Nature," to borrow Richard St. Victor's definition for our own ends.[7] When we consider the other great properties or perfections of the Divine Reality—Almighty God's Goodness or Unicity—we encounter the Forms or Subsistences of Deity, God's existence as Person. We need not develop an argument for a threefold Personal Being of God; indeed in my theology we could not. Trinity, I say, is Divine Mystery and dogma, given to us in Holy Scripture and the deliverances of the early Church; we do not prove or "demonstrate" it. Like Truth Itself, Trinity is Sublime, not contrary to but above reason, Hyper-rational and Super-celestial, and again, like Substantial Truth, the full and worthy goal of all our intellectual striving.

Now these Persons, the One, the True, the Good, exist each and altogether as God, and these Persons bear relation One to the Other. This relation does not lie behind God but rather simply is the Divine Reality: the Persons are Identical to One Another, yet Distinct. This odd relationship, Unique to Deity, is what some scholastic theologians called Conversion. The Persons are "convertible" One with Another: Truth is convertible with Goodness; these in turn are convertible with Oneness. And these Three convertible with Being, Being Itself, the Sublime, Ever Rich, Majestic Reality that is God. Now those familiar with scholastic doctrine will recognize the language I have used here without comment: it is the grammar of the Transcendentals, those ineffable predicates of Being that accompany, measure, and give rise to every category of reality, in this world and beyond.

Rooted in Aristotle's *Categories*, the scholastic Doctrine of the Transcendentals equipped the Christian mind to contemplate with great technical sophistication the relation of Divine Persons to Divine Being, and

---

7. Richard St. Victor, *De Trinitate*, book IV, ch. 18. English translation: *Trinity and Creation* (ed. B. T. Coolman, D. M. Coulter; Hyde Park, NY: New City Press, 2011), 282.

the Divine Reality to the creatures It has made, and ordered, and saved. The relation of God as Creator to creatures, the relation that perfects and ennobles and trues them, I shall call the "Transcendental relation," and it is the unique and glorious work of the Creator to illumine, elevate, and consecrate his creatures in this way. In the Transcendental Relation, God *descends* to his creatures, enters down into them, their creaturely truths and unity and blessings; but he is not exhausted by them. These two relations, Conversion and Transcendence, do not exhaust the Divine Concourse with creatures.

More wonderful still, Almighty God is Savior, Helper, Deliverer. He is the Incarnate One, mighty to save, and in this glorious work of sheer grace, Almighty God has also this relation: Incarnation, Embodiment as the world's Savior, the *Salvator Mundi*. So we are led by our reflections on Transcendent Truth to these three: Conversion, Transcendence, Incarnation. Almighty God is Tri-Personal, each Person convertible One with Another; God is Creator, Exemplar of Transcendent Perfections, transcendentally communicated to creatures; and God is Incarnate Lord, embodied as Savior of the world. In Jesus Christ, the One Truth of God is incarnate as Savior and Lord, the surpassing Good given to a sorrowing world.

Our scholastic vocabulary now in order, we can turn once again to a Christology drawn from the Gospel of John, guided and illumined by Scripture's light of Truth. We need not work out here how we might regard the delicate interplay of scholastic or rational argument to Scriptural revelation, but rather content ourselves with the axiom that Holy Scripture grounds and guides Christian doctrine, and because Truth is One, the Light of Scripture will not contradict, make otiose or irrational, nor wall itself off from the truths given, upheld, and ordered by the True and Good God. To borrow once again from the insights of Karl Barth: the relation between our truths and the One Truth given by Holy Scripture is "asymmetrical" and ordered, so that revelation governs reason, even while upholding it and exemplifying it as creaturely truth. (It is this lesson and not many others thought to be taught there that I see elaborated in Barth's landmark study, *Fides quaerans Intellectum*.) So we turn our eyes once again explicitly to Christology, to this Good God, the Truth Incarnate who is Jesus Christ.

Consider, first of all, that the dogma of the Incarnation teaches us that it is a Person who becomes flesh, not simply God *simpliciter*, God in his Ineffable Being and Nature. In my view, much theology of the Incarnation pays scant attention to the salience of the Divine Person, rather than

Divine Nature per se, as Subject of the Incarnation. In this I follow traditional Reformed instincts in Christology: the Person of Jesus Christ is the Subject and thus, Object, of our study and worship and contemplation; not the "natures," divine and human. Reformed polemicists such as Turretin advance this point strenuously under the rubric of opposing "abstract natures" in Christological reflection. Such danger he spotted in Lutherans, who gave extended consideration to such Alexandrian themes in Christology as the *communicatio idiomata*, the communication of properties in Christ's natures, and most especially—and dangerously, Turretin said— to the *genus majestaticum*, the form of majesty of Christ's human nature, joined as it was to his Divine, omnipresent Nature.[8] Now I should be quick to say that I think there is much to be admired in the *genus majestaticum*, and indeed believe that Christ's humanity was glorified by its union with Divine Truth. But I feel special sympathy for the Reformed position here as I believe it points our attention and worship to the very heart of the Incarnation, the descent of the Divine Person into human flesh.

The Divine Person incarnates, bringing the Deity concomitantly; Truth Itself descends, entering into the world, becoming Incarnate Word for us. Now I put matters in this rather elaborate way because there are high matters of doctrine caught up in small places when we speak of the Incarnation of the Word of God. Is it the case, we might ask, that any Person of the Trinity could have been Incarnate? This is the scholastic form of this high matter in doctrine. If so, some modern theologians charge, we have learned nothing about God's Personal Life by the Incarnation, nothing distinctive, particular, and unique about the Second Person of Trinity. The great names of Rahner, Pannenberg, and Jenson come to mind here.

Yet, others say, were we to say that *only* the Son could be incarnate, we would affirm a difference, a salient difference, in the Deity of the Son—and that is the ancient and never fully eradicated danger of Arianism in Christology. I believe the danger of subordinationism in Christology—Jesus Christ as the lesser, visible god—is a persistent, abiding, and deeply caustic impulse in Christology; and by no means an ancient impulse alone. So great is this danger that I believe we Christians should teach that the Divine Oneness, the Divine Goodness as well as Divine Truth, could have been Incarnate; and that also to the saving health of the

---

8. Francis Turretin, *Institutes of Elenctic Theology* (trans. G. M. Giger; Phillipsburg, NJ: Presbyterian & Reformed, 1994), 13th Topic, Q 8. 1:321332. "The question concerns communication in the abstract or of nature to nature—whether the properties of the divine nature were really and truly communicated to the human nature by the hypostatical union. This the Lutherans hold; we deny."

whole world. And I do not consider this a "bare counterfactual," a claim that something could be true—perhaps logically only—but in fact is not the case. Rather, the possibility of any Person of the Trinity becoming Incarnate Lord is living, real, and metaphysical, and belongs to the proper dignity, equality, and unity of the Divine Triunity. So it must be, I believe, that Divine Truth entered into our poor frame for what Leibniz called "sufficient reason": this act of Divine condescension was not necessary but rather an act full of grace, the fitting, proper, and glorious election of Truth as the Personal Agent of our salvation. Such Truth can never be without its own Unicity nor its own Goodness—they are convertible One with Another—yet it pleased Almighty God to deliver us in the Form of Wisdom, the Plenitude of Divine Rationality, Knowledge and Word. Or, perhaps better: Divine Omniscience is the Personal Form, Incarnate for us and for our Salvation.

Now because this is true, because it is the highest Truth and the very best, we may give over our hearts and minds, our entire life, to the investigation of this Infinite Good. Why would God desire to save us through Truth, Truth Itself? Now, there can be no simple answer to this question; indeed in the high things of God, there can be only the Divine Simplicity as answer, the very Fullness, Plenitude, and Majesty of the One God, beyond all saying and all praise. So, instead of answer, there is self-offering: we offer our whole selves, our souls and bodies, to be our rational worship, our intellectual self-giving in the exploration of the very great Mystery that is Divine Truth among us.

We notice first that it is possible to be wrong about these high matters; indeed very wrong, benignly but also culpably ignorant and foolish and blind about this great Gift. It is possible to doubt, seriously doubt, deny, repudiate, scorn this Measureless Truth. Every encounter in our world tells us plainly that it can be considered a higher good, a more pleasant, yes, but also a higher *moral* good, to deny the Divine Truth, to be resolute citizens of this earth, utterly satisfied with it, fully enmeshed in this world's sorrows and puzzles and delights, and consider life exhausted by commitment to this earth and its material realms. Increasingly in our Western cultures, the old citadels and high towers of Christendom, it is fully possible, indeed in some places likely, to be wholly indifferent to Divine Omniscience and Being, to never feel, stealing over one, the Sublime Music of that Other Shore, the touch of that Light and Sweetness that can never fade away. It is possible now to belong to educated classes, to be worldly, sophisticated, and humane, without a tinge of nostalgia for the old ways of God and true religion, or haunted ever by a hollowness at the core of things, the "fear of a rustling leaf," as Calvin puts it so well,[9] when life finds its broken and violent and cruel habits laid bare. All these forms of denial of Divine Truth are possible; indeed we encounter them, when we are honest at our prayers, as possibilities sadly and all too emphatically realized, within our own very hearts and lives.

Just this we see in the life of Jesus Christ, the Saving Truth of the world. Salient to the witness of the Gospels is the truth that Jesus Christ can be and is ignored, denied, rejected and scorned, doubted and ridiculed and misunderstood, by outsiders—by the powerful, the sophisticated and worldly—but even more by insiders, by the crowds and bystanders, by his family and townspeople, by his disciples, by the Twelve. "Show us the Father and we will be satisfied," Philip says, betraying more than Judas Iscariot, more than Judas the Less, more than Peter or Pilate or Caiaphas, the error and confusion and blindness that human life, our lives, bring to the Incarnate Truth. Of course there has been and, under the grace of Almighty God, will be faithfulness, sometimes very great faithfulness, understanding and true confession among the followers of Jesus Christ; these are the saints of God, the human lives sanctified and lit up by Truth. But this is a holiness always bounded by a great darkness, the frailty, ignorance, and uncertainty that bounds our brief compass on earth. So, we must say that this odd freedom of ours over against Christ, this distance, sometimes painful, sometimes indifferent, from the Brilliant Light that is come into the world, is permitted as witness, despite itself, to the Truth that sets us free.

The Incarnate Truth comes to us in the mode and manner of humility, as the slave, bending down to those at table. Holy Scripture shows us that True, Absolute and Perfect Truth, has a Way all its own, a Path the world does not know. It can be silent; it can be hidden; it can be lowly and without domination: Divine Truth can be like this. Not a denial of Deity, not an emptying or constraint, but rather a full expression and Divine exercise of Truth is the Way of humility and hiddenness. Divine Truth is content to be the Light by which all creatures see their own truths: content to illumine all cultures with its highest and most prized goods, all learning

---

9. John Calvin, *Institutes of the Christian Religion* (ed. John T. McNeil; trans. Ford L. Battles; Philadelphia: Westminster, 1960), 1.3.2 (p. 45). "You may see now and again how this also happens to those like him [Gaius Caligula]; how he who is the boldest despiser of God is of all men the most startled at the rustle of a falling leaf [cf. Lev 26:36]. Whence does this arise but from the vengeance of divine majesty, which strikes their consciences all the more violently the more they try to flee from it?"

and science and literature and art; content to be the Subject that bathes all mind with the haunting beauty of Truth even when denied, or ignored, or hurried by on the other side. Jesus Christ comes to us in this Way.

He is content, Perfect Truth, to enter into a human life, to become a human life in such a Way that he knows only our own good, our own salvation. Jesus Christ looks on the heart; he sees us truly, as we are in all our shabbiness, yes, but also in our creaturely goodness; he is Judge, True and Exhaustive Knowledge of us and our kind. And to this end, Divine Truth will graciously bow down to and become human truth, a human life that knows only this: the food and drink that is the Father's will. Divine Truth is Omniscience, limitless, perfect, and whole; wholly Good; wholly Wise; and in its Way of humility, It is also the human life that is perfect and whole Redeemer, limited and constrained and dedicated to this one work, this one zeal, to lose nothing the Father has given him but to gather it up and raise to new life. The historical limitation of Jesus' knowledge, his growth in wisdom and stature, his seeking after the Father's will and pleasure, his own concrete and particular commandments that he gives us: these are not the denial but rather the confirmation of his Perfect Truth as human truth, saving truth. He is *for us* in just this. These traits are the communication of majesty to the human person of Christ.

Jesus Christ saves, gives Eternal Life, through his own Incarnate Truth. He reveals to us who we are: those free in the Truth but also against It. He elevates us, raises us up to the Divine Life, through our entrance into his Truth and participating in his Wisdom. Because Truth is Itself Substantial, Real, and Effective, these gifts of Jesus Christ as not merely exemplary, not merely lessons he teaches us, showing us a higher truth. No, this Truth that the Incarnate Word bestows on us is Itself God, communicated transcendentally—the Way of Descent—to fallen creatures.

We participate in Christ; this is our own sanctification and deliverance; but even more he participates in us, communicates himself in lowliness and freedom to his own flock. Jesus Christ feeds us with his own flesh, heavenly food, that is the Truth of his own abundant Life. And he lays down that Life, the Life he has in himself, to be the Sacrifice for sin, for error, for cruelty and folly, and to raise us up on the last day. Divine Truth, the Person of the Word, does not die on that Paschal Day long ago; Christ's Truth can never die. Yet It can be *joined* to death, can enter into it completely, wholly, truly, so that our death, which we never see in its fullness, can be known for what it is, the last misery of sinners, and transformed, shot through, with Eternal Life. Such Self-sacrifice, the Way of the Son of Man into the Far Country, is in just this act, made the Truth of all creaturely life: to give ourselves, and to give ourselves away is to die into the death of Christ. This is the Substantial, Saving, and Eternal Truth, the One Good Word, of every life. In all these Ways, but in so much more, infinitely more, Jesus Christ is the Way, the Truth, and the Life.

CHAPTER 4

THE OBEDIENCE OF THE ETERNAL SON

Catholic Trinitarianism and Reformed Christology[1]

SCOTT R. SWAIN AND MICHAEL ALLEN

I

One of the most interesting dogmatic theses to emerge from the twentieth century is the claim that the Son's obedience to the Father in accomplishing the work of salvation is not merely a consequence of the humble existence he assumed in the incarnation but rather constitutes his *opus proprium* within the *opera Trinitatis ad extra*, the Son's distinctive manner qua Son of executing God's undivided saving will. This thesis originates with Karl Barth, who gives it penetrating exposition in *Church Dogmatics* IV/1 §59.1, and it enjoys wide acceptance, both among those who are self-consciously indebted to Barth's theological program and among those who are not. In each instance, warrants for this *theologoumenon* are drawn from the broad New Testament witness to the one who declares: "I have come down from heaven, not to do my own will but the will of him who sent me" (John 6:38).[2]

Affirming the obedience of the only begotten Son has in many cases entailed significant revisions to classical trinitarian metaphysics. Whether in Barth's historicizing of the doctrine of God, the significance of which remains fiercely debated among his interpreters,[3] or in von Balthasar's

---

1. This essay was originally published in IJST 15 (2013): 114–34.

2. A survey of the NT witness to this theme may be found in Richard N. Longenecker, *Studies in Hermeneutics, Christology and Discipleship* (Sheffield: Sheffield Phoenix, 2004), ch. 6.

3. For an early assessment of Barth's historicized doctrine of God, see Eberhard Jüngel, *God's Being Is in Becoming: The Trinitarian Being of God in the Theology of Karl Barth* (trans. John Webster; Grand Rapids: Eerdmans, 2001). More recently, see the debate between Bruce McCormack, Paul Molnar, George Hunsinger, and others, essays of which are collected in Michael T. Dempsey, ed., *Trinity and Election in Contemporary Theology* (Grand Rapids: Eerdmans, 2011).

lavish metaphysics of trinitarian kenosis,[4] identifying obedience as the Son's personal property has led theologians to reconfigure the nature of the Father-Son relation and to reformulate traditional understandings of the divine being. In evangelical circles, revision has often meant replacing eternal generation with obedience as the Son's distinguishing personal property (usually identified as the Son's "role" in the Trinity), and adopting (a sometimes unreflective) social trinitarianism, which affirms three centers of self-consciousness and willing within the triune God.[5]

Such revisions seem inevitable in view of the history of trinitarian doctrine, where the Son's obedience is most commonly attributed to the *forma servi* that he assumed in the economy, as opposed to the *forma Dei* that he eternally shares with the Father or the personal *modus essendi* whereby he is and acts "from the Father."[6] Thus Gregory of Nazianzus states: "in his character of the Word he was neither obedient nor disobedient.... But, in the character of the form of a servant, he condescends to his fellow servants, nay, to his servants, and takes upon him a strange form."[7] Similarly Augustine: "in the form of a servant, he did not come to do his own will, but the will of him who sent him."[8] If obedience can only qualify as a human attribute within the metaphysical complex of pro-Nicene trinitarianism, as a form that is "strange" in relation to the *forma Dei*, then the apostolic witness to the Second Person's obedient saving embassy seemingly demands that dogmatics develop a more thoroughly evangelized metaphysic than that on offer in the tradition. On the basis of the apostolic witness to Jesus' divine filial obedience, we must conclude that obedience is proper to God's being, with all the metaphysical revisions that this entails.[9] Doctrinal development in this vein

---

4. Hans Urs von Balthasar, *Theo-drama* (San Francisco: Ignatius, 1998), 5:236–39.

5. Representative examples of these moves may be found in Wayne Grudem, *Systematic Theology: An Introduction to Biblical Doctrine* (Grand Rapids: Zondervan, 2000), ch. 14 and appendix 6; J. Scott Horrell, "Toward a Biblical Model of the Social Trinity: Avoiding Equivocation of Nature and Order," JETS 47 (2004): 399–421; and Bruce Ware, *Father, Son, and Holy Spirit: Relationships, Roles, and Relevance* (Wheaton, IL: Crossway, 2005).

6. This threefold classification of biblical descriptions of Christ is found throughout patristic writings. For representative examples, see Athanasius, *Orations against the Arians* 3.29–36, in *The Christological Controversy* (ed. Richard A. Norris Jr.; Philadelphia: Fortress, 1980), 87–96; Gregory of Nazianzus, *Oration* 29.18; 30.20, in *Christology of the Later Fathers* (ed. Edward R. Hardy; Louisville: Westminster John Knox, 1954), 172–73, 190–92; Augustine, *The Trinity* (trans. Edmund Hill; Brooklyn, NY: New City Press, 1991), 2:2–4.

7. Gregory of Nazianzus, *Oration* 28.6, in *Christology of the Later Fathers*, 180.

8. Augustine, *The Trinity* 1.22. Compare the above-cited quotation, however, with Augustine's comments on John 5:19 in *The Trinity* 2.5, and also with his treatment of John 5:19–30 in his *In Johannis evangelium tractatus*, helpfully discussed in Keith E. Johnson, "Augustine's 'Trinitarian' Reading of John 5: A Model for the Theological Interpretation of Scripture?" JETS 52 (2009): 799–810.

9. Thus Karl Barth, *Church Dogmatics*, 4 vols. in 13 pts. (ed. and trans. G. W. Bromiley and T. F. Torrance; Edinburgh: T&T Clark, 1956–75) (hereafter *CD*), IV/1, 192–210.

takes the form of sending the classical Catholic and Reformed trinitarian tradition packing.

The purpose of the present article is to question the seeming inevitability of this form of modern doctrinal development. Note well: we do not wish to challenge the claim that obedience constitutes the proper form of the Son's divine work in the economy of salvation.[10] We wish to challenge what is perceived to be the necessary *implication* of this claim, i.e., that affirming the obedience of the eternal Son requires a revision of traditional trinitarian metaphysics in the classical Catholic and Reformed tradition.[11] Our strategy for issuing this challenge is not primarily critical but constructive. We do not intend to engage directly the various modifications of trinitarian theology that have emerged in the wake of our modern *theologoumenon*, but to demonstrate how this *theologoumenon* fits—indeed, supremely so—within the orbit of traditional trinitarian metaphysics, and to address some of the most significant objections that might be posed against this claim in the current theological climate. In so doing, we will argue that the church's tradition of trinitarian reflection, and specifically its Thomist representation, has resources that actually enable this development to proceed (e.g., the distinction between common and proper attributes of the triune persons, the distinction between

---

10. This is not to say, however, that we endorse the lush kenotic approaches to the Trinity *in se* as proposed by Balthasar and others; for helpful concerns on this front, see Bruce D. Marshall, "The Unity of the Triune God: Reviving an Ancient Question," *The Thomist* 74 (2010): 26–31. Marshall wisely suggests that a recovery of the distinction between divine processions and divine missions enables us to avoid the "unhappy results" of Balthasar's trinitarian maneuvers (p. 30). We would add that the distinction between the common and proper attributes of the divine persons must also be recovered, as well as the necessary redoubling that must mark any faithful characterization of the particular divine persons (see below).

11. Cf. Steven D. Boyer, "Articulating Order: Trinitarian Discourse in an Egalitarian Age," *ProEccl* 18 (2009): 255–72; and Thomas Joseph White, "Intra-Trinitarian Obedience and Nicene-Chalcedonian Christology," *NV* 6 (2008): 377–402. Boyer engages some of the issues raised in the present article and argues that certain (mainly) patristic precedents provide warrant for thinking about the obedience of the divine Son. Conversely, White engages Barth's thesis and argues, from a Thomistic perspective, against the current thesis, though he does propose a reformulated version of pretemporal "obedience" of the Son (construed as a statement about the mission, though not the procession of the Son). White has expanded his case in two more recent essays: "Classical Christology after Schleiermacher and Barth: A Thomist Perspective," *ProEccl* 20 (2011): 229–63; "On Christian Philosophy and Divine Obedience: A Reply to Keith L. Johnson," *ProEccl* 20 (2011): 283–89. The *Pro Ecclesia* exchange with Keith L. Johnson and Fritz Bauerschmidt does not really move the conversation regarding this topic forward, precisely because it ranges so widely over the terrain of modern theology after Schleiermacher and Barth. For a somewhat similar attempt to understand the theological implications of the Son's economic obedience within a Thomistic metaphysics, see Michael Waldstein, "The Analogy of Mission and Obedience: A Central Point in the Relation between *Theologia* and *Oikonomia* in St. Thomas Aquinas's *Commentary on John*," in *Reading John with St. Thomas Aquinas: Theological Exegesis and Speculative Theology* (ed. Michael Dauphinais and Matthew Levering; Washington, DC: Catholic University of America Press, 2005), 92–112; cf. Keith L. Johnson, "When Nature Presupposes Grace: A Response to Thomas Joseph White, O.P.," *ProEccl* 20 (2011): 264–82: "The obedience of Jesus of Nazareth on the cross cannot be held at a distance from God, as if it does not tell us something essential about God's being as God; rather, this obedience reveals God's innermost being" (268).

the divine processions and divine missions). We envision this argument as an attempt at Catholic and Reformed *ressourcement*—neither mere repristination nor rejection of this classical tradition, but traditioned reasoning within this tradition in fresh and faithful form.

Our thesis, then, is as follows: The obedience of the eternal Son in the economy of salvation is the proper mode whereby he enacts the undivided work of the Trinity "for us and for our salvation." More fully, the obedience of the Son is the economic extension of his eternal generation to a Spirit-enabled, creaturely life of obedience unto death, and therefore the redemptive foundation for his bringing of "many sons to glory" (Heb 2:10). We will endeavor to establish this thesis in two steps. First, we will consider the relationship between the Son's eternal generation and his economic obedience following the direction of the medieval dictum: *modus agendi sequitur modus essendi* (sections II-III). Second, we will attempt to address three major objections that might be raised against our proposal: two classical and one modern (section IV).

II

As the economic extension of his eternal generation, the Son's obedience to the Father in the economy of salvation constitutes the proper filial mode whereby he executes the Trinity's undivided work of salvation. The present claim is a particular application of the more general trinitarian rule: mode of acting follows mode of being (*modus agenda sequitur modus essendi*). Attempts to follow this rule—by grounding trinitarian missions in processions or by considering God's inner-trinitarian depths prior to the economic acts that flow there from—are commonly regarded as excessively speculative, even "disastrous" for trinitarian theology.[12] Such endeavors, it is argued, transgress the boundary of evangelical revelation within which alone God's being may be known. Even among those who would affirm the aforementioned trinitarian rule regarding the ontological priority of the divine being over the divine works, it is often assumed that the order of knowing (*ordo cognoscendi*) follows an order different from that of the order of being (*ordo essendi*): first, we come to know God's works; then, we infer the nature of God's being on the basis of those works.[13] We wish

---

12. See Robert W. Jenson, *The Triune Identity: God according to the Gospel* (Philadelphia: Fortress, 1982), 125–31.

13. Bruce McCormack discusses this strategy and its attending logic in *Orthodox and Modern: Studies in the Theology of Karl Barth* (Grand Rapids: Baker, 2008), 58; and more fully in *Karl Barth's Critically Realistic Dialectical Theology: Its Genesis and Development 1909–1936* (Oxford: Clarendon, 1997), 350–58.

to dispute both perspectives, and this on the basis of the apostolic order of teaching (*ordo docendi*).

That the Son's mode of acting follows from his mode of being is not merely a statement about the order of being. As strange as it may seem to Kantian sensibilities, it is also a statement about the order of knowing insofar as the order of knowing follows the scriptural order of teaching, which in many instances presents the *identity* of the Son as propaedeutic to understanding the *action* of the Son. As Thomas Aquinas observes, the apostle John's contemplation of the Word was "full" because he was able to consider "not only the essence of the cause, but also its power":

> Since John the Evangelist was raised up to the contemplation of the nature of the divine Word and of his essence when he said, "In the beginning was the Word; and the Word was with God," he immediately tells us of the power of the Word as it extends to all things, saying, "Through him all things came into being." Thus his contemplation was full.[14]

In other words, the "order"[15] of the Fourth Evangelist's contemplative teaching is to reveal to us the *nature* of the divine Word in order that we may appreciate both the character and the consequence of his *action*. Because the Word is the Father's perfect self-communication (John 1:1), dwelling in eternal repose at the Father's side (1:18), his mission can result in the perfect revelation of the unseen God (1:18), and not simply the witness to a greater light (cf. 1:6–8).

The Gospel of Mark also provides a key example of the scriptural *ordo docendi* in this regard. Though the nature of Jesus' messianic sonship remains a riddle to human characters within the narrative until the end of the Second Gospel, the truth of his divine filiation is made known to Mark's readers from "the beginning" (Mark 1:1, 11). At the beginning, middle, and end of his gospel, Mark identifies Jesus the Messiah as "the Son of God" (1:1, 11; 9:7; 15:39),[16] as one whose filial way is "the way *of the Lord*" (1:3).[17] The structural location of these identifications within Mark's narrative lends support to Kingsbury's argument that the primary secret

---

14. Thomas Aquinas, "Prologue to the Gospel of John," in *Commentary on the Gospel of John, Chapters 1–5* (trans. Fabian Larcher and James A. Weisheipl; Washington, DC: Catholic University of America Press, 2010), 3.

15. Ibid., 3.

16. Joachim Gnilka, *Das Evangelium nach Markus* (Zürich/Neukirchen-Vluyn: Benziger/Neukirchener, 1979), 2:171.

17. On Jesus' identity as Israel's one Lord in Mark's gospel, see Richard Bauckham, *Jesus and the God of Israel: God Crucified and Other Studies on the New Testament's Christology of Divine Identity* (Grand Rapids: Eerdmans, 2008), ch. 8.

that Mark seeks to disclose to his readers is not so much the so-called "*messianic* secret" as it is the secret concerning Jesus' "divine sonship." [18] This is the secret that God knows, that Jesus knows, and that the unclean spirits know as well (1:11; 3:11; 5:7; 9:7).

This is, moreover, the secret that is not revealed to human characters in the Gospel of Mark until Jesus breathes his last on the cross. In his lordly self-offering as a ransom for many (cf. Mark 10:45), wherein he fulfills the role scripturally patterned for the beloved Son in the Binding of Isaac (the *Aqedah*),[19] the Gentile centurion comes to see what Mark has made known to his readers from the beginning: "Truly this was the Son of God!" (15:39). Mark's story of the wicked tenants thus summarizes in parabolic form the characteristic pattern of evangelical revelation: the Father *has* a beloved Son; the Father *sends* a beloved Son; and the ensuing rejection and vindication of the beloved Son constitute the *realization* of the divine counsel, a counsel graciously unveiled to us through the evangelical witness in order that we might understand that "*this* was *the Lord's* doing," and that this as the Lord's doing might be "marvelous in our eyes" (12:1–12).

To be sure, the knowledge of the Trinity rendered in the sacred writings is ectypal theology, not archetypal theology, with all the limitations that this entails. However, the distinction between these two modes of knowledge is not to be understood as a distinction between epistemology and metaphysics, or as a distinction between phenomenal form and transcendental condition. No, God reveals *both* his triune being and his action to us through his prophetic-apostolic Word. And this revelation—delivered by the divine rhetor in a form wisely suited to the needs of creaturely wayfarers[20]—enables an ectypal contemplation of the relation between trinitarian being and action as that relation obtains in its archetypal foundation. It is the Father's sovereign good pleasure to reveal unto babes both his unique knowledge of the Son and his unique knowledge of the Son's status as one fully invested with all things requisite to our salvation (Matt 11:25–27).

These assertions run contrary to contemporary assumptions about the nature of trinitarian revelation. Contrary to what is commonly supposed,

---

18. Jack Dean Kingsbury, *The Christology of Mark's Gospel* (Philadelphia: Fortress, 1983), 14.

19. See Ernest Best, *The Temptation and the Passion: The Markan Soteriology* (2nd ed.; Cambridge: Cambridge University Press, 2005), 167–72. For other associations of the *Aqedah* with divine sonship, see *Testament of Levi* 18.6–7; John 3:16; and Romans 8:32.

20. That is, a form that "imparts to us wayfarers as much knowledge of the First Principle as we need to be saved" (Bonaventure, *Breviloquium* [Works of Saint Bonaventure 9; Saint Bonaventure, NY: Franciscan Institute, 2005], 1.1.2).

Holy Scripture does not portray the economic Trinity as the more accessible starting point from which we may infer the more inaccessible depths of the immanent Trinity.[21] According to scriptural testimony, neither God in himself (*theologia*) nor God's economy (*oeconomia*) is transparent to naked reason in its fallen state. Both are "hidden" from the wise; and both are "revealed" only to babes (Matt 11:25; cf. 11:1ff).[22] The meaning of Jesus' saving work is not so transparent that it can be "read off" the surface of that work in any straightforward manner. His enigmatic work repeatedly provokes *questions*—"Who then is this . . . ?" (Mark 4:41). And answers are not easily found by either friend or foe in the evangelical narratives, or among auditors of the apostolic preaching (cf. 1 Cor 1:23). An understanding of Christ's person, and the appreciation of his work that accompanies it, is a gift rendered by the Gospels' "omniscient" narrators, who invite Spirit-illumined readers to understand the nature of Jesus' messianic action by unveiling to them the secret of his messianic identity.

Some will no doubt worry that the present line of thought threatens to saddle the biblical portrait of the drama of the divine persons (*dramatis Dei personae*) with an alien "essentialism" or "substance ontology." We will address this worry in due course. The point to emphasize at present, however, is that the apostles, not Aristotle, direct theological reason to the conclusion that mode of operation follows mode of being.[23] T. F. Torrance well summarizes the canonical pointers in this regard:

> What Jesus is toward us he is antecedently and eternally in himself, in God. . . . Were that not so, the revelation we are given in Christ would not have eternal validity or ultimate reality. That is why the fourth Gospel

---

21. In emphasizing the present point, we do not wish to deny that when it comes to the knowledge of God available through general revelation there is a sense in which the "things visible" are better known to us than the "things invisible" (Rom 1:20), and therefore that "from the effect we proceed to the knowledge of the cause" (Thomas Aquinas, *Summa theologiae* [trans. Fathers of the English Dominican Province; 5 vols.; New York: Benziger Bros., 1948], 1a.2.2). However, when it comes to the knowledge of the divine persons, and therefore to a knowledge that is not available to us through general revelation, Scripture's characteristic order of teaching is to instruct us concerning the identity of the divine persons in order that we may fully appreciate the action of the divine persons, which would otherwise remain shrouded in mystery. As Aquinas says, a revealed knowledge of the divine persons is necessary if we are to arrive at right ideas about the divine acts of creation and salvation (*Summa theologiae*, 1a.32.1).

22. In this (and only this) sense, we move from economy to theology, namely, that God's revelation of his own identity occurs within his works (and, thus, that revelation is a part of the divine economy). So the context of our knowledge is surely an economic form of knowledge—we did not exist or commune with God apart from this economy. But the shape of revelation within the economy—following the scriptural order of teaching—moves from his identity in himself (*theologia*) to his works (*economia*).

23. For further exegetical argumentation along these lines (see, e.g., John 13:14; 15:26; 16:28; 17), see Gilles Emery, "*Theologia* and *Dispensatio*: The Centrality of the Divine Missions in St. Thomas's Trinitarian Theology," *The Thomist* 74 (2010): 543–44 (515–61).

begins with the wonderful prologue of the eternity of the Word in God, for it is from the eternal God that the Word proceeded, and all that follows in the Gospel—all that Jesus said and was in his dependence as the incarnate Son upon the Father—goes back to and is grounded in that eternal relation of Word to God within God. Similarly, the Epistle to the Hebrews begins its exposition of the high priestly work of Christ by teaching that the Son came forth from the Godhead, the Son by whose word all things were created. It is that Son who came and manifested himself, and now in the incarnation stands forth as the divine servant Son to fulfill his work of atonement in entire solidarity with man, eternal Son of God though he was. But all that Jesus did has reality and validity just because it rests upon that eternal relation of the Son with the Father, and therefore reaches out through and beyond the span of years in his earthly ministry into God. Again, what Christ is in all his life and action, in his love and compassion, he is antecedently and eternally in himself as the eternal Son of the Father.[24]

It is this canonical directive that must be our guide for dogmatic reasoning, regardless of what metaphysical ancillaries might have proven or may yet prove serviceable to theological reason in bearing witness to the one who came to do his Father's will.[25]

III

In light of the general rule that guides our discussion, it is time to focus our attention directly and specifically on the relationship between the Son's eternal generation and his economic obedience.[26] As we will see, the Son's distinctive *modus essendi* as the Father's only begotten determines his distinctive *modus agendi* as the Father's obedient emissary. In order to appreciate this link between the Son's eternal generation and his economic obedience, it will be helpful to turn a brief glance to John's initial characterization of the Word in his Prologue as the one "through whom" all things were created. This brief glance, along with the important trinitarian concept that it provides, will serve us well as we then turn to consider one of the primary biblical texts that establishes our thesis: John 5:19–30.

---

24. T. F. Torrance, *The Incarnation: The Person and Life of Christ* (ed. Robert T. Walker; Downers Grove, IL: InterVarsity Press Academic, 2008), 176–77.

25. For further criticism of the strategy of deriving necessary transcendental arguments about God's being *in se* from God's actions *pro nobis*, see Nicholas M. Healy, "Karl Barth, German-Language Theology, and the Catholic Tradition," in *Trinity and Election in Contemporary Theology*, 240–43.

26. Space forbids a lengthy discussion and defense of the doctrine of eternal generation. For a fuller consideration of the doctrine, see John Webster, "The Eternal Begetting of the Son," in *God without Measure: Essays in Christian Doctrine* (London: T&T Clark, forthcoming).

Aquinas begins his commentary on John 1:3 with a statement that recalls his earlier observation about the "fullness" of John's contemplation of the Word: "After the Evangelist has told of the existence and nature of the Divine Word, so far as it can be told by man, he then shows the might of his power."[27] In other words, having considered the Word's subsistence in relation to God ("the Word was with God") as God ("the Word was God" [John 1:1]), John considers the Word's agency in creation: "All things were made through him" (1:3). Aquinas immediately rules out a number of possible misinterpretations of this verse, including, for example, those that would take the Word as God's "instrumental cause" for creating (as when a man makes a bench "through" a hammer) or that would take the Word as God's "efficient cause" for creating (as when a man makes a bench "through" the direction of a carpenter). He also surveys a number of orthodox alternatives by which the meaning of this verse might be illumined. Among these, he mentions Augustine's suggestion that texts like 1:3 reflect a common pattern of trinitarian "appropriation" whereby the undivided work of the Trinity *ad extra* is considered to flow "from" the Father "through" the Son "in" the Spirit.[28] He concludes, however, that John's statement in verse 3 should not be taken as mere appropriation but rather as referring to a mode of divine agency that is "proper to the Word." Creation comes into being "through" the Word because the Word performs the common trinitarian work of creation in a manner consistent with his distinctive mode of being: "the statement, 'The Father does all things through the Son,' is not [mere] appropriation but proper to the Word, because the fact that he is a cause of creatures is had from someone else, namely, the Father, from whom he has his being."[29]

Aquinas's interpretation of the Word's activity in John 1:3 invokes the theologically fundamental distinction between what is "common" versus what is "proper" to the persons of the Trinity. According to this distinction, whereas the Father, the Son, and the Spirit hold in common one divine substance, wisdom, will, and activity, they are distinguished from one another by the unique or proper way in which they hold the one divine substance, wisdom, will, and activity in common. Each person's

---

27. Aquinas, *Commentary on the Gospel of John*, 30.

28. Ibid., 30–34. Cf. also Gregory of Nyssa: "there is one motion and disposition of the good will which proceeds from the Father, through the Son, to the Spirit" (*An Answer to Ablabius: That We Should Not Think of Saying There Are Three Gods*, in *Christology of the Later Fathers*, 262).

29. Aquinas, *Commentary on the Gospel of John*, 34. Cf. Aquinas, *Summa theologiae*, 1a.39.8: "the word *by* is not always appropriated to the Son, but belongs to the Son properly and strictly, according to the text, *All things were made by him* (Joh. i. 3); not that the Son is an instrument, but as the *principle from a principle*."

unique or proper way of being God is indicated by the personal names themselves: i.e., Father, Son, and Spirit. As Aquinas observes, the personal names "signify *processions*,"[30] or what we may characterize as "communicative relations." It is proper to the Father to father/beget the Son and, with the Son, to spirate/breathe the Spirit. It is proper to the Son to be fathered/begotten of the Father and, with the Father, to spirate/breathe the Spirit. And so forth.

These processions, it must be emphasized, do not involve the coming into being of a product by a producer (contra Arianism). Nor do they involve the transition of a cause into a new relationship with its effect (contra modalism). The processions of the divine persons are *internal* to the simple and indivisible being of God.[31] They signify the unique ways in which the one divine being of God is eternally *communicated* to or by each person within the eternal fecundity that is the triune God.[32] With reference to the Son, eternal generation thus refers to "a communication of essence from the Father (by which the Son possesses indivisibly the same essence with him and is made perfectly like him)."[33] The Son's personal property—that which is "proper" to him and to him alone within the Godhead—is finally nothing other than the *subsisting filial relation* in which he eternally stands to the Father *as a receptive communicant* in the undivided divine essence.[34]

This discussion sheds light on the nature of a "proper" act. For Aquinas, a proper act is one in which a divine person "acts in the distinct mode of his relation with the other persons" in carrying out the undivided work of the Trinity.[35] This concept, found not only in the Dominican master but also in Reformed orthodoxy, is a direct application of the principle,

---

30. Aquinas, *Summa theologiae*, 1a.27.1.

31. Ibid., 1a.27.1.

32. Ibid., 1a.27.5.

33. Francis Turretin, *Institutes of Elenctic Theology* (ed. James T. Dennison Jr.; Phillipsburg, NJ: Presbyterian & Reformed, 1992), 1:293. Cf. Aquinas, *Summa theologiae*, 1a.41.3.

34. Because it is intrinsic to God's eternal and wholly realized identity, the Son's "receptive" stance in relation to the Father involves no passivity or passibility. The Son has "by nature what he receives" (*Summa theologiae*, 1a.33.4). Gilles Emery states: "The fact of being begotten does not imply any 'passivity' in the Son. To be begotten is an action. And when one says that the Son 'receives the divine nature from the Father,' this 'reception' refers to a pure relation of the Son to the Father; this is the relation of origin" ("The Immutability of the God of Love and the Problem of Language concerning the 'Suffering of God,'" in *Divine Impassibility and the Mystery of Human Suffering* [ed. James F. Keating and Thomas Joseph White; Grand Rapids: Eerdmans, 2009], 69 n. 139). For further reflection, see Aquinas, *Summa theologiae*, 1a.27.1–3.

35. Gilles Emery, *Trinity, Church, and the Human Person: Thomistic Essays* (Naples, FL: Sapientia, 2007), 129. In contrast to a "proper" act, an "appropriated" act or attribute is one that is common to all three persons but that, because of its affinity with a particular person, leads "to a better understanding and knowledge of what is proper" (Bonaventure, *Breviloquium* 1.6.1).

modus agendi sequitur modus essendi. When it comes to the external works of the Trinity, there can be no distinction between the works of the persons. Because they share one being, they also share one principle of action. Nevertheless, there can be—indeed must be—distinctions *within* the common work of the persons in their external operations.[36] Because they share one being in tripersonal modification, they also share one principle of action in tripersonal modification. Thus Zacharias Ursinus: "The works of the Trinity are indivisible, but not in such a sense as to destroy the order and manner of working peculiar to each person of the Godhead."[37] With respect to the Son, therefore, the concept of a "proper" act requires us to confess that "as the Son is from the Father, so he works from the Father."[38] As the Son's proper mode of being God consists in the pure relation wherein he receives his being from the Father, so the Son's proper mode of acting as God consists in the pure relation wherein he receives his actions from the Father. "Receptive filiation" is the Son's proper mode of being and acting as the one true and living God.

How does this concept illumine the matter under discussion? We may gather an answer to this question by looking at John 5:19–30, a text devoted to vindicating Jesus' right to perform his Father's works. The occasion for this defense is a Sabbath healing described earlier in John 5, which has provoked the ire of "the Jews" and which Jesus defends as a work performed in imitation of his Father: "My Father is working until now, and I am working" (5:17). To the minds of his accusers, Jesus' defense amounts to claiming that God is "his own/proper Father [πατέρα ἴδιον]," and therefore that he is "equal with God" (5:18). The *topos* of this passage, then, concerns the way in which Jesus' *manner of working* follows from the fact that God is his *proper Father*.

In expanding on this theme, Jesus juxtaposes two claims that, taken together, present a perennial challenge to Johannine interpreters. The first claim is that Jesus does *nothing* on his own initiative, but *only* what he sees the Father doing. The second claim is that Jesus, in following his Father's lead, does *everything* that his Father does. "The Son can do nothing of himself, unless it is something he sees the Father doing; for whatever the Father does, these things the Son also does in like manner" (John 5:19).

---

36. Cf. Eugene F. Rogers, *After the Spirit: A Constructive Pneumatology from Resources Outside the Modern West* (Grand Rapids: Eerdmans, 2005), 11–16, 45–46.

37. Zacharias Ursinus, *Commentary on the Heidelberg Catechism* (trans. G. W. Williard in 1852; repr. Phillipsburg, NJ: Presbyterian & Reformed, n.d.), 120.

38. Turretin, *Institutes*, 1:282. The principle on which the above-quoted statement rests: "the order of operating follows the order of subsisting" (1:281).

The problem facing interpreters is not that the Fourth Gospel would make a claim implying the Son's inferiority to the Father. Nor is it that the Fourth Gospel would make a claim implying the Son's equality with the Father. Taken in isolation, these claims could be understood as evidence of different redactional layers or of authorial inconsistency. The problem facing interpreters is that the Fourth Gospel makes these seemingly contradictory claims *within the same context*.[39] Indeed, John 5:19 insists that the former claim is the basis for the latter claim: *because* the Son always only follows the Father's initiative, he always performs all of the Father's works. The remainder of the passage focuses on one particular divine work that Jesus performs with his Father at his Father's behest, a work that far outstrips any Sabbath healing (5:20), and whose power to perform lies uniquely with the one true God of Israel: the power to kill and to make alive (5:21–29).[40] John 5:19–30 concludes by recapitulating the principle that explains Jesus' *modus operandi*: "I can do nothing on my own. As I hear, I judge, and my judgment is just, because I seek not my own will but the will of him who sent me" (5:30).

Some interpreters take our text's description of the Son's manner of working as solely indicative of his humble mediatorial state. John Calvin provides a rather forthright example of this interpretive stance. He regards both the Arian and the orthodox exegesis of John 5:19–30 as misguided. According to Calvin, the Arians were wrong to conclude that this text revealed the Son's inferiority to the Father, while the orthodox fathers were wrong to conclude that this text revealed the Son's distinctive personhood as one who is simultaneously "from the Father" and yet "not deprived of intrinsic power to act." Indeed, the Genevan reformer considers a properly trinitarian exegesis of this passage as "harsh and far-fetched." In his judgment, the proper subject matter of John 5:19–30 is the Son of God only "so far as he is manifested in the flesh."[41]

Although our text makes undoubted reference to the Son's mediatorial

39. C. K. Barrett summarizes the interpretive challenge thusly: "those notable Johannine passages that seem at first sight to proclaim most unambiguously the unity and equality of the Son with the Father are often set in contexts which if they do not deny at least qualify this theme, and place alongside it the theme of dependence, and indeed of subordination" (*Essays on John* [Philadelphia: Westminster, 1982], 23).

40. See Deut 32:39; Isa 26:19; with Marianne Meye Thompson, *The God of the Gospel of John* (Grand Rapids: Eerdmans, 2001), 118–19; and Andrew Lincoln, *Truth on Trial: The Lawsuit Motif in the Fourth Gospel* (Peabody, MA: Hendrickson, 2000), 210.

41. John Calvin, *Commentary on the Gospel according to John* (trans. William Pringle; repr. Grand Rapids: Baker, 1998), 1:198–207. On Calvin's general reticence toward trinitarian reflection in his exegesis of classical trinitarian proof texts, see Arie Baars, *Om Gods verhevenheid en Zijn nabijheid: De Drie-eenheid bij Calvijn* (Kampen: Kok, 2004), 291–308.

office—he executes judgment "because he is the Son of Man" (John 5:27), the eschatological agent of God and representative of God's people (cf. Dan 7:13–14)—an interpretation such as Calvin's seems too modest, and that for at least three reasons. First, the language used in the present passage to describe the manner in which the Son follows the Father's initiative, thereby performing the Father's works, is exactly the same as the language used in later passages to describe the manner in which the Spirit follows the initiative of the Father and the Son, thereby performing their works. As the Son can do nothing ἀφ' ἑαυτοῦ, but only what he sees the Father doing (John 5:19), so the Spirit will not speak ἀφ' ἑαυτοῦ, but only what he hears: drawing forth the truth from the common wellspring of the Father and the Son and distributing it to Jesus' disciples (16:13–15). Because this language cannot be reduced to the Spirit's *forma servi*—he has no *forma servi* (!)—so it should not be reduced to the Son's *forma servi*.[42]

Second, part of the rationale provided in this passage for the Son's manner of working is that the Son is doing the bidding of the one who "sent" him (5:30; cf. 4:34; 5:36–37; 6:38–39; etc.). And, as Augustine long ago observed, the Son's sending *precedes* his incarnation.[43] The Son is "consecrated and sent *into* the world" (10:36). Thus, the manner in which the Son works in obedience to his Father's commission is not simply indicative of the state in which he assumed the *forma servi* but of his own proper filial relation to the Father, which precedes his assumption of the *forma servi*.

Third, and most telling for the present discussion, John 5:19–30 follows the pattern of contemplative reflection exhibited in John's Prologue, which, as we have seen, grounds the might of the Word's power (1:3) in the Word's existence and nature (1:1). The Son shares the Father's unique and sovereign power to *give life* to those he will (5:21) because he shares the Father's unique and sovereign power to *live*: he has "life in himself." Moreover, both of these powers that the Son shares with the Father are powers that he has received from the Father: "as the Father has life in himself, so he has granted the Son also to have life in himself" (5:26; cf. 10:18). And therefore: Just as it is the Son's proper *modus essendi* to have life in himself and to have it from the Father who begets him, so it is the Son's proper *modus agendi* to raise the dead and to have this power from the Father who sends him.

In light of the preceding discussion, we are in a position to appreciate how the concept of a "proper" act illumines the topic at hand. The fact

---

42. Augustine, *The Trinity* 2.5.
43. Ibid., 4.27.

that the Son does not pursue his own initiative but that of the Father who sends him is not merely a consequence of the human form he assumed in the incarnation. The fact that the Son does not do his own will but the will of the Father who sent him is a consequence of his distinctive *modus agendi*, which follows from his distinctive *modus essendi*. More briefly stated: "'to send' implies authority, and 'to be sent' implies subordination to authority [*subauctoritatis*] *in the order of eternal production in the Godhead*."[44] In this sense, the obedience of the Son to the Father who sends him constitutes the Son's *opus proprium* within the undivided *opera Trinitatis ad extra*.[45]

IV

The present interpretation raises at least three questions, two that would have animated classical theologians (and that continue to animate contemporary theologians working faithfully within the Thomist tradition), the other that animates modern theologians. The first question is: Does such an assertion threaten to divide the common will of the Father and the Son into two separate wills? Thomas Joseph White suggests that this is the primary problem with the obedience of the eternal Son: "It would seem that one must forfeit either the notion of a unity of will in the persons, or reinterpret Barth's notion of a distinction of persons in God derived through obedience."[46] White suggests that the Son's identity as Wisdom—his unique personal nature—manifests his possession of a "unique spiritual Will" that is shared with the Father; indeed, he argues that this is part and parcel with Athanasius's polemics against those "fourth century 'Arian' or anti-Nicene theologians [who] appealed to New Testament examples of the obedience of Christ in order to argue for a preexistent, ontological subordination of

---

44. Bonaventure, *Breviloquium* 1.5.5 (italics ours).

45. Based on his eternal procession from the Father and the Son, should we also speak of the Spirit's "obedience" to the Father and the Son in the economy of salvation? One might take our methodological approach and say that the sending of the Spirit implies that his "proper" identity ought to be spoken of as enacting obedience in the economy or as receptive filiation within the immanent life of the Godhead (the latter effectively introducing two sons within the Godhead). In other words, one might take our approach as potentially undermining our ability to differentiate the proper characteristics of the second and third persons of the Trinity. But this is precisely why the *filioque* is important: the Spirit's movement in both the missions and the processions is similar to the Son's movement, yet the Spirit is sent by and proceeds from the Father and the Son, whereas the Son is sent by and proceeds from the Father *alone*. Even if one took the proposal that this double procession occurred from the Father through the Son, there would still be a distinction in terms of proper relational characterizations. We do not claim to be expressing everything there is to say about the Son's properties (or for that matter the Spirit's), which exceed his receptive relation to the Father, but we do believe that our approach in no way nullifies the theologian's ability to distinguish Son from Spirit.

46. White, "Intra-Trinitarian Obedience and Nicene-Chalcedonian Christology," 393.

the Logos to the Father."[47] In light of White's concern, then, we must ask: Does the obedience of the eternal Son undermine the shared divine will? Aquinas asks and answers this question in his commentary on John 5:30:

> But do not the Father and the Son have the same will? I answer that the Father and the Son do have the same will, but the Father does not have his will from another, whereas the Son does have his will from another, i.e., from the Father. Thus the Son accomplishes his own will as from another, i.e., as having it from another; but the Father accomplishes his will as his own, i.e., not having it from another. Thus he says: I am not seeking my own will, that is, such as would be mine if it originated from myself, but my will, as being from another, that is from the Father.[48]

In other words, the Son's obedience to the Father in the work of salvation is not indicative of a *second will* alongside that of the Father but of *the proper mode whereby Jesus shares the Father's will as the only begotten Son of the Father.*[49]

The second question is similar, though it involves a worry about divine omnipotence rather than the divine will. White suggests that the obedience of the eternal Son "risks to undermine the intelligibility of Barth's own soteriological affirmation that God, in order to save us, must in no way be alienated from his own prerogatives of omnipotence in the Incarnation."[50] White argues that obedience necessitates a lack of power—so that "one can therefore plausibly suggest that either we must rethink the claim to eternal obedience in the Son, or else qualify in important ways any affirmation of his omnipotence."[51] Are these the only options or is there an excluded middle? It seems at this point that the answer is to go deeper into the Thomist tradition rather than further from it. Indeed, the notion of redoubling/reduplication (*redoublement*) provides the conceptual framework for finding our way to the middle excluded by White's question. The eternal Son exists receptively as one whose self-existence (*auto-theos*) and Almightiness are granted to him by the Father.

As noted above, trinitarian theology requires the use of two forms of attribution: essential characteristics (common terms) and personal characteristics (proper terms). Gilles Emery has employed the term "redu-

---

47. Ibid., 389.

48. Aquinas, *Commentary on the Gospel of John*, 294–95; cf. Aquinas, *Summa theologiae* 1a.42.6, ad 3. For analysis of Aquinas's exegesis of John 5:30, see Thomas Joseph White, "The Voluntary Action of the Earthly Christ and the Necessity of a Beatific Vision," *The Thomist* 69 (2005): 497–534.

49. This is not to deny dyothelitism, but to suggest that the Son's obedient human will is determined by and expressive of his obedient divine will, i.e., the proper filial manner in which he executes the undivided divine will *ad extra*. See Aquinas, *Summa theologiae* 3a.48.6.

50. White, "Intra-Trinitarian Obedience and Nicene-Chalcedonian Christology," 389.

51. Ibid., 395.

plication" or "redoubling" (*redoublement*) to describe this linguistic rule impelled by the very nature of a trinitarian metaphysics: "To express the Triune mystery, one must use two words, two formulas, in a reflection that joins the aspect of the unity of the divine substance to that of the distinction of the persons."[52] The Son is divine, yes, but he is also generated eternally from the Father. The first characteristic is common and can be attributed to the Father and Spirit as well; the second trait, however, is proper to the Son and can be attributed to him alone. It is crucial, though, to see that, while different proper terms can be applied only to one or another divine person, some terms must be applied to every divine person. In other words, there is no genuine knowledge of a divine person unless the common (what it means to be the one God) is matched by the proper (what it means to be the one God in this distinctive relation).[53]

Aquinas argues that this redoubling is impelled by biblical language *a la* John 5:

> Hilary calls our attention to the remarkable relationship of the passages so that the errors concerning eternal generation can be refuted. Two heresies have arisen concerning this eternal generation. One was that of Arius, who said that the Son is less than the Father; and this is contrary to their equality and unity. The other was that of Sabellius, who said that there is no distinction of persons in the divinity; and this is contrary to their origin.
>
> So, whenever he mentions the unity and equality, he immediately also adds their distinction as persons according to origin, and conversely. Thus, because he mentions the origin of the persons when he says, "the Son cannot do anything of himself, but only what he sees the Father doing" (John 5:19), then, so we do not think this involves inequality, he at once adds: "for whatever the Father does, the Son does likewise." Conversely, when he states their equality by saying: "For just as the Father raises the dead and grants life, so the Son grants life to those to whom he wishes," then, so that we do not deny that the Son has an origin and is begotten, he adds, "the Father himself judges no one, but he has given all judgment to the Son."[54]

Again, exegesis pressures Aquinas to speak in redoubled language about God: witness about the common life of the Trinity matched by testimony to the proper characteristics of each divine person.

---

52. Gilles Emery, *The Trinitarian Theology of St. Thomas Aquinas* (trans. Francesca Aran Murphy; New York: Oxford University Press, 2007), 46.

53. Denial of this point necessarily leads to the view that the divine essence is a fourth person behind the three divine persons, inasmuch as it requires the divine essence be viewed in an abstract and discrete manner. The divine essence is abstract, if that means shared by the three, but it is always concrete in the person of Father, Son, or Spirit, and never existent in any other way.

54. Aquinas, *Commentary on the Gospel of John*, 282.

With respect to the issue at hand, the obedience of the eternal Son is not contrasted with his omnipotence; rather, the two exist at one and the same time.[55] Steven Boyer shows that this approach was followed by Athanasius in his opposition to the Arians and anti-Nicenes:

> The Son eternally comes from and is eternally dependent upon the Father, yet in a manner that in no way entails the Son's being less than or inferior to the Father. To connect dependence to inferiority is in fact to accept an axiom of Neoplatonism that the fourth-century Fathers who knew Neoplatonism best went out of their way to reject.... And by rejecting this tenet of Platonism, the Fathers paved the way for a full-blooded Trinitarian tradition that speaks over and over not of equality *or* order, but of equality *and* order.[56]

As possessor of the divine nature, the Son is equal in power to the Father; as receptive to the Father's gift of life in himself, the Son is ordered to the Father. There is a personal order in the one true God. Almighty power is possessed by all three divine persons, though it is not possessed in the same way. The Son possesses Almightiness (omnipotence) in a filial way, whereas the Father possesses this same attribute in a paternal manner. Equality cannot be reduced to the opposite of order; rather, equality is the setting for a triune order. So the Son's obedience cannot be construed as a reason to jettison the traditional Christian claim that the Son is omnipotent.[57] Indeed, the wind and the waves hearken to his Almighty power, even as his power is exercised to do the will of the one who sent him.

Briefly it should be noted that the two questions raised by Thomas Joseph White are joined together in a single Johannine text, where the

---

55. For further analysis of how "redoubling" language of the Trinity affects theological reflection on the economy of salvation, see Gilles Emery, "The Personal Mode of Trinitarian Action in St. Thomas Aquinas," *The Thomist* 69 (2005): 31–77. For reflection on how an eternally generated person can share the one divine essence, see John Duns Scotus, *Lectura* I, d.2, p. 2, q. 3 (no. 148) in *Opera omnia*, vol. 16 (ed. C. Balić et al.; Città del Vaticano: Typis Polyglottis Vaticanis, 1960).

56. Boyer, "Articulating Order," 260. While affirming Boyer's substantive point, we will not follow him in employing the terminology of "dependence" to describe the obedience of the eternal Son. We will use the term "receptivity" to remain closer to the biblical language of receiving life in himself as a gift from the Father and, thus, to avoid adding terminology that may unduly distort. Given its widespread usage in psychological and therapeutic contexts, and cognizant of the influence of therapeutic conceptualities in the wider contemporary scene, "dependence" likely brings unhealthy conceptual baggage to the analogical task—baggage not present in use of the less frequently employed term "receptivity."

57. A related worry would be whether or not the obedient Son and his commanding Father can share in the divine simplicity given those distinct personal properties. It is crucial to see that the patristic use of the doctrine of divine simplicity took the form of nuancing its pagan employment to fit this kind of trinitarian grammar, on which see Andrew Radde-Gallwitz, *Basil of Caesarea, Gregory of Nyssa, and the Transformation of Divine Simplicity* (New York: Oxford University Press, 2009).

will and power of Christ are yoked with his obedience to his heavenly Father. "For this reason the Father loves me, because I lay down my life that I may take it up again. No one takes it from me, but I lay it down of my own accord. I have authority to lay it down, and I have authority to take it up again. This charge I have received from my Father" (John 10:17–18).

Jesus here notes that his cruciform obedience flows from his own will and authority. First, he affirms that he surrenders himself to the forces of death "of my own accord" and not because something "takes it from me." Second, he reminds the disciples that he has authority to lay down his life and then to take it up again. The term employed here, ἐξουσία, refers to authority or power. Jesus reiterates that his willed submission to the forces of death is not powerlessness—it is the very exercise of authoritative power. Aquinas comments:

> In Christ, his own nature and every other nature are subject to his will, just like artifacts are subject to the will of the artisan. Thus, according to the pleasure of his will, he could lay down his life when he willed, and he could take it up again; no mere human being can do this. . . . This explains why the centurion, seeing that Christ did not die by a natural necessity, but by his own [will]—since "Jesus cried again with a loud voice and yielded up his spirit" (Matt. 27:50)—recognized a divine power in him, and said: "Truly, this was the Son of God" (Matt. 27:54).[58]

Yet the concluding line pairs the will and power of the incarnate Son with the charge (ἐντολή) received from his Father. The Father commands the Son—there is an economic receptivity here. But the charge and command of the Father does not negate the will and power of the Son—in trinitarian fashion, they are both not only valid affirmations but necessary aspects of the gospel proclamation. Jesus wills to do this, and he exercises real authoritative power in so doing, and yet his action in this regard is according to his Father's charge.[59] There is a noncompetitive relationship between his powerful will and his submission to the paternal will.[60] Karl Barth will say of the incarnate Son: "This man wills only to be

---

58. Aquinas, *Commentary on the Gospel of John, Chapters 6–12* (trans. Fabian Larcher and James Weisheipl; Washington, DC: Catholic University of America Press, 2010), 203.

59. See Augustine, *Homilies on the Gospel of John* 31.6 (trans. Edmund Hill; Hyde Park, NY: New City Press, 2009), 508–9.

60. Paul N. Anderson refers to John's "dialectical reflection" regarding a number of "Christological tensions" in his "On Guessing Points and Naming Stars: Epistemological Origins of John's Christological Tensions," in *The Gospel of John and Christian Theology* (ed. Richard Bauckham and Carl Mosser; Grand Rapids: Eerdmans, 2008), 311–45.

obedient—obedient to the will of the Father, which is to be done on earth for the redemption of man as it is done in heaven."[61]

The third question, mentioned already in section II, ranges over wider formal territory than the previous two and can be stated as such: Does not all this smack too much of a "substance ontology" or an unevangelized "essentialism"? Once again, we may address this question with the aid of the Fourth Gospel. John's Prologue distinguishes the being of the Word, who "was [ἦν]" and "is [ὤν]"[62] with the Father (John 1:1–2, 18), from the becoming that characterizes the economy of creation and redemption (1:3, 6, 10, 14, 17 [ἐγένετο throughout]).[63] In so doing, the Prologue exhibits "the doctrine of Jews and Christians which preserves the unchangeable and unalterable nature of God" over against the changeable nature of the creature (cf. Ps 102:25–27).[64] This being of the Word, however, is not that of Aristotle's Unmoved Mover, who remains forever locked in self-enclosed contemplation over against all worldly becoming. This is the being of the Word who lives in eternal active relation to his Father and who temporally extends his active relation to others[65] through his obedient execution of the Father's will. The only begotten Son "who is at the Father's side" (1:18) came into the world in order to extend to his creatures "the right to become children of God" (1:12).

The distinction between the divine procession (in this case, the eternal generation of the Son) and the divine mission (the obedient journey of the Son) is crucial if the doctrine of the obedience of the eternal Son is to be affirmed within a classical Catholic and Reformed trinitarian metaphysics. However, the purpose for distinguishing the unchanging being of the Word *ad intra* from his temporal work *ad extra* is not to separate the only-begotten Son from those who become his brothers and sisters but to indicate both the character and the consequence of the mission whereby his Father becomes their Father, and his God becomes their God (cf. 20:17).

With respect to the character of his mission: distinguishing the Son's eternal generation, which is natural and necessary to his identity, from his saving mission, which is contingent to his identity, preserves the free and

---

61. Barth, CD, IV/1, 164; cf. Matthew Levering, "Augustine and Aquinas on the Good Shepherd: The Value of an Exegetical Tradition," in *Aquinas the Augustinian* (ed. Michael Dauphinais et al.; Washington, DC: Catholic University of America Press, 2007), 237.

62. John 1:18 is possibly an allusion to Exod 3:14 [LXX]. Cf. Rev 1:8; 4:8; etc., which certainly are.

63. See Barth's exegetical comments on John's Prologue in *CD*, I/2, 159–60.

64. Origen, *Contra Celsum* (trans. Henry Chadwick; Cambridge: Cambridge University Press, 1980), 1:21.

65. In a mode suitable to their creaturely natures, which does not elide his singular identity as the Father's μονογενής.

gracious character of his mission.[66] Only because the economy "was not motivated by any need of completion in the being of the Word" can it be an act of "incomparable generosity." [67] "The Word became flesh," according to Athanasius, "not for the sake of any addition to the Godhead"—or as he elsewhere states, "not for the Word's own improvement"—"but so that the flesh might rise again." [68] Furthermore, the distinction between eternal generation and economic action preserves not only the free and gracious character of the Son's economic action but also its distinctive filial shape. The counsel to collapse eternal filiation into temporal mission,[69] a counsel designed to secure the real presence of the second hypostasis in history, ironically threatens to rob that history of that which makes it distinctive as the history of the only begotten. Apart from Jesus' metaphysically prevenient identity as God's beloved Son, we are unable to appreciate that which distinguishes his embassy from the embassy of the Father's other servants (Mark 12:1–12). Apart from his metaphysically prevenient identity as God's own/proper Son, we are unable to appreciate that which distinguishes his gift from the Father's other gifts (Rom 8:32). To put the point positively, Jesus' identity as God's beloved Son is what characterizes his actions as properly divine filial actions and not simply as actions of an unspecified historical agent.

With respect to the consequence of the Son's mission: distinguishing eternal generation from economic mission not only preserves the free and gracious character of the economy as an economy of the Father's only begotten Son, but it also helps us appreciate the final cause of the Son's economic mission, which is to communicate to creatures a distinctly creaturely fellowship in the Son's eternal relation to the Father, through union with him who is the head and firstborn of many brothers and sisters.

---

66. Space forbids unpacking the metaphysical distinction between "natural/necessary" and "contingent." For the sense that we assume, a sense common among Reformed Orthodoxy, see Andreas J. Beck, "Gisbertus Voetius (1589–1676): Basic Features of His Doctrine of God," in *Reformation and Scholasticism: An Ecumenical Enterprise* (ed. W. J. van Asselt and Eef Dekker; Grand Rapids: Baker Academic, 2001), 205–22; and more extensively J. Martin Bac, *Perfect Will Theology: Divine Agency in Reformed Scholasticism as against Suárez, Episcopius, Descartes, and Spinoza* (Leiden: Brill, 2010).

67. Robert Sokolowski, *The God of Faith and Reason* (Notre Dame, IN: University of Notre Dame Press, 1982), 34.

68. Athanasius, "Letter to Epictetus" 9, in John McGuckin, *Saint Cyril of Alexandria and the Christological Controversy* (Crestwood, NY: St. Vladimir's Seminary Press, 2004), 387. Cf. McGuckin's comments on Cyril of Alexandria's understanding of the incarnational economy: "The Logos had no need whatsoever to appear as man. Two deductions thus followed inevitably about the incarnation: firstly that it was an entirely free act of divine power, a Charis, or gracious act, of God. Secondly, that it was not for God's benefit but for mankind's" (ibid., 184).

69. Thus recently Robert Jenson: "The Father's sending and Jesus' obedience *are* the second hypostasis in God" ("Once More the *Logos asarkos*," *IJST* 13 (2011) : 133).

The fact that the Son's relation to the Father is always fully realized and that our filial relation to the Father is a matter of temporal realization, "an economy for the fullness of time" (Eph 1:10; cf. 1:5), does not mean that the divine and the human offspring of the Father are related to one another as Platonic form to temporal shadow. Rather, the Son's economic obedience is the means whereby other sons and daughters come to share as creatures in his filial relationship to the Father. Economic obedience, the free and gracious overflow of the Son's natural and necessary generation, is the means whereby the Son's prayer is answered: "I desire that they may be with me where I am" (John 17:24; cf. 17:5; 1:1, 18). "He put on our flesh," says Calvin, "in order that having become Son of Man he might make us sons of God with him."[70] This "with him" is the final cause of the Son's economic embassy and the manner in which his perfect filiation comes to perfect ours.

V

We have seen that a trinitarian account of divine agency must speak by means of redoubling or reduplication. This is not the same as speech by means of appropriation, which tethers particular actions to specific divine persons (normally for reason of emphasis). Rather, this is to say that the external works of the Trinity are indivisible (*opera ad extra trinitatis indivisa sunt*), though they are performed by all the persons in their own person-specific, "proper" ways. Dogmatic reasoning aids exegetical reflection in noting the common and proper engagement of each triune person in the various acts of the divine economy. Only in such a context does the obedience of the eternal Son fit within a classical Catholic and Reformed trinitarian metaphysics—such a setting, however, is surely in need of this doctrinal development if it is to remain attentive to the ever-fresh prompting of the living Word.

We have seen that the divine missions do extend the divine processions: the mode of being shapes the mode of acting. The relationship between processions and missions indicates that the divine freedom and self-sufficiency is not to be misinterpreted as divine aloofness; quite the contrary, as Dorner says, "God is not merely distinct from the world, but also distinguishes Himself from it and it from Himself ... and by means of this absolute inalienable Self-mastery of God, this doctrine opens the prospect that God can communicate Himself to the world without det-

---

70. I. John Hesselink, *Calvin's First Catechism: A Commentary* (Louisville: Westminster, 1997), 23.

riment."[71] God is not aloof, and the shape of his communicative communion with us is not arbitrary. The three persons act in union with one another—indivisibly—though this union is a harmony of activity drawing on the active manner proper to each person. Thus, the divine missions flow forth and manifest the temporal extension of the divine processions; the relations of origin within the triune life, then, shape the form of external works performed by the three persons together.

One such extension has been considered here: the eternal Son's receptivity in relation to his Father—expressed poignantly in the doctrine of eternal generation—provides the metaphysical and relational grounds for his free enactment of his proper activity in the divine economy, which is time and again characterized as obedience. T. F. Torrance is surely right: "The perfect human life of Jesus in all his words and acts reposes entirely upon the mutual relation of the Son to the Father and the Father to the Son."[72] Yet this "mutual relation" must be clarified in ways appropriate to the canonical witness, which identifies that relation as one of receptivity and obedience on the part of the incarnate Son. Making use of distinctions deep within the classical trinitarian tradition—hammered out by Thomists and drawn upon by classical Reformed thinkers—we have shown that the obedience of the eternal Son is not only exegetically necessary, but dogmatically coherent with the classical trinitarian metaphysics of this Catholic and Reformed tradition.

---

71. Isaak A. Dorner, *A System of Christian Doctrine* (trans. Alfred Cave; Edinburgh: T&T Clark, 1885), 1:338. Cf. the exposition of Richard Sibbes: "God's goodness is a communicative, spreading goodness.... If God had not a communicative, spreading goodness, he would never have created the world. The Father, Son and Holy Ghost were happy in themselves and enjoyed one another before the world was. But that God delights to communicate and spread his goodness, there had never been a creation nor a redemption" ("The Successful Seeker," in *Works of Richard Sibbes* [ed. Alexander B. Grosart; Edinburgh: Banner of Truth, 1983], 4:113).

72. Torrance, *The Incarnation*, 127.

CHAPTER 5

EXALTATION IN AND THROUGH HUMILIATION
Rethinking the States of Christ

JEREMY R. TREAT

IN JOHN'S ACCOUNT of the life of Christ, everything moves toward the climactic "hour" when Jesus, being "lifted up" on the cross, is truly being enthroned in glory (John 12:23–32; cf. 3:14; 8:28). The cross becomes not only the center of redemptive history, but the fulcrum on which the logic of the world is turned upside down. Shame is transformed into glory, foolishness into wisdom, and humiliation into exaltation. The cross becomes the throne from which Christ rules the world.[1]

The kingship of Christ on the cross, however, has been downplayed by

---

1. Although this theme may be most explicit in the gospel of John, the crucifixion as enthronement has been recognized as an important feature of all four Gospels. Matthew: W. D. Davies and D. C. Allison, *A Critical and Exegetical Commentary on the Gospel According to Saint Matthew* (ICC; Edinburgh: T&T Clark, 1988), 3:598–606; D. A. Carson, "Matthew," in EBC (ed. Frank Gaebelein; Grand Rapids: Zondervan, 1995), 8:573; Mark: Joel Marcus, "Crucifixion as Parodic Exaltation," JBL 125 (2006): 73–87; Frank Matera, *The Kingship of Jesus: Composition and Theology in Mark 15* (SBLDS; Chico, CA: Scholars, 1982); Luke: Yong-Sung Ahn, *The Reign of God and Rome in Luke's Passion Narrative: An East Asian Global Perspective* (Leiden: Brill, 2006); Joshua Jipp, "Luke's Scriptural Suffering Messiah: A Search for Precedent, a Search for Identity," CBQ 72 (2010): 260; John: Mavis Leung, *The Kingship-Cross Interplay in the Gospel of John: Jesus' Death as Corroboration of His Royal Messiahship* (Eugene, OR: Wipf & Stock, 2011); Martin Hengel, "The Kingdom of Christ in John," in *Studies in Early Christology* (Edinburgh: T&T Clark, 1995), 343–44; N. T. Wright claims that all of the Gospels emphatically intertwine kingdom and cross (*How God Became King: The Forgotten Story of the Gospels* [New York: HarperOne, 2012], 225).

the over-categorization often employed in the doctrine of the two states of Christ (humiliation and exaltation).[2] Unfortunately, the atoning death of Jesus is commonly relegated solely to the state of humiliation, with the unfortunate consequence of rending asunder the kingship of the Messiah and his atoning death on the cross. In this essay I will present an argument for the kingship of Christ on the cross, followed by a reconsideration of the doctrine of the two states of Christ in light of Scripture and theology. In place of a strictly linear view of exaltation *after* humiliation, I propose that the states are best understood as exaltation *in* humiliation within the broader progression of exaltation *through* humiliation. One important implication will be that while the themes of the kingdom and the cross are often set at odds, we will see that the messianic mission of Christ culminates on Golgotha, where the crucified king establishes the kingdom by way of the cross.

THE KINGSHIP OF CHRIST ON THE CROSS
THE BIBLICAL WITNESS TO THE KINGSHIP OF CHRIST

Jesus was declared king in his birth (Matt 2:2); anointed as king and empowered by the Spirit for his kingly mission at his baptism (3:13–17); recognized as king in his ministry by his disciples (John 1:49; 6:15), his enemies (19:14), and himself (Luke 23:2); and ultimately entered Jerusalem to die on the cross with the acclamation, "Your king is coming to you" (Matt 21:5). During his trial, Jesus spoke of "my kingdom" (John 18:36); received a crown of thorns (John 19:2); and was presented for crucifixion with the announcement, "Behold, your king!" (John 19:14). Although mocked as king by the soldiers and Pharisees, the sign above his head— "The King of the Jews" (Mark 15:26)—ironically expressed a truth recognized by the criminal beside him (Luke 23:42) and the centurion below (Mark 15:39). Jesus rose from the dead, being declared king to a broken creation (Rom 1:3–4) and inaugurating his kingdom as the firstfruits of the new creation (1 Cor 15:20–25). He ascended into heaven, where he sat down at the right hand of God, demonstrating the completion of his earthly task (Ps 110:1; Heb 10:11–12) and continuing his reign on earth through his Spirit (Acts 2:33).

---

2. A similar discussion could be had regarding the offices of Christ. Although my focus here is on the states of Christ, the overlap of the two is inevitable, for in Scripture kingship is intricately bound up with glorification (Ps 24:7–10; Dan 4:30; 5:18; Luke 19:38; 1 Tim 1:17) and exaltation (1 Sam 2:10; Ps 47:2; Dan 4:17). In other words, God/Christ is exalted and glorified as king.

Throughout his incarnation, life, death, resurrection, and ascension, Jesus is king. But does this mean that there is no development in his kingship, no process of *becoming* king? Certainly not. In order to answer this question properly, two areas must be addressed, namely, the distinction between Jesus' divine and human kingship, and the Old Testament *process* of becoming king.

THE KINGSHIP OF CHRIST ON THE CROSS

As the divine Son of God, Jesus *is* king—yesterday, today, and forever. "Enthronement," says John Webster, "cannot mean acquiring an honour or jurisdiction not previously possessed; indeed, the kingly rule of the Son is not some accidental status or role external to his being, but rather is what he is: he is king."[3] However, as God promised David, the one to establish the kingdom would be a Son of God *and* a descendant of David (2 Sam 7:12–14). As a human, a second Adam, a descendant of David, Jesus came in the likeness of sinful flesh with the task of restoring human vicegerency over all the earth. Therefore, while Jesus *is* king as the divine Son of God from the beginning of his life, his human kingship is a process of establishing his Father's throne on earth as it is in heaven. Thus, his human kingship is grounded in his divine kingship. How does he become king as a representative of a new humanity? The Old Testament provides the proper background for the process of enthronement.

Becoming a king in biblical times was a process, the high points of which were anointing and enthronement (the latter often associated with establishing the king's throne through a decisive victory over enemies). In the Old Testament, "royal anointing is part of the more comprehensive act of enthronement ... with various parts."[4] The anointing, however, "is the most important or the most distinctive of the individual acts."[5] The reason anointing is *the* distinctive act in the enthronement process is because it is what affects the *identity* of the anointed one.[6] To be anointed *as king* is to be authorized by God as the chosen ruler, bringing about a "change of status"[7] (highly significant for a discussion on the *states* of Christ). How-

---

3. John Webster, "One Who Is Son: Theological Reflections on the Exordium to the Epistle to the Hebrews," in *The Epistle to the Hebrews and Christian Theology* (ed. Richard Bauckham et al.; Grand Rapids: Eerdmans, 2009), 91; cf. 82, 92.

4. Franz Hesse, "χρίω κτλ.," *TDNT*, 9:498.

5. Ibid.; cf. Tryggve Mettinger, *King and Messiah: The Civil and Sacral Legitimation of the Israelite Kings* (Lund: Gleerup, 1976), 185.

6. To be anointed is to be anointed *king* ("They anointed David king," 2 Sam 2:4; 5:3).

7. John Walton, Victor Matthews, and Mark Chavalas, eds., *The IVP Bible Background Commentary: Old Testament* (Downers Grove, IL: InterVarsity Press, 2000), 327; cf. 305.

ever, this new identity as king is for a purpose, "a specific commission is given to the king with his anointing."[8] In other words, anointing the king serves the greater purpose of establishing his kingdom.

What, then, does this reveal about Christ's human kingship? First and foremost, Jesus' baptism is his public anointing to kingship. The Spirit descends on Jesus, and he is declared to be God's beloved Son, the anointed one of Psalm 2. Although his rule will be misunderstood, rejected, and even hidden, from this point forward Jesus *is* king. Furthermore, just as in the Old Testament, Jesus' anointing to kingship carries with it a commission. In the baptism, Jesus is not only declared the royal Son of God, but he is also empowered by the Holy Spirit to carry out his messianic mission of establishing God's kingdom (Mark 1:9–11; cf. 2 Sam 7:12–14; Ps 2; Isa 42:1). Jesus, therefore, approached the cross as king, seeking to establish his kingdom. As Michael Horton says, "Jesus embraced the cross precisely as a king embraces a scepter."[9]

Although Jesus *is* king before the cross, there yet remains something to be done for his kingship. As the second Adam, sent to restore God's mediatorial reign on earth, Jesus must dethrone the unrightful king of the fallen creation in order to establish his throne over the new creation. This takes place primarily at the cross, where Jesus fulfills the core promises of the kingdom; namely, victory over Satan (Dan 2:44; Col 2:15), the forgiveness of sins (Isa 40:2; Eph 1:7), and a new exodus (Isa 52:12; Mark 1:2–3). Jesus establishes God's kingdom on earth "because of" and "through suffering" (Heb 2:9–10). I conclude, then, as is clear in Mark's gospel, that Jesus' baptism is his anointing to kingship, and his crucifixion is his enthronement over the new creation.[10]

In sum, before the cross Jesus is king in at least two senses: (1) as the divine Son of God who is in union with the Father, and (2) as the human publicly anointed as king in his baptism. And yet, before the cross Jesus is *not* king in the following two senses: (1) he has yet to definitively defeat Satan and establish God's kingdom, and (2) he has yet to restore human vicegerency. The way I have proposed to understand these different facets of Jesus' kingship is by arguing that Jesus approaches the cross as king seeking to establish his kingdom. There is an "already and not yet" quality

---

8. Hesse, "χρίω κτλ.," 9:499.

9. Michael Horton, *Lord and Servant: A Covenant Christology* (Louisville: Westminster John Knox, 2005), 254.

10. Ardel Caneday, "Christ's Baptism and Crucifixion: The Anointing and Enthronement of God's Son," *SBJT* 8 (2004): 70–85..

to Jesus' kingship. Before the cross, he is already king, but he is yet to establish his kingdom.

CROSS AND RESURRECTION

The kingship of Christ on the cross challenges the dominant view that Jesus became king in the resurrection or session.[11] Although the resurrection and session are essential in Jesus' kingdom mission, they should not rule out Christ's kingship before and on the cross. The resurrection is not the beginning, but the revelation of Christ's kingship and the inauguration of his kingdom on earth. As Barth said, "His resurrection revealed Him as the One who reigns in virtue of His death."[12] Jesus' death is not a defeat that needs to be made right by the resurrection, but a victory that needs to be revealed and implemented in the resurrection. Likewise, Christ's session does not begin his reign but completes his earthly task and continues his reign through the Spirit.[13] It is "the repetition in time of his eternal being."[14] Jesus rises from the dead and is seated on the throne not *in order to* be king, but *as* king.

JESUS REIGNS FROM THE CROSS

Inasmuch as the person and work of Christ are inseparable, to say that Jesus *is* king on the cross is also to say that he *reigns* from the cross. This emphasizes the *active* nature of Christ's atoning death. While active and passive obedience are often wrongly divided among Christ's life and death, John Murray has demonstrated that they are complementary aspects throughout Christ's work: "In his sufferings he was supremely active."[15] The cross, therefore, is the pinnacle of Christ's obedience (Phil 2:8), in both its passive and active aspects. He obediently fulfills his mission of bringing the kingdom (active) by means of obediently suffering as a servant (passive). Jesus himself interprets the laying down of his life as an act of authority (John 10:18), and although he suffers at the hands of others, he does so sovereignly because he has voluntarily given his own life: "No one can take it from me, but I lay it down of my own accord" (John 10:18; cf.

---

11. See, e.g., Wolfhart Pannenberg, *Jesus— God and Man* (2nd ed.; trans. Lewis Wilkins and Duane Priebe; Philadelphia: Westminster, 1977), 365–77.

12. Karl Barth, *Church Dogmatics* (ed. G. W. Bromiley and Thomas Torrance; trans. G. W. Bromiley; Edinburgh: T&T Clark, 1958), IV/2, 291.

13. G. Dautzenberg, "Psalm 110 im Neuen Testament," in *Liturgie und Dichtung* (ed. H. Becker and R. Kacyznski; St. Ottilien: Eos, 1983), 1:141–71.

14. Webster, "One Who Is Son," 92.

15. John Murray, *Redemption Accomplished and Applied* (Grand Rapids: Eerdmans, 1978), 20 (cf. 20–25).

19:30). Despite being bound, he is in complete control, for at any moment he could have appealed to his Father to send legions of angels (Matt 26:53).

The fathers of the early church championed the kingship of Christ in all things, especially his atoning death on the cross.[16] In the first century, Barnabas declared that "the kingdom of Jesus is based on the wooden cross" (*Epistle of Barnabas* 8:5).[17] Justin Martyr promoted the mantra, "The Lord hath reigned from the tree."[18] Irenaeus says, "He whom the Jews had seen as a man, and had fastened to the cross, should be preached as the Christ, the Son of God, their eternal King."[19] According to Augustine, "The Lord has established his sovereignty from a tree. Who is it who fights with wood? Christ. From his cross he has conquered kings."[20] The widespread understanding of Jesus as the "the immortal king, who has suffered on our behalf,"[21] is exemplified in the early artistic portrayals of the crucifixion, which often place on Jesus' head a golden crown.[22]

This great tradition of Christ reigning from the cross was also preserved through the theologically rich hymnody of the early church. The *Vexilla Regis*, by Venantius Fortunatus (530–609), is sung by Roman Catholics on the Feast of Exaltation of the Cross:

> That which the prophet-king of old
> Hath in mysterious verse foretold
> Is now accomplished, whilst we see
> God ruling the nations from a tree.[23]

This hymn, written hundreds of years after Justin, still upholds the theme

---

16. See Per Beskow, *Rex Gloriae: The Kingship of Christ in the Early Church* (Stockholm: Almqvist & Wiksell, 1962).

17. Michael Holmes, ed., *The Apostolic Fathers in English* (trans. Michael Holmes; 3rd ed.; Grand Rapids: Baker Academic, 2006), 186.

18. Justin Martyr, *First Apology* 41 (ANF 1:176); Justin claimed that the original text of Ps 96:10 read, "Let them rejoice among the nations. The Lord reigns from the wood," but that the Jews removed the key phrase "from the wood" because the crucifixion of the Messiah on a tree was incomprehensible in the light of Deut 21:23, which says, "Anyone who is hung on a tree is under God's curse" (*Dialogue with Trypho* 73 [ANF, 1:235]). Whether Justin was right or not, the early church clung to the slogan "the Lord reigns from the tree," as well as the theology of the kingship of Christ on the cross.

19. Irenaeus, *Against Heresies* 3.12.6 (ANF 1:432).

20. Augustine, *Exposition of Psalm 95* (Works of St Augustine 18; Brooklyn, NY: New City Press, 2002), 425.

21. From the Sibylline books, quoted in Alois Grillmeier, *Christ in Christian Tradition* (trans. John Bowden; Atlanta: John Knox, 1975), 71.

22. Richard Viladesau, *The Beauty of the Cross: The Passion of Christ in Theology and the Arts from the Catacombs to the Eve of the Renaissance* (New York: Oxford University Press, 2008), 111.

23. Quoted in Paul Gavrilyuk, "God's Impassible Suffering in the Flesh: The Promise of Paradoxical Christology," in *Divine Impassibility and the Mystery of Human Suffering* (ed. James Keating and Thomas Joseph White; Grand Rapids: Eerdmans, 2009), 130.

of Christ's reigning from the tree. Jesus' life-bringing death is understood as the accomplishment of the reign of God, the fulfillment of the prophecy of old.

The Orthodox Church has preserved a hymn that is sung on Good Friday, from the Byzantine *Lenten Triodion*:

> Today he who hung the earth upon the waters is hung upon the
>   cross;
> He who is king of the angels is arrayed in a crown of thorns;
> He who wraps the heaven in clouds is wrapped in purple mockery.[24]

This hymn reveals the paradoxical nature of Christ's kingship on the cross. Rather than diminishing the royalty of Christ's kingship or softening the severity of his death, this hymn upholds both in a way that makes Christ's majesty more splendid and his death more appalling.

Lastly, the hymn "Sing My Tongue" (sixth century) eloquently summarizes the paradoxical nature of Christ's kingship on the cross within the history of redemption.[25] While the lengthy hymn tells the story of Christ's obedience on the tree in Golgotha, recapitulating Adam's disobedience on the tree in Eden, it speaks of Christ as both the "dying King" and the "lamb upon the altar of the cross." It is within the expansive vision of God's reign in the Old and New Testaments that Christ the king reigns on the cross by offering himself as a sacrificial lamb.

THE TWO STATES OF CHRIST: HUMILIATION AND EXALTATION

The idea of the kingship of Christ on the cross often finds resistance because it does not fit within the common understanding of the two-state doctrine, which places the cross as an act of humiliation preceding exaltation. Wayne Grudem's definition is representative: "The doctrine of 'the twofold state of Christ' is the teaching that Christ experienced *first* the state of humiliation, *then* the state of exaltation."[26] Having divided Christ's work into two successive temporal categories, Grudem then customarily allocates Christ's incarnation, suffering, death, and burial to the

24. Mother Mary and Kallistos Ware, trans., "The Service of the Twelve Gospels," in *The Lenten Triodion* (South Canaan, PA: St. Tikhon's Seminary Press, 2001), 587.

25. Philip Schaff, ed., *Christ in Song: Hymns of Immanuel* (London: Sampson Low, Son, and Marston, 1870), 125–28.

26. Wayne Grudem, *Systematic Theology: An Introduction to Biblical Doctrine* (Grand Rapids: Zondervan, 1995), 620 (italics mine); cf. idem, "States of Jesus Christ," *Evangelical Dictionary of Theology* (ed. Walter Elwell; Grand Rapids: Baker, 1989), 1052–54.

state of humiliation, and his resurrection, ascension, session, and parousia to the state of exaltation.[27]

The problem with this interpretation, as neat as it is categorically, is that it does not take into account the whole witness of Scripture. While at times Scripture certainly presents humiliation and exaltation in terms of a general progression (Acts 2:33–36; Phil 2:6–9; Heb 2:9–10; 1 Peter 1:10–11), it also reveals a more organic and overlapping relation between the two states (John 12:23–33; Rev 5:5–6). After providing a brief historical survey of the doctrine of the two states, I will offer a constructive proposal for better understanding the whole witness of Scripture regarding Christ's humiliation and exaltation.

HISTORY OF THE DOCTRINE OF THE STATES OF CHRIST

The systematic distinction between Christ's states of humiliation and exaltation was first employed by the Lutherans in the late sixteenth century and developed in the ensuing debates with the Reformed. The Lutherans, seeking to uphold the union of Christ's two natures by means of the *communicatio idiomatum*, interpreted the exaltation of the human nature of Christ as the revelation of his previously possessed *divine* glory.[28] The Reformed criticized the Lutherans for wrongly divinizing Christ's humanity, and therefore sought to explain the exaltation in terms of Christ's newly gained *human* glory.[29] In short, for Lutherans, exaltation is the revelation of previously possessed divine glory. For the Reformed, exaltation is the reward for prior obedience of newly acquired human qualities.

One of the strongest developments in the Reformed tradition was not merely arguing for a temporal transition from humiliation to exaltation but defining the relationship in terms of cause or reward. Herman Bavinck, for example, says, "The entire state of exaltation from the resurrection to his coming again for judgment is a reward for the work that he accomplished as the Servant of the Lord in the days of humiliation."[30] Humiliation is "the meritorious cause of the exaltation."[31] Although the

---

27. For similar treatments, see Millard Erickson, *Christian Theology* (2nd ed.; Grand Rapids: Baker Academic, 1998), 788–97; Louis Berkhof, *Systematic Theology* (Grand Rapids: Eerdmans, 1979), 331–55.

28. For a survey of the Lutheran view of the two states, see Marvin Hoogland, *Calvin's Perspective on the Exaltation of Christ in Comparison with the Post-Reformation Doctrine of the Two States* (Kampen: Kok, 1966), 11–44.

29. For a survey of the Reformed development of the two states, see ibid., 45–94.

30. Herman Bavinck, *Sin and Salvation in Christ*, vol. 3 of *Reformed Dogmatics* (ed. John Bolt, trans. John Vriend; Grand Rapids: Baker Academic, 2003), 433.

31. Ibid., 434.

two-states doctrine has persisted at some level in Reformed theology,[32] it was largely put into disrepute by Friedrich Schleiermacher in the nineteenth century.[33] Because Schleiermacher rejected the preexistence of Christ, it made no sense to speak of Christ's life in terms of humiliation.[34] "Accordingly," says Schleiermacher, "we are perfectly entitled to set this formula aside; it may justly be entrusted to history for safe keeping."[35] Barth also rejected the traditional distinction between humiliation and exaltation, although, as we will see, for quite different reasons.[36]

EXALTATION IN AND THROUGH HUMILIATION

In response to the common understanding of exaltation *after* humiliation, I propose that the proper view is exaltation *in* humiliation within a broader progression of exaltation *through* humiliation. By "exaltation in humiliation" I am breaking down the typical dichotomy by demonstrating that Christ is exalted supremely in his redemptive suffering, the apex of which is his death on the cross. By "exaltation through humiliation" I am maintaining a general progression from humiliation to exaltation while at the same time showing how they overlap and interrelate.

The argument will be based on Scripture and theology and draw from Calvin and Barth in order to revise the interpretation of humiliation and exaltation as strictly successive temporal states. Calvin and Barth both differ from the linear schema and offer a middle way between the Reformed and Lutheran positions, affirming the simultaneity of humiliation and exaltation with the idea that Jesus is humbled in his divinity and exalted in his humanity.[37] Though drawing from both in arguing for exaltation in humiliation, I will part ways with Barth—as he ultimately dismisses the doctrine—and follow Calvin in maintaining a broader temporal progression.

EXALTATION IN HUMILIATION: INTEGRATING THE STATES

The primary mistake of the standard view of the states of Christ is that it polarizes humiliation and exaltation. The strictly linear view of humiliation *then* exaltation simply does not do justice to the breadth of Scripture's witness, namely, that Christ is exalted before the resurrection and remains

---

32. Some use the doctrine as a framing device for the work of Christ (e.g., Berkhof, *Systematic Theology*, 331–55), and others as an individual doctrine (e.g., Grudem, *Systematic Theology*, 620).

33. Friedrich Schleiermacher, *The Christian Faith* (Edinburgh: T&T Clark, 1986), 473–75.

34. Ibid., 475.

35. Ibid.

36. Barth, *CD*, IV/1, 133; *CD*, IV/2, 106, 110, 135–36.

37. Hoogland, *Calvin's Perspective on the Exaltation of Christ*, 214–15.

humble after the crucifixion. Not only do humiliation and exaltation overlap in Christ's work, but they both find their apex in his atoning death.

EXALTATION BEFORE THE RESURRECTION

From the cradle to the cross it is plain to the human eye that the life of Jesus is one of humiliation. However, Scripture reveals, and the eye of faith perceives, that even during his time of humiliation Jesus is being exalted, glorified, and enthroned as king. The most common and explicit way Scripture speaks of Christ's pre-Easter exaltation is with the language of glorification. Far from being reserved for his resurrection and ascension, the glory of Christ is displayed from the moment of the incarnation, for as John declares, "The Word became flesh ... and we have seen his glory" (John 1:14). Though hidden to sinful eyes, "He *is* the radiance of the glory of God" (Heb 1:3, italics mine). In Cana Jesus "manifested his glory" through his first "sign" (John 2:11), and through the transfiguration he "received honor and glory from God the Father" (2 Pet 1:17). Jesus himself says, "My Father ... glorifies me" (John 8:54) and later speaks of "the glory that you have given me" and even "my glory" (17:22, 24). Finally, and ultimately, Jesus refers to his own death as "the hour ... for the Son of Man to be glorified" (12:23) and "lifted up" (12:32), thereby combining glorification and exaltation and centering them on the cross. As Paul would later say, they "crucified the Lord of glory" (1 Cor 2:8). Clearly in Scripture, Christ is glorified and exalted as king before the resurrection.

Rightly understanding the person of Christ is essential for his pre-Easter exaltation. In accordance with Chalcedonian Christology, Jesus is not only truly God and truly man, but his two natures are *united* in his one person (the hypostatic union). This means, first of all, that he as the God-man *is* exalted and glorious in his divinity. The majestic glory of Christ's divinity, though "concealed and not exerting its force,"[38] was by no means absent from his person during his ministry on earth.[39] His humanity need not be subsumed into his divinity (the Lutheran tendency) nor treated in isolation from his divinity (the Reformed tendency) but in

---

38. John Calvin, *Calvin's Commentaries* (trans. Calvin Translation Society; Grand Rapids: Baker, 1999), comment on John 12:27.

39. This, of course, goes against kenotic Christologies, which argue that Christ emptied himself of divine attributes. For a survey of kenotic Christologies, see Sarah Coakley, "Kenosis and Subversion: On the Repression of 'Vulnerability' in Christian Feminist Writing," in *Powers and Submissions: Spirituality, Philosophy and Gender* (Malden, MA: Blackwell, 2002), 3–39.

union with it. As the eternal Son of God he does not need to be exalted, but as the incarnate Son of God he is exalted for us.

Christ is also exalted before the resurrection in his human nature. Although truly human, Jesus was not just *any* human. According to Calvin, Christ was the human who was exalted above every other human because he was completely "without sin" (Heb 4:15) and uniquely empowered by the Holy Spirit, which was evident in his miracles and proclamation of the kingdom.[40] Barth discusses the exaltation of the human nature of Christ under the title "the royal man," highlighting an often overlooked point: Christ's kingship is attributed primarily to his humanity.[41] God's rule over the earth is mediatorial, and Christ is the second Adam and the Son of David who will establish God's kingdom and restore his people to their proper place of dominion over the earth.

HUMILIATION AFTER THE CROSS

Not only is Christ exalted before the resurrection, but he retains many features of his humiliation after the cross. Although his atoning sacrifice is finished (John 19:30) and need not be repeated (Heb 9:26), his identity and reign continue to be shaped by his servant form and cross work. Even after his resurrection, he remains the crucified one (Mark 16:6) and appears to his disciples in his glorified state still bearing the scars from the cross (John 20:27). When John is granted a vision into the heavenly throne room, he shockingly sees Christ as a slaughtered lamb still being praised for his redemptive death (Rev 5:5–12). Even after his ascension and session, Jesus remains a humble king who intercedes on behalf of his people (Rom 8:34), graciously gives the gift of the Holy Spirit (Acts 2:33), and will ultimately hand the kingdom over to the Father (1 Cor 15:24).

Calvin says Christ's kingship remains humble because his kingdom still "lies hidden in the earth, so to speak, under the lowness of the flesh."[42] Marvin Hoogland elaborates Calvin's view, saying, "In so far as the Kingdom or Church of Christ is not yet fully glorious in the world, the glory of Christ Himself is not yet complete, and in this sense His humiliation is not yet a matter of the past."[43] Barth concurs: "Neither the Gospels nor the New Testament as a whole see and know and attest the risen and living

---

40. Hoogland, *Calvin's Perspective on the Exaltation of Christ*, 100–27.
41. Barth, *CD* IV/2, 156–268.
42. John Calvin, *Institutes of the Christian Religion* (ed. John McNeill; trans. Ford Lewis Battles; LCC 20; Louisville: Westminster John Knox, 2006), 2.16.17.
43. Hoogland, *Calvin's Perspective on the Exaltation of Christ*, 192.

and exalted man Jesus except as the man who had this end and outcome, whose story is finally the story of His passion."[44]

THE OVERLAP OF HUMILIATION AND EXALTATION IN CHRIST

Based on the two sections above, any simplistic successive interpretation of the two states—humiliation *then* exaltation—must be rejected. Temporally, there is overlap. More importantly, as aspects of Christ's person and work, humiliation and exaltation are deeply intertwined. Barth refers to this as the "inter-connexion" between humiliation and exaltation and helpfully shifts the emphasis from temporal succession to Christological simultaneity:

> The exaltation of the Son of Man begins and is completed already in and with the happening of the humiliation of the Son of God; and conversely ... the exaltation of the Son of Man includes in itself the humiliation of the Son of God, so that Jesus Christ is already exalted in his humiliation and humiliated in His exaltation.[45]

How can these apparently contradictory aspects be simultaneous in Christ? The key for Calvin and Barth is that Jesus is the God-man who is simultaneously humbled in his divinity and exalted in his humanity.[46] According to Barth, "As God he was humbled to take our place, and as man he is exalted on our behalf."[47] Furthermore, the simultaneous humiliation and exaltation of Christ is not a contradiction because Christ always humbles himself (Phil 2:8; cf. Luke 14:11) and is exalted by the Father (Acts 2:33; Phil 2:9). In other words, Christ is not in two static states of humiliation and exaltation but is constantly humbling himself and being exalted by the Father. Calvin adds that Christ is able to retain his exalted status because he takes on the form of a servant *voluntarily*.[48] In other words, Christ sovereignly accepts a mission of servitude. Thomas Torrance correctly asserts that "we are not to think of the humiliation and exaltation of Christ simply as two events following one after the other, but as both involved in appropriate measure at the same time all through the incarnate life of Christ."[49]

---

44. Barth, *CD*, IV/2, 250.
45. Ibid., 110.
46. Hoogland, *Calvin's Perspective on the Exaltation of Christ*, 214–15.
47. Barth, CD, IV/1, 141; for Calvin's view, see Hoogland, *Calvin's Perspective on the Exaltation of Christ*, 125.
48. Hoogland, *Calvin's Perspective on the Exaltation of Christ*, 132–33.
49. Thomas Torrance, *Atonement: The Person and Work of Christ* (ed. Robert Walker; Downers Grove, IL: InterVarsity Press, 2009), 210; cf. Horton, *Lord and Servant*, 254.

EXALTATION IN HUMILIATION: THE MAJESTIC GLORY OF THE CROSS

The humiliation and exaltation of Christ, in both their temporal and Christological dimensions, come to an apex on the cross of Christ. While in the Roman world the cross was an instrument of shame and humiliation,[50] Jesus declared it to be his glorious exaltation. This is most explicit in the gospel of John, when Jesus, speaking of his death, says, "The hour has come for the Son of Man to be glorified" (John 12:23). He continues, revealing that the glorification is also exaltation: "And I, when I am lifted up from the earth, will draw all people to myself" (12:32). Although such language initially sounds more fitting for the ascension or session, in the next verse Jesus makes it clear that he is referring to being "lifted up" in his death. Lest the reader mistake this as a mere blip in Jesus' mission or John's theology, this "hour" (ὥρα) of suffering and glory is on the mind of Jesus from the beginning of his ministry (John 2:4), is used by John to focus the mission of Jesus to Golgotha (John 7:30; 8:20; 13:1), and culminates the night before the crucifixion when Jesus prays, "Father, the hour has come" (John 17:1).

Within this movement to the cross, Jesus speaks of his being "lifted up" on three separate occasions (John 3:14; 8:28; 12:32). For John, everything is moving toward this climactic hour, when Jesus, being "lifted up" on the cross, is truly being enthroned in glory. Barth concludes, based on this passage in John, that "the exaltation of the One who humiliated Himself in obedience (Phil 2:9) is not the divine act towards this man which takes place after His humiliation, but that which takes place in and with His humiliation."[51] Calvin says, "In all the creatures, indeed, both high and low, the glory of God shines, but *nowhere has it shown more brightly than in the cross*."[52] Hoogland's summary of Calvin captures well the essence of exaltation in humiliation: "Jesus Christ was exalted in His very humiliation unto death, in which He supremely manifested His divine glory and power by His triumph on the cross."[53]

Interestingly, many proponents of the strictly successive view acknowledge John's picture of the glory and exaltation of the cross, but then simply ignore or cast it aside as a glitch in the otherwise neat categories of humili-

---

50. Martin Hengel, *Crucifixion in the Ancient World and the Folly of the Message of the Cross* (Philadelphia: Fortress, 1977).
51. Barth, *CD*, IV/2, 256.
52. *Calvin's Commentaries*, comment on John 13:31, italics mine.
53. Hoogland, *Calvin's Perspective on the Exaltation of Christ*, 187.

ation *then* exaltation.[54] A closer look, however, will reveal that John is not merely a wildcard in an otherwise uniform system; he is on to something more broadly attested in Scripture. That which John states explicitly— Christ is exalted on the cross—Mark says through irony (Mark 15) and Paul through concepts of wisdom/foolishness and power/weakness (1 Cor 1:18–25). Martin Hengel says, "The '*doxa*' of the Son of God cannot be separated from the shame of his cross," a truth which he finds not only in John but in Paul, Mark, and Hebrews.[55]

How could Christ be exalted *in* humiliation? First, his suffering is glorious because it accomplishes salvation. Exaltation is "the bright side" of humiliation, says A. B. Bruce, for "while it is a humiliation to die, it is glorious to die for others."[56] Second, Christ is exalted in humiliation because his humiliating death reveals the glorious character of God. Calvin combines both points:

> For the death of the cross, which Christ suffered, is so far from obscuring his high rank, that in that death his high rank is chiefly displayed, since there his amazing love to mankind, his infinite righteousness in atoning for sin and appeasing the wrath of God, his wonderful power in conquering death, subduing Satan, and, at length, opening heaven, blazed with full brightness.[57]

Exaltation *in* humiliation is foolishness to the human eye, but to the eye of faith it is the wisdom of God. According to Calvin, "Since only weakness appears in the cross, death, and burial of Christ, faith must leap over all these things to attain its full strength."[58] While the carnal eye looks at the cross and sees only humiliation, the eye of faith perceives glory in the shame and exaltation in humiliation. This raises an interesting point: the servant form of Christ both hides and reveals his kingship. Christ's servant form veils his majesty because people look at a man dying a criminal's death and would never assume him to be a king. Yet his servant form also reveals his majesty, for his sovereignty can be expressed in servitude. As Webster says, "The 'humiliation' of the Word is thus by no means the contradiction of his exaltation; it is, rather, the chosen mode of his exaltation."[59] How, then, can Christ's kingship be hidden and

---

54. See, e.g., Bavinck, *Sin and Salvation in Christ*, 423.

55. Martin Hengel, *The Cross of the Son of God* (London: SCM, 1986), 85.

56. A. B. Bruce, *The Humiliation of Christ: In Its Physical, Ethical, and Official Aspects* (Grand Rapids: Eerdmans, 1955), 30.

57. *Calvin's Commentaries*, comment on John 13:32.

58. Calvin, *Institutes*, 2.16.13.

59. John Webster, *Word and Church: Essays in Church Dogmatics* (New York: T&T Clark, 2001), 137.

revealed? It is hidden to fallen eyes, yet by faith one can see the gracious majesty of God in the crucified Christ.

EXALTATION THROUGH HUMILIATION: MAINTAINING THE BROADER PROGRESSION

Thus far I have argued against a strictly linear understanding of the two states and sought to replace it with a view that acknowledges the temporal overlap and places at the forefront the Christological simultaneity of humiliation and exaltation. In short, Christ's exaltation is not simply *after* but also *in* his humiliation. Exaltation *in* humiliation, however, does not rule out a broader movement from humiliation to exaltation. Such a progression is irrefutable in light of Scripture. Peter, for example, speaks of "the sufferings of Christ and the *subsequent* glories" (1 Pet 1:11, italics mine). The author of Hebrews says Christ was made "perfect through suffering" (Heb 2:9). Such statements indicate that although the states are tightly intertwined throughout Christ's work, there is an irreversible transition that takes place at the resurrection of Christ.

Perhaps it is a transition from exalted humiliation to humble exaltation, but a transition nonetheless. The resurrected Christ is no longer "in the likeness of sinful flesh" (Rom 8:3). He will never offer himself as a sacrifice again (Heb 9:26). His majesty is no longer veiled (Rev 1:10–18). Taking this into account, along with what has been argued above, we can say that the doctrine of the two states of Christ is properly interpreted as exaltation *in* humiliation within the broader framework of exaltation *through* humiliation. Below, I will demonstrate the validity of this temporal progression by discussing the new glory of Christ's resurrection and the significance of Christ's exaltation as "for us."

I have argued against the dominant position in contemporary Reformed theology by appealing to two of its tradition's greatest theologians — Calvin and Barth. At this point, however, in maintaining the place of an overall progression, I will part ways with Barth, whose critique of the successive view of the two states causes him to interpret it solely in terms of Christological simultaneity.[60] The matter at hand is the fundamental difference between the Lutheran and Reformed positions on the states. For the Lutherans the exaltation of Christ is a *revelation* of his previously held divine glory, whereas for the Reformed it is the *acquiring* of new glory in his human nature. The genius of Calvin is that before these reactionary

---

60. Barth, *CD*, IV/1, 133; *CD*, IV/2, 106, 110, 135–36.

debates led to such polarized positions, he was able to uphold both aspects of exaltation.[61] Exaltation is a revelation of previously held divine glory *and* the acquiring of new human glory.[62] Although Calvin's view on the states was certainly not systematized, I will follow him in order to move beyond the Lutheran/Reformed dichotomy.

REVELATION OF PREVIOUS GLORY

For Calvin, the resurrection is the revelation of Christ's previously held glory *and* his newly acquired human glory. Before speaking of the new glory, however, it must be emphasized that, for Calvin, the revelation of Christ's previously held glory is the primary emphasis. In Hoogland's words, "The honor which comes to Christ in His new exaltation is the honor which is displayed in His death."[63] This puts Calvin closer to the Lutheran view, but because it is a matter of emphasis, he differs with the Reformed only formally rather than materially. The key here for Calvin, though, is that the *revelation* of the previously held glory is itself a new glory. This is possible because revelation is not merely revelatory but effective. In the much later words of Gustaf Aulén, the resurrection "reveals ... *and realizes* the victorious deed contained in his finished work."[64] In other words, not only is the kingship of Christ revealed, but the kingdom of Christ is inaugurated.

EXALTED AS A HUMAN "FOR US"

Regarding the revelation of Christ's new human glory, Calvin does not dwell on how this affects Christ himself, noting primarily the glorification of his physical body.[65] The key is that Christ's human exaltation is ultimately "for us." According to Hoogland, "The 'for us' appears in Calvin's view to be fully as significant for the resurrection as it is for the death of Christ, and thus as significant for the exaltation as for the humiliation of Christ."[66] This stands in contrast to the later Reformed view that Christ's exaltation is primarily *his* reward for humiliation. Calvin asks, "What

---

61. Hoogland, *Calvin's Perspective on the Exaltation of Christ*, 206, 215–16.

62. This does not deny the basic continuity between Calvin and Reformed orthodoxy on the states of Christ (see ibid., 206; Richard Muller, *Christ and the Decree: Christology and Predestination in Reformed Theology from Calvin to Perkins* [Durham, NC: Labyrinth, 1986], 10). The point, rather, is that within broad agreement with Reformed orthodoxy, Calvin shared the Lutheran emphasis on the exaltation of Christ primarily as the revelation of divine glory, even during his life and death.

63. Hoogland, *Calvin's Perspective on the Exaltation of Christ*, 175.

64. Gustaf Aulén, *The Faith of the Christian Church* (Philadelphia: Muhlenberg, 1948), 245, italics mine.

65. Hoogland, *Calvin's Perspective on the Exaltation of Christ*, 156.

66. Ibid., 180.

need was there for God's only Son to come down in order to acquire something new for himself?"[67]

Yet while Calvin said Christ merited nothing for himself,[68] Bavinck said that he did.[69] Is this an irreconcilable difference? Is Christ's exaltation either for himself or for us? I contend there is a third way that can uphold Calvin's and Bavinck's concerns. Although Scripture certainly implies that humiliation is the cause of exaltation, or exaltation the reward of humiliation (Isa 53:10–12; Matt 23:12; Phil 2:9; Heb 2:10), this is penultimate to the goal of Christ's exaltation "for us." In other words, the exaltation that Christ acquired in himself was not because *he* needed to be exalted but because we need to be exalted; it was "for us." He acquired glory "for himself" as a king *so that* it could be given "for us" in his kingdom.

Douglas Farrow sheds further light on the "for us" of Christ's exaltation. According to Farrow, Christ enters into the human cycle of descent and ascent, and where humanity has fallen short of its destiny of ascent to God, Christ has fulfilled it as a second Adam and thereby leads humanity upward toward their original purpose of vicegerency with God over the earth.[70] In Farrow's words, "Through his own U-shaped history (baptism, death, resurrection, and ascension) Jesus recapitulates the entire experience of fallen man."[71] The salient feature is that Christ is exalted "for us"; his exaltation is the recapitulatory precursor for our exaltation. "Jesus' destiny is our destiny; or rather that, in reaching our destiny, he has reached it not only for himself but also for us."[72]

Jesus was not exalted because he was in need of glory or royal status, but *so that* he might pour out the Holy Spirit for the building up of his church (Acts 2:33–36; Eph 4:8–12). While Philippians 2:9 is often referenced for the exaltation of Christ, many neglect the following verses that reveal the purpose of the exaltation: "*so that* at the name of Jesus every knee should bow ... and every tongue confess that Jesus Christ is Lord" (Phil 2:10–11, italics mine). Christ's exaltation as *king* is ultimately aimed at his work of advancing his *kingdom* on earth as it is in heaven, for, as Far-

---

67. Calvin, *Institutes*, 2.17.6.

68. Ibid.

69. Bavinck, *Sin and Salvation in Christ*, 433.

70. Douglas Farrow, *Ascension and Ecclesia: On the Significance of the Doctrine of the Ascension for Ecclesiology and Christian Cosmology* (Grand Rapids: Eerdmans, 1999), 15–40; idem, "Ascension," in *Dictionary for Theological Interpretation of the Bible* (ed. Kevin Vanhoozer; Grand Rapids: Baker, 2005), 65–67; idem, *Ascension Theology* (New York: T&T Clark, 2011), 1–14.

71. Farrow, "Ascension," 67.

72. Farrow, *Ascension Theology*, 10; cf. Calvin, who says, "the cross will be, as it were, a chariot, by which he shall raise all men, along with himself, to his Father" (*Calvin's Commentaries*, comment on John 12:32).

row says, "His ascent to heaven, like his ascent to the cross, is a journey undertaken on behalf of God's people and with a view to the realization of their kingdom hopes."[73]

CONCLUSION: THE KINGDOM AND THE CROSS

Jesus is king on the cross, establishing God's kingdom on earth as it is in heaven. As Barth said, it is "supremely in His cross that He acted as the Lord and King of all men, that He maintained and exercised His sovereignty."[74] This understanding of the kingship of Christ on the cross demands a reconsideration of the commonly over-compartmentalized doctrine of the states of Christ. Though this doctrine is helpful inasmuch as it distinguishes between aspects of Christ's person and work, it does more harm than good when it relegates Christ's death only to his humble state. I have argued against a strictly linear view of exaltation *after* humiliation and for an understanding that focuses on exaltation *in* humiliation within the broader progression of exaltation *through* humiliation. This accounts for the kingship of Christ on the cross, for it was during those dark, shameful hours that Christ's majestic glory shined forth to the world.

We would do well to return to the roots of this doctrine, especially as expressed by Calvin, in seeking to integrate rather than divide the aspects of Christ's work. Horton seems to reflect Calvin's thought and thereby pave a way forward, by expressing the proper relation between the states (and offices) of Christ as they express his kingship.

> While there is a general progression from the state of humiliation to exaltation and from prophet to priest to king, they are all present simultaneously in the unity of Christ's person and work. Even as he was hanging on the cross in dereliction as the enemy of God and humanity, Christ was winning our redemption as our conquering King.[75]

The strictly linear view of the states of Christ unfortunately contributes to the even broader problem of the severance of the themes of the kingdom and the cross.[76] While many Christians either champion the kingdom or cling to the cross, Scripture presents a mutually enriching

---

73. Farrow, *Ascension and Ecclesia*, 23.

74. Barth, *CD*, IV/2, 291.

75. Michael Horton, *The Christian Faith: A Systematic Theology for Pilgrims on the Way* (Grand Rapids: Zondervan, 2011), 524.

76. For the relationship between the coming of God's kingdom and Jesus' atoning death on the cross, see Jeremy R. Treat, "Crown of Thorns: Interweaving Atonement and Kingdom in Biblical and Systematic Theology" (Ph.D. diss., Wheaton College, 2013).

relationship between the two that draws significantly from the story of Israel and culminates in the crucifixion of Christ the King. In short, the kingdom and the cross are held together by the Christ—Israel's Messiah—who brings God's reign on earth through his atoning death on the cross. The kingdom is the ultimate goal of the cross, and the cross is the means by which the kingdom comes. The cross is not the failure of Jesus' messianic ministry, nor simply the prelude to his royal glory, but the apex of his kingdom mission, the throne from which he rules and establishes his kingdom. The shocking paradox of God's reign through Christ crucified certainly appears foolish to fallen human logic, but perceived through faith, it is the very power and wisdom of God (1 Cor 1:18–2:5). May we ever follow Calvin's exhortation to imitate even the penitent thief on the cross, who "adores Christ as a King while on the gallows, celebrates His kingdom in the midst of shocking and worse than revolting abasement, and declares him, when dying, to be the author of life."[77]

---

77. *Calvin's Commentaries*, comment on Luke 23:42.

CHAPTER 6

"WE SAW HIS GLORY"

Implications of the Sanctuary
Christology in John's Gospel

PETER J. LEITHART

SINCE THE FOURTH AND FIFTH CENTURIES, ecumenical creeds have provided the touchstone of Christological orthodoxy. Before the councils, there were no creeds, and the church fathers relied on biblical categories, concepts, and images to set the boundaries of Christian discourse, confession, and belief. Before the creeds, typology controlled Christology.

Typology did not disappear after the councils. Though Athanasius argues that extrabiblical terminology is legitimate insofar as it captures the sense of Scripture, even after Nicea he uses the Nicene *homoousios* infrequently. He commonly resorts to a set of biblical images that he describes as paradigms.[1] There are four: The Son is the "radiance" of the Father's glory (Heb 1:3); the Father is the "fountain of living waters" and the Son the stream from that fountain (Jer 2:13); the Son is son to the Father (many passages); and the Son is the Word and Wisdom of the Father (John 1:1–3; Prov 8).

From these raw materials, Athanasius constructs anti-Arian polemics. Fathers by definition have sons, and those sons are of the same nature as the father; therefore, if the Father is eternally Father, He must have a consubstantial, eternal Son. Light cannot exist without radiance, and so if the Father is eternal light and glory, He must have an eternal Radiance.

---

1. For more, see my *Athanasius* (Grand Rapids: Baker, 2011), ch. 2.

That Radiance is the Son. Unless we wish to blaspheme the Father by saying He was once silent and foolish, we must say that Word and Wisdom of God are coeternal with Him. Scripture identifies that Word and Wisdom with the Son. A fountain without a stream is barren, and so as source the Father must eternally flow out in the Son.

These analogies do not work at every point, of course. Athanasius insists that an apophatic interval separates the created paradigm and the uncreated Father-Son relation. Analogies exist, but, Athanasius declares, "the divine generation must not be compared to the nature of men" (*Discourses* 1.8.28). Athanasius appeals to axioms concerning the eternity and immutability of God to distinguish legitimate from illegitimate implications of his paradigms. The Son is Son, Radiance, Stream, Word, Wisdom in all the ways that it is possible to be so for an eternal, immutable God. To say that the Son is a son does not imply that the Father existed before the Son, as it would if they were human. That would be inconsistent with God's changelessness. But saying that the Father and Son share the same nature is not inconsistent with God's immutability; in fact, quite the opposite. By denying the legitimate force of these paradigms, Arians not only reject the eternity of the Son but destroy God Himself because they imply that God is subject to change (from non-Father to Father). If there is a temporal or ontological interval between Father and Son, then before the Son the Father was an absurdity—a unradiant light, a divine fool, a speechless God, a Father without a Son.[2]

Athanasius also uses biblical paradigms constructively to work out a fuller understanding of Christ's Person and Work. Drawing on New Testament texts like John 2:21, Athanasius suggests that the temple provides a particularly fitting model of incarnation. From the reference to the "founding" of Wisdom (Prov 8:23), he expounds the incarnation as a construction project, and this leads immediately to a description of the church as a temple built on Jesus the Cornerstone:

> according to His manhood He is founded, that we, as precious stones,
> may admit of building upon Him, and may become a temple of the Holy
> Ghost who dwells in us.... He is founded for our sakes, taking on Him
> what is ours, that we, as incorporated and compacted and bound together

---

2. For Gregory of Nyssa's use of tabernacle imagery in Christology, see Ann Conway-Jones, "Filled with the Glory of God: The Appropriation of Tabernacle Imagery in the New Testament and Gregory of Nyssa," in *Torah in the New Testament* (ed. Michael Tait and Peter Oakes; London: Continuum, 2010), 228–38, esp. 231–35.

in Him through the likeness of the flesh, may attain unto a perfect man, and abide immortal and incorruptible. (*Discourses* 2.22.74)[3]

In founding His Wisdom through the incarnation, the Father also founds the church as a temple of the Spirit.

Note what Athanasius does in these passages. The biblical paradigms do not function as poetic window dressing for a prior Christology. Rather, the substance of his Christology emerges from his elaboration of biblical paradigms. Paradigms answer "technical" questions about the eternity of the Son, the nature of the Son, and the consubstantiality of Father and Son. Of course, when rightly elaborated, the biblical paradigms support and prove the creed, but Scripture plays the determining role. For Athanasius, typology controls Christology.

At some point in the history of the church, this mode of Christological reflection fell out of fashion. Typology and technical Christology went their separate ways. I will not trace the history, but will merely point to Thomas Aquinas's various discussions of the tabernacle to document the *fact* of a divergence.

Thomas can spin off sanctuary typologies with the imaginative verve of an Origen or a Bede. According to Thomas, "the figurative reason" for the specific features of the tabernacle and its furnishings "may be taken from the relation of the tabernacle to Christ, who was foreshadowed therein." Christ is typified by the "propitiatory" or mercy seat, which, in Thomas's understanding, was borne aloft above the cherubim, figuring the angels who exalt Jesus. Jesus is the new ark: "As the ark is made of setim-wood, so is Christ's body composed of most pure members," and as the ark is overlaid with gold, so "Christ was full of wisdom and charity, which are betokened by gold." The golden pot inside the ark represents Christ's "holy soul" and is full of manna because "all the fullness of the God" dwells in Him. Since Jesus possesses priestly power, He is fittingly represented by the rod of Aaron; since He is a lawgiver, He is foreshadowed in the tables of Torah. That "Christ is signified by the candlestick" is evident from John 8 ("I am the light of the world"), and the seven lamps on the stand represent the seven Spirits of God that come from the Lamb in Revelation. Jesus is the table of

---

3. See also, "And as a wise architect, proposing to build a house, consults also about repairing it, should it at any time become dilapidated after building, and, as counselling about this, makes preparation and gives to the workmen materials for a repair; and thus the means of the repair are provided before the house; in the same way prior to us is the repair of our salvation founded in Christ, that in Him we might even be new-created. And the will and the purpose were made ready 'before the world,' but have taken effect when the need required, and the Saviour came among us" (*Discourses* 2.22.77).

showbread, since He says "I am the living bread." Christ is figured by the two altars of the tabernacle, since all our works are offered to God through Him. In Christ we offer our afflictions to God on the altar of holocausts, and perfected Christians offer their spiritual desires to God in Christ "on the altar of incense."[4] Nearly every detail of the tabernacle serves as a type of the incarnate Son in His Person and His work of propitiation and intercession.

Yet there is another hand. In his commentary on John, Thomas Aquinas follows Chrysostom and Hilary in seeing John 1 as an anticipation of Chalcedonian orthodoxy and a pre-refutation of heretics. John says that the "Word was made flesh" to "exclude any assumption" of human nature that did not terminate "at a oneness of person." Having escaped that error, though, it is easy to fall into another, namely, that the Word "was converted into flesh" to produce "only one nature compounded from the human and divine natures." To head off this Eutychean, Monophysite error, John declares that the Word "made his dwelling among us." That statement distinguishes the humanity and divinity, since "to dwell implies a distinction between a dweller and that in which it dwells."[5] The Word's dwelling in the temple of His body is unique: God dwells in us too, but that indwelling is by grace while the Word "dwells in Christ according to a union in the person" that includes both body and soul. Thus John does not endorse the errors of Nestorius, who "claims that the Word of God was joined to human nature only by an indwelling," and who implies that "the person of God is distinct from that of man in Christ." To avoid that error, it is essential to insist that "God's indwelling in Christ refers to the nature" and not to the person.[6]

In Thomas's exegesis of John 1, the typological riffs on the tabernacle furniture are entirely absent.[7] And the divergence of Christology and

---

4. *ST* I–II, 102, 4, repl. obj. 4. Thomas appears to be in the mainstream of medieval exegesis here. For Bede, the ark is Christ, in whom are hidden all the treasures of wisdom and knowledge (1.3); the two cubits of the ark's length represent the double ministry of Christ in word and deed, and the additional half-cubit represents human frailty (1.4); the ark is gold inside and out to present the inner power of the Spirit and the outer display of the Spirit's work (1.4); the propitiatory or mercy seat is Christ (1.5), and so is the shaft of the lampstand (1.7) (Bede, *On the Tabernacle* [trans. Arthur Holder; Liverpool: Liverpool University Press, 1994]. See also Bede, *On the Temple* [trans. Sean Connolly; Liverpool: Liverpool University Press, 1995).

5. Thomas Aquinas, *Commentary on the Gospel of John* (trans. James Weisheipl; Albany, NY: Magi Books, 1998), at 1:14. The commentary is available online at http://dhspriory.org/thomas/SSJohn.htm.

6. Ibid., at 2:21.

7. According to Thomas, Jesus' human nature is indwelt by the Spirit, and thus He can be viewed as the perfect tabernacle. By a special mode, God indwells human being in knowledge and love, and in this sense is it true to say that God dwells in the soul "as in His own *temple*" (ST 1, 43, 3). See the discussion in Matthew Levering, *Christ's Fulfillment of Torah and Temple: Salvation according to Thomas Aquinas* (Notre Dame, IN: Notre Dame University Press, 2002), 187 fn 62. Levering is more cautious than Thomas when he writes, "it would be misleading to describe Christ as the perfect Temple of God because Christ is God." Thomas is able to draw more from the tabernacle than Levering because he focuses on the specifics of the tabernacle furnishings, rather than on the tabernacle as dwelling place.

typology is more pronounced, even *startling*, in Thomas's treatment of the incarnation in the *Summa*. In the first twenty-six questions of the *Tertia pars*, Thomas *never* refers to the sanctuary as a paradigm of incarnation. Astonishingly, he cites John 1:14 only *once*, and then only partially ("the Word became flesh," not "He tabernacled among us") in support of his own Christological views (III.16.6). Even there the verse is used only to prove the fact of the incarnation and not to explicate the *mode*.[8] This is in dramatic contrast to his overt use of tabernacle imagery in discussing the sanctification of Mary (III.27.2).[9]

For Thomas, the omission of sanctuary typology from formal Christology is deliberate.[10] One must beware not only of Nestorius but also of the error of Apollinaris, who "said that the body of Christ was inanimate matter because the temple was inanimate." Thomas rebuts this claim by stressing the metaphorical character of the claim that "the body of Christ is a temple," which means that "a likeness does not exist in all respects, but only in some respects, namely, as to indwelling."[11] Athanasius too recognizes discontinuities in his paradigms, but this is something different. The tabernacle imagery that earlier in the *Summa* is a rich source of reflections on Jesus' life and ministry has been reduced to a monochrome metaphor of divine indwelling. Thomas says nothing about how the fact that the tabernacle and temple had two chambers might figure into a theology of incarnation, and nothing about how the furniture of the tabernacle—altars, lamp, table, ark—might explicate the Person of the

---

8. In the section on the incarnation in the *ST* (III, 2–26), he mentions the temple model only to criticize it. It is the position of Nestorius and Theodore of Mopsuestia and their heretical followers to describe the union as a union of indwelling, as if "the Word dwelt in the man, as in a temple" (III, 2, 6). He makes a handful of references to the literal temple of the Jews. He cites John 1:14 in an objection to III.5.3 ("Whether the Son of God assumed a soul") as a basis for the objection that the Son assumed flesh and not soul, and he quotes another part of the verse ("we saw His glory ... full of grace and truth") several times (e.g., III.7.7, 9, 10, 12; III.8.1, III.10.4; III.15.3; III.23.4; III.26.2). Not until he is more than halfway through his treatise on the Incarnation does he use the verse to prove that "God was made man" (III.16.6), and even there he cites only "The Word was made flesh" without referring to the tabernacle imagery. Near the end of the section, he defends relic veneration on the grounds that the saints bodies are "temples, and organs of the Holy Ghost, dwelling and operating in them" (III.25.6).

9. Thomas writes, "The things of the Old Testament were figures of the New.... Now the sanctification of the tabernacle, of which it is written (Psalm 45:5 [46:4]): 'The most High hath sanctified His own tabernacle,' seems to signify the sanctification of the mother of God, who is called 'God's tabernacle,' according to Psalm 18:6: "He hath set His tabernacle in the sun. But if the tabernacle it is written ... 'After all things were perfected, the cloud covered the tabernacle of the testimony, and the glory of the Lord filled it.' Therefore also the Blessed Virgin was not sanctified until after all in her was perfected."

10. His commentary on John 1:14 is at a disadvantage because the Vulgate does not make a direct reference to the tabernacle, employing the verb *habitavit*. Nothing in this part of his commentary indicates that he consulted the original Greek.

11. Thomas, *Commentary on John*, at 2:21.

incarnate Son or the mode of His becoming flesh or the character of His work.

Thomas's interpretation of John 1 points to some of the reasons for the divergence of typology and Christology, especially with respect to the imagery of indwelling. It is partly a result of the boundary-marking work of the early councils, whose formulae came from ecumenical councils and came to serve in place of overt biblical statements as practical summaries of orthodoxy. The divergence is also due to the heretical uses to which biblical paradigms were put. Athanasius freely employs the Johannine typology of Jesus as the new temple, but that paradigm is looked on with disfavor after the Nestorian controversy took sanctuary Christology in an extrinsicist direction. According to the received interpretation of Nestorius, he claims that the "Word was united to human nature only by an indwelling through grace."[12]

In his "Third Letter" to Nestorius, Cyril of Alexandria acknowledges that the language of indwelling is used Christologically in the New Testament, but the thrust of his statement is to distinguish the Word's becoming-flesh from God's indwelling in the saints. Rather, the Word is united "according to nature" and indwells the flesh "as the soul of man too may be said to [indwell] its own body." The eleventh of the twelve anathemas appended to Cyril's letter rejects all who say that Christ's flesh is "possessed of divine indwelling *only*," since that would undermine the uniqueness of Jesus.[13] Over the centuries, the sanctuary comes to be seen as a more appropriate model for the church, believers, or Mary than for Jesus.[14] Orthodoxy demands something more than a Word indwelling flesh; after Nestorius, Christologies of divine indwelling are dismissed as Christologies of *mere* indwelling, and the mode of union is explicated

---

12. This is the summary from ibid. at 1:14. Whether or not Nestorius held to the view expressed here is questionable. See Grillmeier, *Christ in the Christian Tradition* (Louisville: Westminster/John Knox, 1975), vol. 1.

13. "Third Letter," available at www.dailycatholic.org/3ecumen2.htm#Third. Cyril returns repeatedly to this point, distinguishing between a Christology of indwelling and a hypostatic union. See John McGuckin, *Saint Cyril of Alexandria and the Christological Controversy* (Crestwood, NY: St. Vladimir's Seminary Press, 2004), 269, 312, 359–60.

14. See Gary A. Anderson, "Towards a Theology of the Tabernacle and Its Furniture," in *Text, Thought, and Practice in Qumran and Early Christianity* (ed. Ruth A. Clements and Daniel R. Schwartz; Leiden: Brill, 2009), 161–94; also idem, "Mary in the Old Testament," *Pro Ecclesia* 16/1 (2007): 33–55. Depending on the circles one travels in, it may be a commendation or the opposite to note Schleiermacher's affinity for a Christology of indwelling. In Christ, "the God-consciousness in His self-consciousness ... continually and exclusively determine[s] every moment" so that the Redeemer enjoys a "perfect indwelling of the Supreme Being ... as His peculiar being and His inmost self" (*The Christian Faith* [London: Continuum, 1999], sec. 94). See Lori Pearson, "Schleiermacher and the Christologies Behind Chalcedon," *HTR* 96:3 (2003): 368–69.

with extrabiblical categories and terms. This substantive shift is accompanied by a methodological inversion: Christological creeds come to control the legitimate uses of biblical paradigms and types that once controlled Christology.[15]

This paper is by no means an assault on creeds. I am not a primitivist longing for the simplicity of early Christianity. Yet one does not have to be a dyed-in-the-wool Protestant (though it helps) to be alarmed by the absence of John 1:14 from Thomas's doctrine of the incarnation. Christology and typology have often gone their separate ways. I would like to reintroduce them.

Is a reintroduction necessary? Can we not just work from and within the creeds? Can Athanasian paradigms or Thomistic allegory produce any Christological fruit? For me, the proof is in the pudding—a fruit pudding. Does *in fact* a typological framework advance our understanding of Jesus and His work? Can we *in fact* work out Christology along Athanasian lines, elaborating biblical imagery and types? Or do the creeds give us our Christological conclusions before we look at Scripture? Do we know what we want the Bible to say before we open the cover? Do we at some point set the Bible aside to change key, to begin speaking in a different idiom?

Today I offer one slice of pudding for your tasting:[16] sanctuary Christology in the gospel of John.[17] The remainder of my paper is divided into three parts. First, I briefly summarize the form and theology of Israel's sanctuaries. Second, I take a speedy tour through John's gospel to show that

---

15. A similar substantive and methodological shift took place in sacramental theology. "Technical" sacramental theology was worked out in terms of substance and accidents, while preaching, mystical writing, hymnody, and catechesis employed biblical typologies.

16. Gary Anderson has developed some aspects of a temple view of the incarnation in "To See Where God Dwells: The Tabernacle, the Temple, and the Origins of the Christian Mystical Tradition," *Letter & Spirit* 4 (2008): 13–45. According to Anderson, "the temple furniture was understood as possessing something of the very being of the God of Israel" (13). He presents intriguing evidence from both the Old Testament and from ancient Jewish sources, but I remain unconvinced. Anderson's readings of the ancient text are not always persuasive (e.g., his interpretation of a passage from *Yoma* on p. 26), and his characterization of early Christological debates is imprecise (cf. p. 38, fn 68.). On John 1, Anderson overstresses the continuity and does not take sufficient account of the fact that John *contrasts* the condition of Israel with that of the disciples who saw glory in Jesus. It is possible, I think, to agree that the Psalms speak of "seeing God" by seeing the temple without identifying God and His house as closely as Anderson does. The tabernacle and temple were made "according to the תבנית," the pattern of glory revealed to Moses and David; to see the temple was to glimpse the glory of God. Yet it is the case that some of the temple furnishings were imbued with a contagious form of holiness, and this might provide background for gospel accounts in which touching Jesus communicates life. Jesus' body and even his garments are charged with the power and life-giving holiness of His divine person.

17. If, as I believe, Revelation is Johannine, we have further evidence from the closing vision: "I saw no temple in [the new Jerusalem], for the Lord God the Almighty and the Lamb are its temple" (Rev 21:22).

sanctuary Christology radically shapes John's presentation of Jesus and His work. Finally, I take up a question posed by N. T. Wright, "What might it do to our systematic Christologies to make the Temple, rather than theories about natures, persons, and substances, central to our reflection?"[18] Wright answers his own question with a firm, "I do not know." In this paper I hope to advance further than that, if only a hesitant step or two!

I. SANCTUARIES IN ANCIENT ISRAEL.[19]

According to the Pentateuch, Israel's tabernacle is a two-room tent surrounded by an open courtyard. The court is encompassed by a white curtain hooked onto poles set in bronze bases. A curtain doorway faces east. Within the courtyard stands a bronze altar for animal offerings and a bronze basin of water that priests use for washing their hands and feet before entering the sanctuary. As a priest moves west through the curtain into the tent itself, he enters the holy place, a rectangular room containing (to the north) a gold-plated table set with twelve loaves of bread, a pure gold lampstand to the south constructed like a stylized burning tree and set with seven removable oil lamps, and a gold-covered wooden incense altar before the western curtain. Once a year, the high priest passes through the west curtain into the Most Holy Place, clothed in a cloud of incense, to sprinkle blood before the ark, the single item of furniture in the Most Holy Place. The ark or coffer is a rectangular wooden box, covered inside and out with gold, with a removable lid consisting of a slab of pure gold on which are carved two golden cherubim.

The floor plan of the temple is similar, though the temple has triple the cubic volume of the tabernacle. Several furnishings are added to the temple. In the court, the major addition is water. The laver is expanded into a monumental bronze sea, elevated from the ground on the backs of twelve bronze bulls. From the temple there runs a gauntlet of ten water "chariots," basins of waters resting on stylized carts decorated with cherubim and other Edenic motifs, five on each side of a pathway leading to the altar. The temple proper is stone, not fabric; the interior walls

---

18. N. T. Wright, "Jesus' Self-Understanding," in *The Incarnation: An International Symposium on the Incarnation of the Son of God* (ed. Stephen T. Davis, Daniel Kendall, and Gerald O'Collins; Oxford: Oxford University Press, 2002), 58.

19. Despite the title of this section, I do not address controverted historical questions that surround the tabernacle and temple. I believe the biblical presentation of those sanctuaries is historically accurate, but for the purposes of this paper I bracket the question of historicity and concentrate instead on the *textual* sanctuaries of ancient Israel. For the sake of space, I also leave out a great deal of specific information concerning the dimensions and materials. My assumption is that all of those details are important, perhaps important even to discovering the Christological import of sanctuary typology. But there is only so much one can do in a short space.

are completely paneled with cedar wood and the floor covered entirely with gold. Doors rather than curtains separate the rooms, and the rooms are given new names. Some furnishings are added inside. In place of the tabernacle's single lampstand there are ten golden lampstands, and in addition to the golden cherubim on the ark cover Solomon constructs two self-standing "oil wood" cherubim, each ten cubits tall with a wing span of ten cubits.

Both tabernacle and temple are described as "sanctuaries," a term that in Hebrew as in English is etymologically related to the word group for "holiness." A sanctuary is holy space sanctified by the presence of the Lord in His glory. Both the tabernacle and temple are houses for the glory or the Name of Yahweh, and the architectural pattern reinforces this domestic symbolism. The court is Yahweh's kitchen, where His bread is prepared on the altar; the holy place is the "living room" equipped with food and light and pleasing incense; and the Most Holy Place is the throne room of the divine king of Israel, who sits above the cherubim. The tabernacle is also a creation model. The verbal blueprint in Exodus 25−31 is laid out in a series of seven speeches that constitute a subtle variation on the creative words of Genesis 1. Josephus and Philo were perfectly biblical in suggesting that the tabernacle was a cosmic tent, complete with a seven-light solar system. Cherubim evoke Eden, as do the fruits carved in the temple walls. Sanctuaries are renewed gardens, priests the new Adamic gardeners.

In Hebrew, architectural terminology overlaps with anatomical, and this along with other hints suggests that the tabernacle is humaniform. In particular, the tabernacle is an architectural replica of the high priest, and vice versa. Layered tabernacle curtains resemble the layered robes of the priest; the Most Holy Place corresponds to the gold flower on the high priest's head, engraven with the words קדש ליהוה, "Holy to the Lord"; the Holy Place with its twelve loaves and lamps is replicated on the high priest's breastplate as twelve precious stones, which sparkle with light. Both the tabernacle and the priestly garments are made after the pattern of glory that Moses glimpses on Sinai, so that the tabernacle is an architectural depiction of a glorified man.

Before moving to the New Testament, we may note at least this: it would be arbitrary to restrict sanctuaries *merely* to "dwelling places." They are that, but they are also holy spaces, sites of new creation, recoveries of Eden, architectural depictions of a perfected human being. Nor are they empty shells, but are adorned and filled with furniture. Israel's sanctuaries are dwelling places of a particular kind. As we consider the Christological significance of sanctuaries, we should be wary of reducing this rich imaginative detail to a single motif.

II. SANCTUARY CHRISTOLOGY IN JOHN[20]

Virtually all commentators agree that John alludes to the tabernacle in the beginning of his gospel. When the word becomes flesh, He "pitches a tent" (σκηνόω) among us, and the arresting force of that verb is reinforced by the tabernacle-fraught terminology that surrounds it. In the tabernacled Word, John says, "we beheld His glory" (John 1:14), which reminds us of the glistening glory-cloud that rested in the tabernacle at Sinai. John mentions Moses by name and contrasts the gifts of the law with the gifts that the Word brings (1:14, 17).[21] The Torah institutes a tabernacle and a liturgical system, but that is not the full realization of grace and truth, which arrive fully only when the Word tabernacles in flesh. "No one has seen God at any time" (1:18), John says, alluding to the dense narrative of Exodus 32–34. On Sinai, Moses alone sees God's glory, and then only His back. In the Word made flesh, however, God *opens* the tabernacle, displaying glory to all who believe. At Sinai, Yahweh reveals His glory by proclaiming, "The LORD, the LORD, compassionate and gracious, slow to anger, and abounding in lovingkindness and truth" (Exod 34:6), which, translated Johanninely, is "full of grace and truth." [22]

---

20. Tabernacle and temple motifs are evident to any careful reader of John's gospel, but recent work has focused attention on them. See Alan R. Kerr, *The Temple of Jesus' Body: The Temple Theme in the Gospel of John* (London: Continuum, 2002); Stephen Um, *The Theme of Temple Christology in John's Gospel* (London: Continuum, 2006); Mary L. Coloe, *God Dwells with Us: Temple Symbolism in the Fourth Gospel* (Collegeville, MN: Liturgical, 2001); idem, "Temple Imagery in John," *Int* (2009): 368–81; Mark Kinzer, "Temple Christology in the Gospel of John," *SPSBL* (1998), 447–464; Scott Hahn, "Temple, Sign, and Sacrament: Towards a New Perspective on the Gospel of John," *Letter & Spirit* 4 (2006): 107–43; Dan Brown, "Temple Christology in the Gospel of John" (M.A. Thesis, Trinity Western University, Vancouver, BC, 2010), which the author kindly provided to me. Yves Congar gives a superb summary of the temple Christology of the Synoptics and John in *Le mystère du temple: l'économie de la presence de Dieu à sa creature de la Genèse à l'Apocalypse* (Paris: Cerf, 1965), 139–80. Some speak of an "anti-Temple Christology" (Raymond Brown, *Community of the Beloved Disciple* [New York: Paulist, 1979], 166–69).

21. John C. Meagher, "John 1:14 and the New Temple," *JBL* 88/1 (1969): 57–68, suggests that 1:14 refers not to the incarnation but to the descent of the Spirit. That smoothes some of the difficulties concerning the arrangement of the prologue, but to make it work Meagher has to substitute πνεῦμα for σάρξ and posit an emendation for which there is no evidence. For discussion of the "tabernacling" as a wisdom theme, see Pamela Kinlaw, *The Christ Is Jesus: Metamorphosis, Possession, and Johannine Christology* (Atlanta: Society of Biblical Literature, 2005), 62–67, 114–17.

22. Craig Evans gives connections between John's prologue and the narrative of covenant renewal in Exodus 33–34 (*Word and Glory: On the Exegetical and Theological Background of John's Prologue* [LNTS; London: T&T Clark, 1993], 79–82). This adds another layer to John's typology, but it does not negate an allusion to the tabernacle. After all, the fact that Moses sees and begins to reflect the glory of Yahweh is a pledge that Yahweh will remain in the midst of Israel and go with them to the land; Moses' experience is the "firstfruits" of the experience that Israel will have when Yahweh descends to take up residence in the tent.

For our later discussion, it is important to note a few details of the prologue. First, what "becomes flesh" is the Word, God's own self-communication, the Word that "exegetes" the Father. This Word is simultaneously distinguished from and identified with God (1:1). He is toward God and He is God. The Word is God's self-communication that is already differentiatedly united, unitedly differentiated from the Father prior to His coming. He, this Word, takes on flesh.

Second, while "flesh" can refer in Scripture to material bodiliness, it more often carries connotations of weakness, frailty, need, mortality. In Paul's understanding, the resurrection is a translation from flesh to Spirit, the former characterized by mutability, dishonor, and weakness. John's "the Word became flesh" accents not merely the embodiment of God's self-communication, but God's entry into that human condition characterized by "fleshliness."

Third, commentators often assume that the analogy works like this: the Word is the Lord who comes into His tent; the tent is the flesh in which He dwells and in which He displays His glory. That matches John's later aside that Jesus' spoke of "the temple of His body" (John 2:19–21), but it seems preferable to take 1:14 more broadly. The Word takes on a body, also a soul and everything that an individual human being possesses, but more generally the Word pitches His tent in the midst of human need and weakness, so that He can share it all, just as Yahweh pitches His tent in the midst of Israel, in spite of Israel's repeated rebellions.

Fourth, we should feel the full force of John's ἐγένετο, "became." When the Holy One took up residence in the tabernacle, the space and its furnishings were infused with His sanctity. Only men sanctified by ordination dare tread on holy ground, minister at holy altars, or manipulate holy things. But the spread of Yahweh's holiness to the tent is a dim shadow of the Word's relation to His flesh. Yahweh comes and goes in His house; He does not *become* tabernacle or temple. In the incarnation the Word "became" the fleshly house, identifying Himself with flesh, taking flesh as the mode of His own existence so that He could raise it to Spirit. (This is one point of superiority to Moses.) Yet, in becoming flesh the Word does not cease to be toward God and God, as Jesus' "I am" statements testify. Finally, the Word pitches His tent in order to display the glory of God *in* flesh. The force of this point becomes clearer in Jesus' later statements about glory. His hour of crucifixion is His hour of glory, the hour when He and the Father engage in a veritable potlatch of glory-giving. In the cross, we see the glory of the Son, which is the glory of His self-dedication to the Father; in the cross too, we see the glory of the Father, which is the glory of the eternal truth and lovingkindness that sends the Son. John's Christology is a theology of glory, but of a glory refracted through a tent of flesh, and so cruciform.[23]

On the surface, sanctuary themes disappear after the first chapters of the gospel.[24] As we look deeper, we find that temple Christology marks nearly every page. The Son of Man, Jesus tells Nathaniel, is a new Bethel ("house of God"), a ladder connecting heaven and earth, with angelic liturgists ascending and descending (John 1). The time has come, Jesus tells the Samaritan woman, when worshipers must worship in Spirit and in truth (John 4). Jesus spends much of the gospel in and around Jerusalem, worshiping and teaching at the temple during festivals. The "signs" He performs in the first half of the book correspond to symbols and themes of Jewish festivals, indicating that He not only fulfills holy space but also the temple's cycle of holy time.[25] During a Passover, Jesus feeds five thousand in the wilderness and describes Himself as heavenly bread. At the Feast of Tabernacles, which includes a water rite, Jesus announces that He provides living water that will flow "out of the belly" of those who believe in Him, an allusion (among other things) to the waters flowing from the rebuilt temple in Ezekiel 47.[26] Arguably at the Feast of Dedication that commemorates the miraculous relighting of the temple lamps, Jesus declares He is the light of the world.

Let me illustrate further by examining a few passages where the temple imagery is more deeply submerged. In John 15, Jesus describes Himself as the true vine, His disciples as branches in the vine. Fruitful branches are pruned, while unfruitful ones are cut off and burned. It is an organic analogy, rooted in Old Testament imagery of imperial and royal trees. At several points, Jesus uses terms that jarringly take us out of the viticultural zone of the discourse's leading metaphor. "You are clean" (John 15:3; καθαρός; cf. 13:10–11), but why would branches have to be clean? Jesus exhorts the

---

23. John 2 continues the explicit sanctuary Christology. After Jesus cleanses the temple, He says, "Destroy this temple, and in three days I will raise it up" (2:19). When the Jews are confused, John clarifies that "He was speaking of the temple of His body" (2:21). Jesus speaks of His death as a temple demolition, but promises also a reconstruction of His glorified temple-body after three days. For a lively analysis of the temple scene in John 2, see Alan R. Kerr, *Temple of Jesus' Body: The Temple Theme in the Gospel of John* (London: Sheffield Academic, 2002), 67–101.

24. If John and Revelation are designed, as I believe, to be read as a two-volume work (analogous to Luke-Acts), then the opening references to the temple are fulfilled in the final chapters of Revelation, when the Lord God and the Lamb become the temple of the bridal Jerusalem that descends from heaven (21:22).

25. Hahn, "Temple, Sign, and Sacrament," 111–14.

26. Raymond E. Brown, *The Gospel of John* (AB; New York: Doubleday, 1995), 1–121, 327.

disciples to "abide" (15:4; μένω) in Him, which might connote persistence through time but commonly speaks of dwelling in space. Further, Jesus speaks of mutual abiding, branches in vine and vine in branches (v. 5), or the word of the Vine in the branches (v. 7). As the discourse continues, the vine begins to resemble a house and the branches resemble residents of the house who must be clean to enter; we are also reminded of prophetic texts in which Israel is a vineyard (Isa 5) and Synoptic parables in which Jesus threatens to take a vineyard from Israel to give it to others who will produce its fruit (Matt 21:33–45). Even the vine and branches image contains a veiled reference to the house of God. As vine, Jesus is a house of wine.

Two scenes from the Passion Narrative employ temple imagery with equal subtlety. Pilate's inscription on the cross identifies Jesus not as *a* but as *the* Nazarene (John 19:19). In John, Nazareth is barely mentioned (cf. 1:45–46), and in John's view Pilate's *titlon* likely alludes not to Jesus' hometown but to Isaiah 11's prediction of a Messianic Branch (*neṣer*) from the stump of Jesse. Pilate's declaration means: "Jesus the Branch, King of the Jews." Qumran texts link Isaiah's Branch to the temple-building Branch (*ṣemaḥ*) of Zechariah 6:12: "Behold the man whose name is the Branch." *Neṣer* and *ṣemaḥ* are synonymous titles for the Messianic King who will build the eschatological temple. With his famous *Ecce homo*, Pilate quotes the first half of Zechariah 6:12 as he presents Jesus to the Jews, and then by putting "Nazarene" in the *titlon* he finishes the sentence and names Jesus as the Messianic temple-builder, a new Solomon.[27]

When Pilate presents Jesus, the Jews warn him that he is on a collision course with Caesar; they cry out for Jesus' execution and proclaim their loyalty to Caesar as their only king (John 19:12–16). All this takes place, John tells us, on the "Pavement" (Λιθόστρωτον, a term for which John provides the Hebrew equivalent, Gabbathah, 19:13). The Greek word is found only once in the LXX, in the Chronicler's account of the temple dedication. When the glory descends into the Most Holy Place, the Israelites fall with their faces on the "pavement" (Heb. רצפה; LXX λιθόστρωτον; 2 Chr 7:3). Pilate's court has become a topsy-turvy temple, where the God of Israel displays His glory in mutilated flesh and where Jews worship Caesar instead of Jesus.[28]

Finally, while dying on the cross, Jesus declares that the Beloved

---

27. Here I am heavily dependent on Coloe, "Temple Imagery," 377–79. Does Pilate know what he's doing? Maybe not; it's all providential irony. But maybe so; in which case, Pilate certainly intends it as cruel mockery of Jewish hope: "Behold your branch; behold what Rome does to your Messiahs." In this case the providential irony is perhaps intensified.

28. The irony of the scene is even richer if verse 13 is translated as "caused him to sit" rather than "sat down." In that case, Jesus is seated as presiding judge at his own trial.

Disciple is Mary's son and Mary his mother. Jesus is not simply being a good Jewish boy by taking care of his bereaved mother. Jesus' double "behold" indicates that He is pronouncing a "prophetic revelation," and the wording suggests an adoption. In the background is Jesus' Upper Room promise to prepare a place for His disciples in His Father's house or household (in John 14, οἶκος yields to οἰκία). At the beginning of the gospel, Jesus describes the doomed temple as "My Father's house [οἶκος]" (2:16), and in the Upper Room Jesus reimagines His Father's house as a living temple, constructed from disciples, indwelt by Father, Son, and Spirit.

When Jesus delivers the Beloved Disciple to Mary and Mary to the Beloved Disciple, He not only creates a relationship between Mary and the disciple but between Himself and the disciple: "If the woman always called 'the mother of Jesus' is presented also as the mother of the Beloved Disciple, then Jesus' sonship is extended to embrace others; the disciple is adopted as Jesus' brother/sister and therefore becomes a child of God." This fulfills the opening promise of the gospel: "To those who believe on Him, He gives power to become *sons of God*" (1:12). And the fulfillment of this promise is intertwined with temple imagery. To become a son of God is to become a member of the temple-house of Jesus' Father. When Jesus dies, He hands on the Spirit to the new family, so that even at the moment of His death, "the Nazarene temple-builder is in the process of raising up a new temple/Household of God" in the Spirit.[29]

Indeed, it is possible to see John's gospel as a whole as a tour through the sanctuary. In chapter 1, John the Baptist introduces Jesus as the "Lamb of God" who takes away the sins of the world, thus bringing the reader to the bronze altar with a sacrificial animal. Chapters 2–5, with their focus on water, take place at the laver. Jesus turns water to wine, tells Nicodemus he must be born of water and the Spirit, discusses living water with the Samaritan woman, and heals a paralytic who has waited thirty-eight years to be healed by the angelic stirring of the pool. Chapters 6–7 center on the feeding of the five thousand, in which Jesus distributes the bread

---

29. Coloe, "Temple Imagery," 379–80. As Coloe points out, the links to the Prologue go deeper: "The scene concludes with the disciple taking her 'to his own' (*eis ta idia*, 19:27), which forms an inclusio with the same expression used of Jesus in the prologue, 'he came to his own' (*eis ta idia*, 1:11). The inclusio indicates that the action of Jesus coming to his own, is now brought to completion. This scene is the climax of the narrative, bringing the plot announced in the prologue to its conclusion, and the narrator confirms this in v. 28, 'After this, Jesus knew that all was now finished.' The personalizing of the temple, begun in the transfer of temple imagery to Jesus (2:21), then continued with the promise of the divine indwellings in the community of believers constituting them as 'my Father's Household' (14:2), is accomplished. This divine filiation is the ultimate revelation of the 'hour' and brings Jesus' mission to its completion."

of the presence from the golden table. In chapters 8–9, Jesus lingers at the lampstand, declaring Himself the light of the world, and the Upper Room Discourse, especially chapter 17, displays Jesus as the intercessory priest, raising his hands before the golden altar. At the climax of the gospel John is at pains to show that the empty tomb is the new Holy of Holies. Like the ark cover, the slab on which Jesus' body once lay is flanked by angels, and Peter, a high priest, is the first to enter this grave of defilement now wondrously illumined with holiness.[30]

Nearly every commentary on John's gospel recognizes that Jesus' "I am" statements echo the divine name given to Moses at the burning bush.[31] These are claims to divinity, Jesus' self-identification with the God of Israel. As Thomas Aquinas understands, many of the "I am" statements also identify Jesus with some piece of tabernacle furniture or some gift that the tabernacle offers to Israel. Jesus' first "I am" is to the Samaritan woman, with whom He has a conversation about the location of temples and living water, which recalls the cleansing water of the tabernacle laver and the temple Sea. "I am the bread of life," Jesus announces to the grumbling crowds after He feeds them in the wilderness (John 6:35, 41, 48). The typological link is most directly with manna: "I am the living bread that came down out of heaven" (6:51; cf. 6:32, 49–50). But tabernacle associations are not far off. A jar of manna is preserved in the tabernacle for a memorial (Exod 16:33; Heb 9:4), and the bread on the table is heavenly bread, "most holy," reserved for priests because it is soaked in the holiness of Yahweh (Lev 24:5–9).

Several chapters later, Jesus is still in the Holy Place, declaring while healing a blind man: "While I am in the world, I am the light of the world" (John 9:5). As "I am," Jesus fulfills the lampstand. During that debate that follows the healing, He announces, "I am the door of the sheep" (10:7, 9), which points to the doorway between the Holy Place and the Most Holy Place (10:9). He is also Yahweh, the "good shepherd," enthroned on the other side of the doorway above the cherubim (10:11, 14; Ps 80:1). "I am the good shepherd" anticipates Jesus' declaration to Pilate: "You say rightly, I am a king" (John 18:37), as well as the inscription: "King of the Jews." "I am" is lifted up not on cherubim but on a cross.

---

30. W. Wiley Richards, *Riches from the Lost Ark: The Gospel of John and the Tabernacle* (Graceville, FL: Hargrave, 1993); James Jordan, *Through New Eyes: Developing a Biblical View of the World* (Eugene, OR: Wipf & Stock, 1999).

31. One among hundreds: Kevin Quast, *Reading John's Gospel: An Introduction* (New York: Paulist, 1991), 35: "In the simple admission 'I am' ... Jesus speaks as God speaks, taking upon himself God's name 'Yahweh.'"

Jesus' "I am" statements are glosses on John's original affirmation that the Word became flesh and pitched his tent among us. Yahweh's Word is light (Ps 119) and bread (Deut 8), the voice of the Shepherd of Israel. Every ἐγώ εἰμι is a variation on "I am Word." All these are specifications of John's opening claims that the Word who was toward God and was God has tabernacled in flesh. The Word is the original of which the tabernacle gifts and furnishings are earthly copies.

There is much, much more to say, but we move on. What does Johannine sanctuary typology tell us about Christology? How, if at all, can we reconcile typology and Christology?

III. THEOLOGICAL AND METHODOLOGICAL DIRECTIONS

Perhaps reconciliation is not worth the trouble. Keeping typology and Christology strangers seems a safe option. On the one hand, as Thomas Aquinas points out, sanctuary Christology has been put to nefarious Nestorian uses, and pressing Johannine typology might lead to heresies of Hegelian vintage. Where might "I am the bread of life" lead us? "I am" means "Yahweh," but if we take Jesus' statement with the full ontological force it seems to carry, we run into difficulties. How can Yahweh's incarnate Word, who *is* God, *be* bread, *be* light? Is He being *defined* over against a world of hunger and darkness?[32] On the other hand, if we avoid these dangers by diluting the ontological force of the "I am" statements, we seem to be diluting what Jesus Himself says. The better part of caution would be to let the creeds answer fundamental exegetical questions for us. "I am the Bread of Life" is not the controlling Christological statement; Nicea's *homoousios* and Chalcedon's "withouts" set the parameters within which it is true that Jesus is "I am the bread of life."

Yet I do not think that keeping typology and Christology apart is healthy for theology or the church. For starters, we run the risk of turning Scripture into a collection of proof texts for creedal statements with an accompany-

---

32. One can resolve this particular problem with two devices, one patristic, one Barthian. The patristic device is the idea of "appropriation," which in Athanasius means that the Word takes flesh and all it entails as His own (*idios*) property. It is His, even though it is acquired; it is He, even though it is acquired. We can thus speak of the Word's own sufferings, even though when we imagine an unincarnate Word, He is incapable of suffering. Thus, Jesus' "living-breadiness" is His; it is true to say that He *is* bread, because in taking flesh He has made "living-breadiness" His own. The Barthian device is to recognize that in election God determines His own being. God is not dependent on creation in any way, and yet He has willed to *be* God-for-us, elected not to be God unless He is the God who saves. "I am Bread" means that in creating the world God freely determined to *be* the world's true food.

ing florilegium of homiletic and mystical poetry. Besides, even in the fifth century, Chalcedon did not provide anything close to complete answers to fundamental Christological questions. Its *Definition* resolved the issues of the Nestorian conflict with the formula "two natures, one person." The natures remain distinct: divinity and humanity are not changed, merged, or mixed, yet neither are they separated. They are united in the one Person. Chalcedon was a notable achievement, but unlike Nicea, it failed to unite the church. Declared heretical, the churches of the East, holding to something more like Nestorian Christology, separated from the churches of the empire, with largely tragic results. Churches in Africa, claiming with some justice to hold fast to the authentic teaching of Cyril, were condemned as heretics on other grounds. Even within the churches that accepted Chalcedon, the consensus was not complete. Still today, many in the East sniff Leo's *Tome* and smell Nestorius.

Not a few modern theologians have charged that the reason for this fragmentation was that Chalcedon failed to address the Christological problems that provoked the council in the first place. Chalcedon left key terms undefined and key questions unresolved. To Schleiermacher, the two-natures doctrine is impossible to reconcile with the unity of the incarnate Son. Bulgakov considers Chalcedon a gift from God's hand, but "by no means a theological achievement," "more a schema than a doctrine," juxtaposing a Yes to a No in response to each of the conflicting Christological schools.[33] Pannenberg complains that the two-nature doctrine implies that God and humanity are species of a genus (nature) that encompasses both.[34]

More recently, Robert Jenson has pointed to what he regards as the fateful influence of Leo's *Tome*. It begins with the "unobjectionable" claim that Jesus is "true God" and "true man," but then adds: "Each nature is the agent of what is proper to it, working in fellowship with the other: the Word doing what belongs to the Word and the flesh what belongs to the flesh. The one shines forth in miracles, the other submits to the injuries." Bitingly, Jenson sums this up as "each nature does its own thing," and he describes Leo's formula as "the Antiochene doctrine or something rather cruder." Jenson sees the council's endorsement of Leo's *Tome* as a standing contradiction to Cyril's main concern, his insistence on "the theological unity of the gospel narrative."

In Jenson's view, the Chalcedon *Definition* itself has similar shortcomings. Since the decree does not say anything about agency of the one *hypostasis*, the natures appear to be the only active agents. *Hypostasis* has little to do,

---

33. Sergius Bulgakov and Boris Jakim, *The Lamb of God* (Grand Rapids: Eerdmans, 2008), 57.
34. Wolfhart Pannenberg, *Jesus: God and Man* (2nd ed.; trans. Lewis L. Wilkins and Duane A Priebe; Philadelphia: Westminster, 1977), 322.

and in Jenson's view the *Definition* diverges even from established Trinitarian usage: "in trinitarian theology, it is a hypostasis that has a 'distinguishing character' and is an agent within the total divine saving history," while for Chalcedon, "these features are attributed instead to the natures." Suspicious readers of Chalcedon have long viewed its affirmation that the natures belong to "one and the same" Person as mere "verbiage," and Jenson thinks "it is hard to say they were wrong, taking the text just as it stands." [35]

I am not citing theologians of the lunatic fringe. And once again I want to stress that I am not opposed to creeds or to the particular *Definition* of Chalcedon. It was offered as a summary of Scripture's teaching, and with all its limitations it is that. Yet, even many who regard Chalcedon as an authoritative creedal statement, who take it as a settled framework for Christology, who affirm what the *Definition* endorses and deny what it excludes, find its *Definition* far too undefined.

What happens if we pursue a Christology that is typological all the way down? What if we do what Wright suggests by starting our systematic Christology from the temple? It's high time to get my pudding off the stove and serve it up.

What is the Christological import of Johannine sanctuary typology? Let me answer by posing a series of fundamental Christological questions, answering them as I think John does:

- Who is the subject of the gospel story? From its origin in the bosom of the Father through the cross and the Word's return to the Father, the adventure story of the gospel has one protagonist: The Word who was with God and was God.
- How does the Word come to us? The Word becomes flesh. As noted, "flesh" designates not the soulless body of a human but subeschatological existence in its totality. [36] "Flesh" includes everything classic Christology includes in the human nature, but adds to it the notes of weakness, vulnerability, and mortality.

---

35. Robert W. Jenson, *Systematic Theology, 1: The Triune God* (Oxford: Oxford University Press, 1997), 1:130–33.

36. Donald MacLeod is particularly vivid at this point: "For the Son of God, the incarnation meant a whole new set of relationships: with his father and mother; with his brothers and sisters; with his disciples; with the scribes, the Pharisees, and the Sadducees; with Roman soldiers and with lepers and prostitutes. It was within these relationships that he lived his incarnate life, experiencing pain, poverty, and temptation; witnessing squalor and brutality; hearing obscenities and profanities and the hopeless cry of the oppressed. He lived not in sublime detachment or in ascetic isolation, but 'with us,' as 'the fellow-man of all men,' crowded, busy, harassed, stressed and molested. No large estate gave him space, no financial capital guaranteed his daily bread, no personal staff protected him from interruptions and no power or influence protected him from injustice. He saved us from alongside us" (*The Person of Christ* [Downers Grove, IL: InterVarsity Press, 1998], 180).

- What is the mode of union? It is a union of indwelling, for the Word "tabernacles" among us and "becomes" flesh. It is a union-by-indwelling that grounds Jesus' twin declarations, "I am the bread of life" (John 6:35, 48), and "the bread which I shall give for the life of the world is my flesh" (6:51). He is the bread of life, His flesh is the bread of life; having tabernacled in flesh, the Word is His flesh and His flesh is He.

Understood along these lines, John gives us a Christology faithful to Nicea and Chalcedon, but one that satisfies legitimate objections of Chalcedon's ancient and modern critics. On the one hand, John's sanctuary Christology does not depend on the controverted, undefined terms of Chalcedon. It thus avoids *some* Monophysite and Nestorian objections and sidesteps Schleiermacher's challenge. On the other hand, Johannine sanctuary Christology is more clearly Cyrillian than Chalcedon itself at the crucial point: it is a single-subject Christology, in which the Word that is God is the sole agent. Yet by taking "flesh" in its full biblical sense, Johannine sanctuary Christology satisfies Antiochene worries about preserving the fully reality of Jesus' humanity and human experience in history. It is an ecumenical advantage, I think, that a sanctuary Christology remains within the conceptualities of the Bible. To contest my sketch of Johannine Christology, one would have to question my exegesis of John and other biblical texts. Exegetical debates are not easy; but they are preferable to becoming embroiled over elusive terms like "person" and "nature."[37]

Johannine sanctuary Christology, worked up from Johannine typology, opens some fresh angles on other Christological concerns. More vividly than some formulas, it highlights the inseparable union of Christ's person and work. Words reveal; when the Word comes He shows the Father. The Word comes in a particular manner, in the way of *tabernacle*, and that means that the Word comes among us as the dwelling of God on earth, the first site of renewed creation, the sacred place, the exclusive location of worship, the glorified man, the place where heaven intersects earth. To come in the way of tabernacle means that the Word comes in the way of sacrifice and incense, with altars, showbread, a lampstand, an ark-throne.

---

37. According to Pannenberg, the earliest patristic writers located the key question about the incarnate Word in his relationship to the Father. For later writers, the question about the incarnate Word moves a step to become a question about the relationship of this being, Jesus, to the eternal Son of God (*Jesus: God and Man*, ch. 9). Jenson (*Systematic Theology*, 127, fn. 6) raises this complaint, calls the later shift a "misstep," and says that Pannenberg's clarity in restoring the earlier consensus is one of his chief contributions to dogmatics. Johannine sanctuary Christology represents a forceful return to the earlier view.

John translates each of these sanctuary vessels into Messianic action: As bread Jesus feeds, as light He opens blind eyes, and as ark He is the place where God is enthroned in glory. The tabernacled Word is "full of grace and truth" (John 1:14), loaded with the true gifts of the covenant. That the Word tabernacles in *flesh* points ahead to Jesus' self-gift in death, and it is above all there that the Word walks in the way of tabernacle—on the cross where He is bread, light, living water, the visibility of the Father's glory. After John has identified Jesus as Word tabernacled in flesh, he does not have to add a second level of reflection to describe His work. What the Word becomes leads, gravitationally we might say, to what He comes to do.

Johannine sanctuary Christology supports Melanchthon's dictum, "To know Christ is to know his benefits." Yet while the Word comes "clothed in His benefits," John teaches that the Word offers *Himself* with and as benefit. The Word is the eternal archetype of all the sanctuary furnishings, which *He* makes accessible in His advent. All the sanctuary gifts that John enumerates exegete John's opening declaration that Jesus is the Word. He, the Word, becomes light, bread, living water, good shepherd, just as He tabernacles to become flesh. But because the tabernacle is *flesh*, the Word offers Himself as light, life, bread, living water, good shepherd by suffering what flesh suffers—agonizing torture and death.

Sanctuary Christology also integrates soteriology, ecclesiology, and eschatology into Christology and sets all these within a Trinitarian framework. Since the fifth century, orthodoxy has hedged on the analogy between the Word's dwelling in Jesus and God's dwelling in believers and the church. It is a necessary distinction, but the hedging tends to push apart what the New Testament blurs together. The Word begins His career in the "bosom of the Father," and Jesus describes this as mutual habitation: "I am in the Father and the Father is in me" (John 14:9–11; 17:21). Because the Word has shown His glory in flesh, human beings see and know the Father, and knowing the Father in the Son is eternal life. By knowing the Father and the Son, the believer himself becomes a temple of the Father and the Son, both dwelling in him by the Spirit.[38] The glory

---

38. We can elaborate this salvific indwelling by reference to the "I am" statements: To say that the Word dwells in us is to say that we are inhabited by light, filled with the living bread, attuned to the voice of the good shepherd. Through death, resurrection, and the outbreathing of the Spirit, the Word who pitches His tent in flesh pitches His tent also in us, who become sons in the Son, and this is eternal life. Paul, of course, picks up the same typology and draws ethical conclusions. Those who are temples of God, one Spirit with Him, should not make themselves one flesh with a prostitute. They should not defile the temple of their bodies with sexual sin.

of the Word is thus displayed in the flesh of the believer, as each follows Jesus in self-immolating obedience to the Father.

This life is an inherently corporate reality, for the Word who pitched His tent in Jesus pitches His tent among *disciples*. As a result of the Word's tabernacling, the Spirit forms a communion of disciples whose unity with one another resembles the communion of the Father and the Son: "That they may be one," Jesus prays, "as you, Father, are in Me and I in You" (John 17:21). Sanctuary Christology has its source in a "sanctuary" Trinitarianism, which spills out in a sanctuary-soteriology and a sanctuary-ecclesiology.

Temple ecclesiology points in turn to a sanctuary eschatology. Creation will reach its consummation in a city that descends from heaven, adorned like a bride and greeted with the shout, "Now the tabernacle of God is among men." The Word is consummately tabernacled among human beings when He comes to dwell in the new heavens and new earth, in which God and the Lamb are the temple. For John, Christology, soteriology, ecclesiology, and eschatology are all variations on a sanctuary theme: the tabernacling of the Word replicates itself with difference in each believer, in the church, in the new Jerusalem.[39]

---

39. Sanctuary Christology focuses attention on the liturgical and sacramental dimensions of the Christian life. If Jesus is the tabernacled Word, He is the house of prayer, the place of sacrifice. All the liturgical practices of Israel are folded into Him, but they are again unfolded in the church as the Word who indwells flesh indwells the church by His Spirit.

CHAPTER 7

THE THEANDRIC UNION AS *IMAGO DEI* AND *CAPAX DEI*

JASON MCMARTIN

INTRODUCTION

Theological anthropology has taken on a Christological cast in recent decades, perhaps due in large measure to the influence of Karl Barth.[1] Contemporary theologians frequently assume that humanity is theologically best understood through Christ as the true human. The conduit supplying a significant measure of the flow from Christology to anthropology is the concept of *the image of God*. Some of the same reasons adumbrated for reasoning from Christology to anthropology are also cited as reasons to resist the opposite direction of reflection, from anthropology to Christology.

My purpose in this paper is not to develop an argument that the relationship between Christology and theological anthropology should be bidirectional. Instead, seemingly contrary to Barth's better judgment, I will develop a model in theological anthropology that I will then apply to Christology. To provide a kind of rationale for this procedure, we might borrow a distinction common in the philosophy of science between the context of justification and the context of discovery. Though I will ostensibly start with anthropological material, we might consider this as a means

---

1. For helpful examples see Marc Cortez, *Embodied Souls, Ensouled Bodies: An Exercise in Christological Anthropology and Its Significance for the Mind/Body Debate* (New York: T&T Clark, 2008), and Stanley J. Grenz, "Jesus as the *Imago Dei*: Image-of-God Christology and the Non-linear Linearity of Theology," *JETS* 47/4 (December 2004): 617–28.

of discovery, the way of forming an initial hypothesis, which then might be later justified by Christology proper.

In this chapter, I will develop a model of the image of God, in both Christ and in humans, as the capacity for relationship with God. Augustine discusses this account of the image as *capax Dei* (capable of participation in God) in his treatise *On the Trinity*. I will use exegetical considerations from Genesis 5 and distinctions from philosophical anthropology to develop the hypothesis further. Next, I will extend the model into Christology by using the Chalcedonian categories of one person in two natures. Finally, I will briefly consider some of the implications the model has for life in Christ and for soteriology. My purpose in this paper is to sketch a core hypothesis around which further investigation might develop. There are too many facets to ground any of the affirmations thoroughly, but my hope is to sketch a line for further exploration.

THE IMAGE OF GOD AS *CAPAX DEI*

From relatively few biblical passages, theologians have wrangled over a wide variety of theories concerning the nature of the image of God in the human person. Three common categories have emerged in the discussion. Substantive or ontological theories have been the most dominant over the course of church history and contend that the image consists in certain qualities possessed by the human person. Relational views find the image in the relation humans bear to God and secondarily to other humans. Functional views perceive the image in human activity, usually dominion or representative regency. Since none of the biblical passages explicitly delineate that in which the image consists, other evidence must be adduced to provide an account of the nature of the image. Endorsement of one theory over and against the others has frequently been driven by a perceived tension in the biblical affirmations concerning the image. For example, the Reformers are frequently interpreted as having moved toward a relational interpretation of the image because they held that the substantive views of their medieval forebears insufficiently grappled with the effects of sin.

Briefly stated, the tension is this: some biblical passages imply that the image is not lost in the fall, while other passages imply that it is. On the one hand, the image remains in fallen humanity. The prohibition of murder in Genesis 9:6 on the basis of human persons being created in the image of God is categorical,[2] which implies that post-fall humanity still

---

2. John H. Walton, *Genesis* (NIVAC; Grand Rapids: Zondervan, 2001), 130.

bears the image, and universal ethical norms follow from that.[3] Similarly, in the New Testament, James 3:9 and 1 Corinthians 11:7 suggest that fallen humans still bear the image of God. On the other hand, most of the New Testament passages describe the way in which redemption brings about a renewal of the image. To become Christlike is to conform to the image, to become human in the way in which we were intended. Redemption makes conforming to the image possible; the implication is that the image was lost in the fall and needs to be restored. None of the biblical references to the image of God describe the effects of sin thereupon; instead, the idea that sin harmfully affected the image is inferred from the need to restore the image.[4]

The tension between the distinct theories arises from varying understandings of the relationship of sin to the image. Theological history has witnessed a wide variety of frameworks that have attempted to express the tension. As Berkouwer explains: "The purpose of all such distinctions is to differentiate between that which remains in man even in sin (man's essence), and that which is lost through sin—his orientation towards God."[5] The impulse of the relational theorists has been toward the erasure or defacement of the image through the effects of sin and the fall. In these theories, the image is righteousness, rectitude, and right relationship to God, which is lost in the fall and restored in redemption. Ontological theories, by contrast, emphasize that the image persists in fallen humanity. Sinful, unredeemed humans are still human. Ontological theories see relational theories as removing the image in fallen humanity. Relational theorists accuse the structuralists of minimizing the effects of sin. These differences concerning how to understand the relationship of sin to the image provide a means for distilling the categories of theories into static (structural/substantive/ontological) and dynamic (relational, functional) theories of the image.

I propose that the image should be understood as the capacity for relationship; in particular, it is the capacity for relationship with God. It is structural, but has the end or purpose of relationship. Although I do not know if other theologians have characterized the image in precisely this way, it bears affinity to the ways many have discussed the topic, including representatives of the major alternative theories.

---

3. G. C. Berkouwer, *Man: The Image of God* (Grand Rapids: Eerdmans, 1962), 44.
4. Robert L. Saucy, "Theology of Human Nature," in *Christian Perspectives on Being Human* (ed. J. P. Moreland and David Ciocchi; Grand Rapids: Baker, 1993), 29; Walton, *Genesis*, 130–31.
5. Berkouwer, *Man*, 40.

Elements of both the structural and relational views can be found in Augustine; his conception of the image as *capax Dei* provides a starting point for development of the model.[6] According to Grenz, even though Augustine inspired the substantive views of the image in the Middle Ages, his view includes enough of the relational view to provide support for the later Reformational rejection of the structural view.[7] For Augustine, the *telos* of the human person is knowledge of and participation with God. The aspect of the human person that enables participation in God is the image. He explains that the image still remains in fallen humanity.

> The mind must first be considered as it is in itself, before it becomes partaker of God; and His image must be found in it. For, as we have said, although worn out and defaced by losing the participation of God, yet the image of God still remains. For it is His image in this very point, that it is capable of Him, and can be partaker of Him; which so great good is only made possible by its being His image.[8]

The capacities of the mind that comprise the image enable the human person to be capable of participation with God and have not been erased by sin. The purpose of this set of capacities is its relationship with God; hence, directedness toward God is its natural and proper orientation.[9] The capacities of the mind can be misdirected; the mind can wrongly and selfishly turn in upon itself and understand, remember, or love itself instead of God. Even when misapplied, the image remains because it is an essential element of the human mind. Its proper application is in the worship of God. "Let it [the mind] remember its God, after whose image it is made, and let it understand and love Him ... let it worship God, who is not made, by whom because itself was made, it is capable and can be partaker of Him."[10] Capacities need to be directed toward their proper end. The proper application of the image is in participation in God. Augustine discusses the fate of those who forget God described in Psalm 94:

> These nations, then, will not so have forgotten God as to be unable to remember Him when reminded of Him; yet, by forgetting God, as though forgetting their own life, they had been turned into death, i.e. into hell.

---

6. Stanley J. Grenz, *The Social God and the Relational Self: A Trinitarian Theology of the Imago Dei* (Louisville: Westminster John Knox, 2001), 162.

7. Ibid., 157.

8. Augustine, *City of God* 14.8, in *NPNF1* (ed. Philip Schaff; Peabody, MA.: Hendrickson, 1994), 2:189.

9. Ibid., 14.12 (2:191).

10. Ibid.

But when reminded they are turned to the Lord, as though coming to life again by remembering their proper life which they had forgotten.[11]

The image is renewed, echoing the New Testament understanding, when the capacities of the mind are properly directed toward participation in God. "It has now come to love itself rightly and not perversely when it loves God, by partaking of whom that image not only exists, but is also renewed so as to be no longer old, and restored so as to be no longer defaced, and beatified so as to be no longer unhappy."[12]

Augustine captures the dynamic qualities of the capacity view by explaining the changeableness of the mind. Without multiple possibilities, how would one explain the fall into sin and subsequent redemption? "If it were not changeable, then, as it could not become wretched after being blessed, so neither could it become blessed after being made wretched."[13] Augustine's view of the image as *capax Dei* unifies structural and dynamic-relational theories, drawing together the strengths of each.

Usually, Genesis 1 is used to support all theories of the image. Frequently, the remaining passages are aligned with one theory over and against the others. For example, a common impression is that the New Testament primarily supports dynamic relational theories, while the Old Testament supports substantive theories.[14] In contrast to this picture, John Walton's discussion of Genesis 5:1–3 suggests that both kinds of theory are united within the passage.[15] He implies that this passage addresses the exegetical tension created by loss or diminishment of the image through sin. Genesis 5 compares the image of God implanted in the original creation of Adam and Eve to the way in which Seth is in the image of Adam. Walton explains that "the image of God in people provides them the capacity not only to serve as God's vice-regents ... but also the capacity to be and act like him."[16] The child possesses the image of her parents, but that image may not be clearly perceived early in the child's life. Through growth and development into maturity, the image of the parent in the child becomes more and more apparent. According to Walton, this passage provides the interpretive key needed to understand the nature of the image. "While we are all in the image of God, we likewise have the capacity to become more and more in the image of God; that is, we were created with the potential

---

11. Ibid., 14.13 (2:192).
12. Ibid., 14.13 (2:193).
13. Ibid., 14.15 (2:194).
14. David Cairns, *The Image of God in Man* (London: Collins, 1973).
15. I thank Ken Way for pointing me to this reference.
16. Walton, *Genesis*, 131.

to mirror divine attributes."[17] He further explains that the various capacities that have been suggested as constituting the image are means toward the goal, rather than the actual image itself. Both Walton and Augustine describe the image as a structured capacity ordered toward an end that it may actualize to a greater or lesser extent.

To develop the model suggested by these historic and exegetical contexts further, it will be useful to explore the way in which the use of the term *capacity* in contemporary English has a kind of ambiguity between two different but connected meanings. It is this set of meanings that, when given analysis and a few additional distinctions, makes capacity a fitting concept for application to the supposed tension in the theological notion of the image of God. Consider the relationship between the concepts of capacity and ability. Suppose you asked whether I have the capacity to speak Arabic. Capacity can mean two different things. The first meaning concerns whether I currently have the ability to speak Arabic. The other connotes my potential to be able to speak it, whether or not I am currently able to do so. The two are related; for example, if I am not now able to speak Arabic, I can learn to do so. Notice, too, that my ability to speak Arabic can be degreed; I may not be able to speak it well and therefore may need to make further progress in my ability. Even a native speaker could grow in his or her ability to speak Arabic. In both instances —ability and potentiality—I have the capacity to speak Arabic; the question concerns whether my capacity to do so has been actualized or not. On the one hand, capacity means potential; on the other, it means actualization of potential.

Ordering capacities into hierarchies unifies the actual and potential aspects of capacities. Potential to speak Arabic is a higher order capacity realized by the lower order capacity (ability) to speak Arabic. My actual or potential ability to speak Arabic requires the higher order capacity to speak a language, which may in turn require a capacity for concept formation, etc. At the top of these chains are ultimate capacities, which can only be realized by the development of lower order capacities. Ultimate capacities are part of the nature of the individual.[18] To have a human nature means to possess a set of ultimate capacities that are structured in an ordered unity. The loss or absence of an ultimate capacity causes the individual that bears a certain nature to cease to exist, because the nature

---

17. Ibid.
18. J. P. Moreland and Scott B. Rae, *Body & Soul: Human Nature & the Crisis in Ethics* (Downers Grove, IL: InterVarsity Academic, 2000), 73.

has been destroyed.[19] The capacity for relationship with God is an ultimate capacity that is an essential constituent of human nature (and is the image of God in the sense of potential).

Capacities have a directedness or means of fulfillment. Since they are fulfilled through action, they fall under ethical evaluation. Have they been used well or poorly, rightly or wrongly? Capacities have a *telos*, in which they find their fulfillment. They are *for* something. In a sense, capacities are empty without expression. Not only is the actualization of specific capacities subject to moral evaluation, but also my own choices about which capacities I exercise are subject to evaluation. I may be blamed if I never exercise my capacity for justice or love, for example. I may choose to exercise my capacity to read at the expense of my capacity to relate to others, or causing me to forgo sleep, resulting in being less patient with others the next day. I could buy yet another book, but perhaps, *per impossible*, I should spend my money elsewhere?

Capacities are also subject to amoral norms of operation—the ways we expect them normally to operate. Eyes are meant to see, but they may not, or their ability to do so may be greatly impaired. Capacities can be obstructed or blocked through my own choices and through circumstances outside my control. My body, my environment, and other people set limits on the exercise of my own capacities. Lower order capacities can be destroyed, while higher order ones remain. A deaf person may not have the lower order capacity to hear, perhaps through physical damage, while still having the higher order capacity to do so. Instances of repair through cochlear implants, which bypass physical damage and send auditory information through radio waves directly to nerve receptors in the brain, strikingly illuminate the continued possession of the higher order capacity to hear.

The full exercise of some capacities can also be blocked through the positive exercise of other capacities. If I choose to employ all of my efforts into becoming a world-class body builder, then I likely will not have many resources also to become a world-class synchronized swimmer (or anything else for that matter). My finitude circumscribes the actualization of my capacities. I may be able to exercise my capacity to learn a language by learning many languages, but surely there is an upper bound on how many I am able to learn and the level of proficiency I am able to attain in each of them.

---

19. Saucy, "Theology of Human Nature," 25–26.

Perhaps the various capacities typically associated with substantive views—reason, morality, freedom—should be understood, in a manner similar to Augustine's view, as capacities, the actualization of which potentially enables relationship with God. Each of these capacities serves the higher order purpose of knowing and relating to God and possesses a higher order goal that makes them meaningful. The ultimate capacity for relationship with God is the essential aspect of our constitution that enables us to commune with God and ought to order our other capacities, both ultimate and secondary. The operation of this capacity can be specified by its purpose and design; it is not simply standing in relation to God, since everything does that by virtue of being created by God.

Specification of the rightful activity of the capacity for relationship with God is a rich topic of theological reflection in its own right. Many biblical images illumine the kind of relationship with God that rightly expresses the capacity to do so: friendship, adoption, marriage, and so forth. Ordered under the ultimate capacity for relationship with God is the ultimate capacity for relationship with other human persons. With God's help and in partnership with our fellow humans we are called to exercise the relationships of dominion over and stewardship of the natural world.[20]

CHRIST AS *CAPAX DEI*

In order to develop the Christological facets of the model, I will consider the intersection between the capacity for relationship with God and the Chalcedonian categories for the theandric union. The image-as-capacity may be most naturally attributable to one of the two natures or to his person. However, if we only have reason to think that Christ bears the image in virtue of his divine nature, then a major motivation for connecting anthropology and Christology will be lost.

Starting with Christ's divinity, some of the New Testament passages concerning the image of God appear to reference his preexistent divine nature. In Colossians 1:15, "he is the image of the invisible God" in whom "all the fullness of God was pleased to dwell" (1:19), and in verse 16, he is the creator of all things. Likewise, in Hebrews 1:3, "he is the radiance of the glory of God and the exact imprint of his nature," and the image is again connected to both creation and preservation. According to these passages, it would seem that Christ bears the image of God as the preexistent second person of the Trinity.

---

20. Ibid., 26–27.

Both Colossians and Hebrews connect Christ's preexistence to his sonship. In Colossians, he is the firstborn; Hebrews develops the sonship motif extensively through interpretation of Old Testament passages. The connection of sonship to the image provides an initial pathway out of a merely equivocal application of the image to both Christ and humans. As interpreted by the Nicene fathers, sonship meant that Christ shared the same nature as the Father.[21] The explication of the analogy with human reproduction is elusive since Christ's sonship consists in an eternal, passionless generation.[22] The strength of the analogy, however, is that human children bear the nature of their parents, which is where Genesis 5 comes to the forefront again. The author of Hebrews uses Psalm 8 to imply that Jesus is the only one to fulfill completely the creation mandate of Genesis 1 (the mandate that many believe is constitutive of the image). The entire created order will be placed in subjection to Christ in a way it never has been at the hands of human agency.

Perhaps we might be warranted in extending the argument of Hebrews by connecting the eternal sonship of Jesus to Genesis 5, but with the qualification that as the "exact imprint of his nature," Christ's capacity for relationship with God is fully actualized. Being eternal, the actualization of his capacity is timelessly in evidence. Moreover, expression of his capacity for relationship with God perfectly fulfills the norms governing that relationship. Sans world, Father and Son deeply love each other. Whether through eternal generation or through reproduction, "children" share the same nature as their "parents," and therefore, they are objects of love and community.[23]

The New Testament also provides reason to think that Christ bears the image in the incarnation in such a way that it applies to humanity soteriologically and is not attributable only to his divine nature. Our pursuit of Christlikeness is linked to bearing the image. If we suppose that 2 Corinthians 4:4, wherein "the light of the gospel of the glory of Christ, who is the image of God," forms the best account of the "Lord" referred to in 3:18, then we "are being transformed into the same image from one degree of glory to another." Our transformation makes us like Christ, the true image of God, and causes us to bear the image. Likewise, "the new self, created after the likeness of God in true righteousness and holiness"

---

21. Donald Macleod, *The Person of Christ* (Downers Grove, IL: InterVarsity Press, 1998), 129.
22. Gregory Nazianzen, *The Third Theological Oration, in Christology of the Later Fathers* (ed. Edward Rochie Hardy; Philadelphia: Westminster, 1954), 161–62.
23. Macleod, *Person of Christ*, 130.

(Eph 4:24), enables us "to attain ... to the measure of the stature of the fullness of Christ" (4:13). In our salvation we are "conformed to the image of his Son, in order that he might be the firstborn among many brothers" (Rom 8:29). In these passages, whatever it is that Christ exemplifies as image bearer, we may also possess. Since we do not become God in a univocal sense, this attribute properly pertains to our humanity.

Although these two sets of passages seem to imply that Christ bears the image in each of his natures, the capacities model also allows for understanding the unity of his person. The unity of the two natures in one person is also the union of two sets of ultimate capacities that belong to the respective natures. The two sides of capacities I delineated above may provide a means to explore the structure of the theandric union. On the one hand, although natures bear potentials and dispositions, as universals, they do not actually do anything when uninstantiated.[24] When instantiated in an individual, then the individual who bears that nature has mental or volitional properties and actualizes capacities; the human individual may only actualize capacities for which he or she possesses the relevant nature. Ultimate capacities are potentialities and thus part of the dispositional, but strictly speaking not active, aspect of a nature.

When the nature is individuated, all of the dispositions and potentials defined by the structure of the nature may be expressed. In fact, it is impossible for none of the capacities of an instantiated human nature to fail to be expressed. The expression or actualization of capacities belongs to the person. When we think of capacity as potential, then Christ has two sets of capacities, one for each nature. When we think of capacity as ability, then the incarnate Christ has one set, which is exercised by his person.

When the second person of the Trinity assumes a human nature, two sets of capacities are expressed in one life, effecting a kind of merger of abilities. When the second person of the Trinity takes on humanity, his humanness changes the way his ultimate capacities are expressed, but it does not alter or eliminate his divine nature because it does not remove those ultimate capacities. Therefore, this hypothesis is not kenotic according to the school of kenotic Christologies in the nineteenth century, wherein Christ ceases being God in the incarnation. Christ is fully God, possessing all the ultimate capacities that are proper to possessing a divine nature.

---

24. Garrett J. DeWeese, "One Person, Two Natures: Two Metaphysical Models of the Incarnation," in *Jesus in Trinitarian Perspective: An Introductory Christology* (ed. Fred Sanders and Klaus Issler; Nashville: Broadman & Holman Academic, 2007), 141–42.

Sketching the role of Christ's embodiment in his bearing of the image may further delineate the model. Historically, theologians have been wary of including the human body within the expression of the image since it appears to imply an affirmation of the corporeality of God.[25] Yet, failing to connect the body to the image has a kind of Gnostic overtone. Middleton contends that excluding the body from the image "continues to perpetuate an implicit devaluation of the concrete life of the body in relation to spirituality."[26] If, as I have suggested, the image is the capacity for relationship, the body finds a natural place in this theory. The body is our primary means for relational connection to God, to others, and to our environment.[27] Proper function of bodily capacities is necessary for the operation of inward relational capacities. This is why we so frequently miss the meaning of emails because we do not receive the bodily cues that comprise the greater part of communication. Bodily capacity mediates relational connection and finds its natural application as a means of relationship. Even if we place various capacities of the human person such as perception, thought, or volition within an inward dimension such as the soul, the body is necessary for the full realization of these capacities. Physical damage to my eyes, for example, prevents me from exercising the capacity to see.

Natures are constituted in part by ultimate capacities. In the incarnation, two natures are joined, resulting in two sets of ultimate capacities. Neither of these two sets of ultimate capacities disappears, but they may not each find full expression in lower order capacities because they are blocked in certain ways. One important constraint on the exercise of Christ's capacities in the incarnation is his possession of a human body. As an individual person, his embodiment defines a whole range of expressed capacities that at the same time prevent the actualization of other capacities. His human nature could have been expressed as a wealthy Southeast Asian woman instead of a poor Middle Eastern male. If he was five foot six inches when fully grown, then he was not six foot five. If he was left hand dominant, then he was not right-handed, and so on.[28]

Under the sway of modernism, we tend to be repulsed by the limita-

---

25. Saucy, "Theology of Human Nature," 23.

26. J. Richard Middleton, *The Liberating Image: The* Imago Dei *in Genesis 1* (Grand Rapids: Brazos, 2005), 24.

27. M. Elizabeth Lewis Hall, "What Are Bodies For? An Integrative Examination of Embodiment," *CSR* 39/2 (Winter 2010): 159–75.

28. David H. Kelsey, *Eccentric Existence: A Theological Anthropology* (Louisville: Westminster John Knox, 2009), 2:1012–16.

tions of being embodied. My finitude constrains which capacities I may actualize, but both my creaturely limitations and (at least potentially) the freely chosen shape of my life are profound goods. Positive expression of one capacity may thwart the expression of another, but this is what it means to be, and is part of the good of being, finite.

The surprising example of the human capacity to echolocate illumines the union of capacities of the incarnation. All things considered, being sighted is the rightful and natural state of the human person. However, there are known instances of humans who are able to echolocate. For example, Ben Underwood lost his eyes to cancer at the age of two, but learned to negotiate his environment by attending to the sounds that returned to his ears from the clicks he made with his mouth. He could roller skate, play foosball, and hit you with a thrown pillow in a pillow fight. Few of us would be able to do those things if we were deprived of our sight. It does not appear that Mr. Underwood had a capacity the rest of us do not have.[29] The reason we are not able to negotiate our environment through echolocation and he could is that he exercised his capacity to do it motivated by a need and desire the rest of us do not have. Probably the ability to echolocate can only be developed to any significant extent if you are blind.[30] One positive and remarkable capacity comes at the expense of another. Christ's full, embodied humanity may limit the expression of his divine capacities while not diminishing his full divinity.

The model of the image as the capacity for relationship with God has the potential to steer a solid course within the Chalcedonian boundaries. Initially, the merger of capacities into one set of personal abilities may sound Eutychian or perhaps Apollinarian. However, given the distinction between ultimate capacities and lower order actualization of those capacities, the model can preserve the plenitude of each of the two natures by eliminating nothing that is essential to each of them. It does, however, in an effort to avoid Nestorianism, and in concert with the Fifth Ecumenical Council, insist on the unity of the person of Christ. Christ's capacities are expressed in one unified life.

The capacities hypothesis can make good use of the an/enhypostatic formula and also shows why Leontius's contribution need not be

---

29. Thomas A. Stroffregen and John B. Pittenger, "Human Echolocation as a Basic Form of Perception and Action," *Ecological Psychology* 7/3 (1995): 181–216.

30. Bo N. Schenkman and Mats E. Nilsson, "Human Echolocation: Blind and Sighted Persons' Ability to Detect Sounds Recorded in the Presence of a Reflecting Object," *Perception* 39/4 (2010): 483–501.

considered a "finer species of Apollinarianism."[31] One might worry that if the second person of the Trinity assumes an anhypostatic human nature, the result would be an overly divinized, quasi-Docetic incarnation. Ivor Davidson, expressing the sentiment of objections of this type, explains that "at first glance, such a theology appears anything but congenial to the affirmation of Jesus' humanity. Does it not go out of its way to deny that Jesus is a human 'person,' and reduce his humanity to the level of a 'nature' only?"[32] By contrast, the capacities hypothesis shows the fruitfulness of the an/enhypostatic thesis. Jesus exhibits all of the humanness ascribed to him in the New Testament in a real and non-Docetic way through the exercise of his human capacities in a human way of life. He bears the marks of true humanity because he is truly human. Instead, even though Christ's human nature was anhypostatic prior to the incarnation, the model may be susceptible to the opposite objection: Jesus is too human in the exercise of his capacities. Stated differently, perhaps the model diminishes the divine nature while emphasizing that the second person of the Trinity (the personal subject of the incarnation) lives a human life.

As formulated, the view may appear monothelitic. If the will is best understood as a capacity, then perhaps Christ has two ultimate volitional capacities, one for each of his natures. In exercise, however, the model I have developed postulates a unified will in the execution and actualization of potentialities. The model may allow for two ultimate volitional capacities pertaining to each of the natures, but a single will in actualization of the capacities. If this cannot be maintained coherently, however, the model will have to shift toward either monothelitism or dyothelitism.[33] The position developed here does have the asset that it can be explicated using analogies of health and well-being to illustrate the operation of capacities in the person of Jesus; that is, positive expression of one capacity displaces another, as in human echolocation. By contrast, the coherence of two minds or two wills Christologies is often supported using the analogies of pathological or abnormal conditions such as dissociative identity disorder, schizophrenia, or commisurotomy.[34]

---

31. H. R. Mackintosh, *The Doctrine of the Person of Jesus Christ* (New York: C. Scribner's Sons, 1912), 218.

32. Ivor Davidson, "Theologizing the Human Jesus: An Ancient (and Modern) Approach to Christology Reassessed," *IJST* 3/2 (2001): 135.

33. Others have ably defended a version of monothelitism as the best way to preserve the insights of Chalcedon and of Constantinople II. While monothelitism may be a liability of this model, it at least seems to be coherent. See the contributions in Sanders and Issler, eds., *Jesus in Trinitarian Perspective.*

34. DeWeese, "One Person, Two Natures," 132, and Thomas V. Morris, *The Logic of God Incarnate* (Ithaca, NY: Cornell University Press, 1986), 105–6.

Implications for Soteriology

The sketch of this model leaves much to be developed, including Christ's suffering and sinlessness, and a more complete explication of the components discussed above. To show the practical value of the model, I will consider two of the implications this hypothesis has for soteriology. First, Christ's example shows that in our pursuit of Christlikeness, we need growth, process, and the movement from potentiality to actuality; even Jesus was not immune from these things (Luke 2:40, 52). This slow and often tortuous movement contrasts starkly with the desire inculcated in us by our culture. We are impatient; we want technological, immediate solutions. We want nonpersonal, nonmessy, less-than-human ways of solving our problems, even with respect to our growth in Christ. We long for supernatural, immediate intervention, in the manner of one of Christ's healings, rather than long-developed strength of character.

Second, the personal expression of Christ's human nature was particular, as all instantiated human natures are. Yet, given the hypothesis concerning the image of God as *capax Dei*, that particularity ought not be seen as something that distances us from Christ and obscures how he provides an example for us. It is true that his capacities find a particular expression, but this is within the positive development of his true and common humanity, which he shares with us. I need not become a carpenter, or Jewish, or male in order to properly pattern my life after his. Instead, I need to actualize my ultimate capacities to love God and love my neighbor while expressing the particularity of the location in which I find myself. Most any particular vocational employment, for example, can be easily hallowed, given this reality of Christ's humanity. This broadens the vistas of what it means to be a Christlike human.

Conclusion

Some may object to the use of metaphysics or to a particular metaphysical scheme in the development of the capacities model of the image. Addressing those kinds of objections falls beyond the scope of this treatment. I have tried to show that natures are not static, or at least not inert, which seems to be one of the major complaints of those who are opposed to essentialist metaphysical programs.[35] Our theological forebears did not

---

35. See, e.g., Bruce L. McCormack, "Karl Barth's Historicized Christology: Just How 'Chalcedonian' Is It?" in *Orthodox and Modern: Studies in the Theology of Karl Barth* (Grand Rapids: Baker Academic, 2008), 211.

approach natures as static; they are dispositional. Natures realize their potential to be set in motion by being instantiated, or, in the case of the incarnation, in-personed (enhypostasized). Our present academic environment tends to be allergic to metaphysics. Many thinkers insist that human identity is constituted by relationships. If, however, humanness has no definable structure, it becomes difficult to describe a reliable path of growth toward health and maturity. One might argue that since such a path can in fact be delineated, nonstructural accounts of the human person are at best misguided.

Although I think the hypothesis that the image of God consists in the capacity for relationship with God has value and that this model can be fruitfully applied to Christ as the true image of God, much work remains to be done. I am optimistic that historical, exegetical, and constructive work can find solid grounding for the hypothesis and perhaps at the same time show why reasoning from theological anthropology to Christology has value.[36]

36. I am grateful to Wesley A. Chambers for bibliographic and editorial assistance on this essay.

CHAPTER 8

CHRISTOLOGY AND CONCILIAR AUTHORITY

On the Viability of Monothelitism for Protestant Theology

JORDAN WESSLING

AT THE SIXTH ECUMENICAL COUNCIL, the Third Council of Constantinople, monothelitism (the doctrine that Christ has only one will or faculty of choice) was condemned and dyothelitism was affirmed (the doctrine that Christ has two distinct wills or faculties of choice, one human and one divine).[1] After rejecting the "heresy of a single will and a single principle of action in the two natures" of Christ,[2] the council continues on to read:

> And we proclaim equally two natural volitions or wills in him and two natural principles of action which undergo no division, no change, no partition, no confusion, in accordance with the teaching of the holy fathers. And the two natural wills not in opposition, as the impious heretics said, far from it, but his human will following, and not resisting or struggling, rather in fact subject to his divine and all powerful will.[3]

---

1. I follow what I take to be the standard characterization of dyothelitism, whereas some suggest that this doctrine concerns not two distinct faculties of choice, but divine and human inclinations/desires, or perhaps, a divine kind of willing and a human kind of willing (which may be properly predicated to one capacity for choice). See Richard Swinburne, *The Christian God* (New York: Oxford University Press, 1994), 198–99, for a "non-standard" understanding of dyothelitism.

2. Norman P. Tanner, S. J., ed., *Decrees of the Ecumenical Councils* (Washington DC: Georgetown University Press, 1990), 1:126.

3. Ibid., 1:128.

151

Despite its condemnation, monothelitism has recently been endorsed by a small group of evangelical Protestant philosophical and systematic theologians. Although many of these monothelites affirm the two-natures doctrine outlined at the Council of Chalcedon, they repudiate dyothelitism as an extrabiblical postulate that threatens to undermine the unity of the person of Christ.[4] Other theologians believe that the deliverances of an ecumenical council possess a high theological authority that should not be contravened without overwhelming theological reason for so doing. Absent that, monothelitism should not be considered a live option for evangelical theology.[5]

In the present paper, I contribute to this debate by exploring a case for the claim that monothelitism should be considered theologically viable for evangelicals, even though it was condemned by an ecumenical council (simply "council" hereafter). I do this by contrasting two recent evangelical perspectives on Christology and conciliar authority and by pointing out what I deem to be significant weaknesses for the position that seeks to dismiss monothelitism via the appeal to the Third Council of Constantinople. My goal is not to contend that monothelitism should in fact be considered theologically admissible, let alone true; rather, I aim for the more modest conclusion of showing that the case against its viability should not be closed.

ON BEHALF OF THE VIABILITY OF MONOTHELITISM

J. P. Moreland and William Craig are paradigmatic representatives of evangelicals who do not fear parting ways with the dyothelitic decree of the Third Council of Constantinople. After explicating and defending a monothelitic model of the incarnation, they state, "This [monothelitic] implication of our model is in our view unobjectionable, since dyotheletism, despite its conciliar support, finds no warrant in Scripture."[6] Similarly, Gar-

---

4. For example, Garrett J. DeWeese, "One Person, Two Natures: Two Metaphysical Models of the Incarnation," in *Jesus in Trinitarian Perspective* (ed. Fred Sanders and Klaus Issler; Nashville, TN: Broadman & Holman Academic, 2007), 114–53; Gordon R. Lewis and Bruce A. Demarest, *Integrative Theology* (Grand Rapids: Zondervan, 1990), 2:317; J. P. Moreland and William Lane Craig, *Philosophical Foundations for a Christian Worldview* (Downers Grove, IL: InterVarsity Press, 2003), 608–12; Thomas V. Morris (implicitly), *The Logic of God Incarnate* (Ithaca, NY: Cornell University Press, 1986), 161–62; and Augustus Hopkins Strong, *Systematic Theology* (Philadelphia: Judson, 1907), 694–95. Other Protestant monothelites who are less concerned with maintaining Chalcedonian Christology include: P. T. Forsyth, *The Person and Place of Jesus Christ* (London: Independent, 1909), 319; H. R. Mackintosh, *The Doctrine of the Person of Jesus Christ* (Edinburgh: T&T Clark, 1962), 470; and Wolfhart Pannenberg, *Jesus— God and Man* (2nd ed.; trans. Lewis L. Wilkins and Duane A. Priebe; Philadelphia: Westminster, 1977), 329–30.

5. As we shall see, Oliver D. Crisp is most explicit on this score; see his *Divinity and Humanity* (Cambridge: Cambridge University Press, 2007), 34–71.

6. Moreland and Craig, *Philosophical Foundations for a Christian Worldview*, 611.

rett DeWeese defends his monothelitism by stating that "while most Evangelicals should and do regard the deliverances of the ecumenical councils as weighty in defining the orthodox faith, they would agree that the councils cannot be accepted uncritically but must themselves be judged by the authority of Scripture."[7] Other evangelical monothelites reason in a similar fashion, arguing (or sometimes just stating) that dyothelitism can be rejected since it's not biblical.[8] So, these monothelites seem to rely on what might be deemed the Conciliar Undercutting Principle—or simply "CUP."

> CUP: The (evangelical) Christian is free to reject a conciliar pronouncement if this pronouncement is not taught or implied by Scripture.

An important assumption for those who use CUP against dyothelitism appears to be the common Protestant conviction that one can legitimately interpret Scripture in such a way that it stands above and corrects traditions of interpretation in the church (though deeply influenced by one or more of these traditions), even a tradition that has been formalized in a council.

Let us for the moment suppose that CUP is right. The correctness of CUP would make what the Bible teaches or implies central to the debate over the obligatory nature of dyothelitism. The question, then, is this: What can be legitimately drawn from the Scriptures?

In his *Fundamentals of Catholic Dogma*, Ludwig Ott adduces no fewer than ten proof texts for dyothelitism.[9] Here we cannot examine them all, but we can briefly look at the most important texts. The results of this investigation will, arguably, apply to the other texts used in support of dyothelitism.

The most central and hotly disputed dyothelitic proof texts during the time of the monothelite controversy were those that depict Jesus' agonized prayer to the Father in Gethsemane: "Father, if you are willing, remove this cup from me; yet, not my will but yours be done" (Luke 22:42; cf. Matt 26:39; Mark 14:36).[10] Although these passages were not uniformly interpreted in a dyothelitic way prior to the seventh century, Maximus the Confessor argued that they strongly support the doctrine. For in the

---

7. DeWeese, "One Person, Two Natures," 148.
8. See, e.g., Strong, *Systematic Theology*, 695.
9. Ludwig Ott, *Fundamentals of Catholic Dogma* (St. Louis: Herder, 1751), 148.
10. Support for this claim comes from Demetrios Bathrellos, *The Byzantine Christ: Person, Nature, and Will in the Christology of Saint Maximus the Confessor* (New York: Oxford University Press, 2004), 140.

Gethsemane scene we find Christ wanting in his human nature to avoid death, while also willing the crucifixion in his divine nature. So we must postulate, thought Maximus, distinct divine and human wills.[11]

Behind Maximus's interpretation of the Gethsemane prayer rests the widely held belief of that day that the Father, Son, and Spirit have the numerically same will. Pope Agatho, who reigned during the time of the monothelite controversy, illustrates the point when he says that the notion that there are three distinct wills within the Godhead is "absurd and truly profane ... it must be consistently understood that there is one natural will, and one natural operation."[12] Given this widespread Trinitarian conviction, we can begin to grasp why one might feel driven toward dyothelitism upon reading Jesus' prayer. If the statement "not my will but yours" is read in a monothelitic way—where the one will of Christ struggles to align itself with the Father's—this implies that the Father and Son have distinct (divine) wills. But this violates the Trinitarian convictions of that time.

The notion that the Godhead has only one will is not as widely held as it once was. If the theologian is open to the idea that there are three distinct wills within the Godhead—one per Father, Son, and Spirit—then he is able to understand Jesus' prayer in a straightforwardly monothelitic manner. DeWeese, himself a monothelite who affirms a *tri*thelitic account of the divine nature, explains: "The one personal will of Christ who, with human nature and a human body was operating as a fully human person, desired the cup of suffering, death, and separation from the Father, to be taken from him. But Christ submitted his (personal) will to the divine will of the Father."[13] In other words, when Jesus says "not my will but yours," the incarnate Logos submits his (distinct) will to the Father's will. Should one worry that this scenario is impossible because it's necessarily the case that the Son cannot make a choice that would contradict the Father's plan, the monothelite can add that the Son nevertheless had to struggle against his natural human desire to avoid suffering and death—hence Jesus' Gethsemane prayer.[14]

---

11. For an excellent overview, see ibid., esp. ch. 2–3.

12. Henry R. Percival, ed., *The Seven Ecumenical Councils*, in *NPNF2* (Grand Rapids: Eerdmans, 1990), 14:332–33. In the words of Gregory of Nazianzus, *Oration* 30.12, "for as we have one Godhead, so we have one will."

13. DeWeese, "One Person, Two Natures," 150. Also see, Moreland and Craig, *Philosophical Foundations for a Christian Worldview*, 611.

14. Richard Swinburne (*The Christian God*, 198) notes that a motive for dyothelitism is its apparent ability to account for conflict between Jesus and the Father's will.

However, let's suppose that we adhere to the more apparently traditional understanding of the Godhead where the Father and Son (and Spirit) have the numerically same will. Even so, it remains unclear that the Gethsemane prayer demands dyothelitism. One way to see this is to note that there is nothing within the text that precludes reading the "my will/your will" language (the word used is θέλω) in terms of two distinct inclinations or desires, rather than distinct wills or capacities of choice. According to the former reading, one might hold that in virtue of his human nature Jesus desired to live, even while *qua* God he was firmly committed to the path that led to the cross.[15] So the phrase "not my will but yours" would read, "not as I desire, but as you have determined."

If the phrase concerns inclinations and desires, though, there is little cause to postulate two wills within Christ. Instead, all one needs to assume is that Jesus had human desires that could in some sense pull him away from his divine mission, something every biblically faithful Christological model must accommodate in light of passages like Matthew 4:1–11 and Hebrews 4:15. Monothelites such as Moreland and Craig try to make sense of these human desires acting on Jesus' one will by crafting a model of the incarnation whereby Jesus (although strictly speaking has only one mind) possesses "a typical human consciousness," so that in his earthly ministry, "Jesus had to struggle against fear, weakness and temptation in order to align his will with that of his heavenly Father."[16] If something like Moreland and Craig's model is acceptable, then monothelites can rephrase Gregory of Nyssa's construal of Jesus' prayer by replacing "will" with "desire" and characterizing the prayer as follows: "Not what I as man [desire], but what thou and so I as God [desire]."[17] Furthermore, and crucially, this understanding of Jesus' prayer appears to be compatible with the existence of just a single will within the Godhead. For if the Gethsemane scene doesn't concern faculties of choice but rather desires and inclinations, it appears that the scene is neutral with respect to the number of wills had by the triune God.

The upshot is that it is far from transparent that Jesus' prayer is best read in a dyothelitic way. Since the biblical passages concerning this prayer

---

15. Explicitly drawing a distinction between will and desires, John Nolland writes in *The Gospel of Matthew* (Grand Rapids: Eerdmans, 2005), 1099–1100: "It can hardly be that Jesus entertains serious doubts about what he has understood to be the Father's will, but a serious gap has opened between what he has understood as his Father's will and what in the reality of his human life he can perceive as *desirable*" (my emphasis).

16. Moreland and Craig, *Philosophical Foundations for a Christian Worldview*, 611.

17. *Antirheticus* 32. Unmodified quote found in Swinburne, *The Christian God*, 198.

aren't explicitly dealing with the number of wills one can aptly predicate to Christ, it seems that this prayer only functions as evidence for dyothelitism insofar as dyothelitism must be postulated to account for the *my will/desire—your will/desire* language. But as we have seen, there are other responsible ways of reading these passages. Consequently, the force of the claim that the Gethsemane prayer supports dyothelitism is significantly diminished.

What's more, our analysis of Jesus' prayer applies to other dyothelitic proof texts as well. To cite just one, Jesus' claim, "I came down from heaven, not to do my will but the will of him that sent me" (John 6:38) can be read, "I came down from heaven, not to act according to my particular human wants and desires, but I came to act according to the Father's plan." One can understand this in such a way that the Father and Son have either the same or distinct wills, yet either understanding is consonant with monothelitism. Although I cannot presently explore this, the monothelite can propose that the same applies to all of the other dyothelitic proof texts.

Of course, there is more to biblically demonstrating something than simply appealing to this or that biblical passage. One can also appeal to the great themes or overarching teachings of Holy Writ to establish doctrine, and perhaps this can be done to secure dyothelitism. One might think, for instance, that the Scriptures teach that the Logos took on a full human nature, and that this implies that the Logos assumed a human will distinct from the divine will.[18] In this case, dyothelitism is biblically based, even if not supported by specific proof texts.

This kind of argument assumes that the capacity for choice is a property of human natures, not persons. Monothelites deny this, however, as DeWeese explains, "Since mental properties inhere in persons and not natures, it follows that the mind and will are faculties or capacities of persons and not of natures. Persons are conscious, natures are not; persons have the capacity of making choices and exercising active power, natures do not."[19] In other words, the monothelite believes it rests on a confusion to think that the human *nature* of Christ requires a distinct will.

But the monothelite can go further yet. She can agree that Jesus could not be fully human without the possession of a human will, but maintain

---

18. We see this reasoning employed in Bathrellos, *The Byzantine Christ*, 141–42.
19. DeWeese, "One Person, Two Natures," 142. Compare with Lewis and Demarest, *Integrative Theology*, 2:317; Strong, *Systematic Theology*, 694.

that the will of the Logos combined with aspects of Jesus' human nature is sufficient for this. To see how this might go, we can draw the common distinction between concrete- and abstract-nature views of the human nature of Christ. The concrete-nature view states that the human nature of Christ is a concrete particular, traditionally a distinct human soul and body. The abstract-nature view, by contrast, holds that the human nature of Christ is a property, or collection of properties, that are sufficient for the possession of a complete human nature.[20] If one adopts the abstractist view, she might say that Christ has both a divine and human will in the sense that he has properties that are sufficient for both wills, even if not two distinct wills. Alvin Plantinga explains:

> Shall we say that duothelitism [sic] is the idea that the will of Christ had both the nature of a human will and the nature of a divine will, in the abstract sense of "nature"? The partisans of the abstract view would happily accept that. Or shall we say that duothelitism is the idea that there are two distinct concrete wills (supposing that in fact a will is a concrete object of some kind)? The concretists would happily accept *that*, and then it looks as if it's the abstractists that are tugging the laboring oar.[21]

So then, the idea would be that the will of the Logos, in virtue of taking on certain human properties—mental and affective properties perhaps—comes to possess everything sufficient for being a human will, even while retaining that which is sufficient for a divine will. To use Thomas Morris's now standard terminology, the incarnate Word would possess a *fully human* will, but not a *merely human* will.[22] According to this schema, monothelitism is retained since Christ has only one capacity for choice and not two as required by Constantinople III; yet this one will can legitimately be characterized as both human and divine.[23]

Certainly the aforementioned considerations on behalf of monothelitism do not demonstrate its truth. However, these considerations might lead us to think that dyothelitism is not supported by Scripture. In that case, given CUP, we should deem monothelitism a live theological option.

---

20. This distinction is delicately explicated in Crisp, *Divinity and Humanity*, 41–49.
21. Alvin Plantinga, "On Heresy, Mind, and Truth," *Faith and Philosophy* 16 (1999): 185. In his *Systematic Theology*, 695, Strong reasons similarly: "Notice that we do not say that Christ's human nature had no will, but only that it had none before its union with the divine nature, and none separately from the one will which was made up of the human and divine united."
22. Morris develops this terminology in *The Logic of God Incarnate*.
23. An interesting question I do not presently have space to explore is whether this monothelitic account of the human will of Christ can fulfill the "two natures *without confusion*" clause in the Council of Chalcedon.

AGAINST THE PERMISSIBILITY OF MONOTHELITISM

But many will want to question CUP. The primary worry is that CUP allows one to cast aside conciliar teachings too quickly, thereby leaving one without a rule of faith by which to interpret Scripture. As history has taught us, this makes it all too easy to reject core Christian doctrines like the Trinity whenever the theologian doesn't find such a doctrine as clearly expressed in the Scriptures as he or she fancies.

Those who think it unwise to embrace monothelitism, therefore, often do not accept CUP. Oliver Crisp, for instance, writes:

> It seems to me that someone dissenting from the findings of an ecumenical council of the Church should have a very good reason—indeed, a very good *theological* reason—for doing so. I can think of no good theological reason for rejecting the findings of the Third Council of Constantinople. This leads me to prefer dyothelite views of Christ's human nature to the monothelite views.[24]

He later elaborates, "A good theological reason for rejecting a conciliar decree would be that it conflicts with Scripture. But, as far as I can see, this does not apply in the present [dyothelitic] case."[25]

So CUP, thinks Crisp, is too lax. Councils possess an authority such that Christians should hold to their decrees provided they don't *contradict* Scripture. In another place Crisp suggests that we should not accept the teaching of a council if it is clearly incoherent.[26] Taken together then, we can draw from Crisp and replace CUP with CAT, the Conciliar Abrogation Thesis.

> CAT. The (evangelical) Christian should reject a conciliar statement if and only if it either: (1) contradicts that which is taught in or implied by Scripture, or (2) is incoherent.

According to Crisp, conciliar statements are not biblically ungrounded decrees. Rather, "those ecumenical councils that touch upon matters Christological are theologically binding because they are repositories of dogmatic *reflection upon Scripture* by the undivided Church, under the guidance of the Holy Spirit."[27] Crisp therefore shares with defenders of CUP a

---

24. See Crisp, *Divinity and Humanity*, 35–36.
25. Ibid., 36, n. 2; cf. 49.
26. Oliver Crisp, *God Incarnate: Explorations of in Christology* (London: T&T Clark, 2009), 14, n. 10.
27. Ibid., 13 (my emphasis).

deep commitment to the primacy of Scripture. Where he differs is in the epistemic weight he places on the councils as an accurate representation of Scripture. For Crisp the councils are Spirit-guided interpretations of God's Word, which are therefore authoritative.

If something like CAT is affirmed, this gives evangelicals excellent reason not to flirt with monothelitism. For it seems that *the most* one can say is that dyothelitism is not the best explanation of Scripture, not that it contradicts it. Nor has one shown, to my knowledge, that dyothelitism is incoherent.

Crisp's support for CAT given is that the councils were guided by the Spirit in a way that secures their true and binding nature. But why believe this? There is no direct biblical warrant for this claim. We are told that Christ gave himself up for the church to make her holy (Eph 5:25–30), and we are assured that the gates of hell will not prevail against her (Matt 16:18), but nowhere are we told that God will ensure that councils will not err. As John Calvin reminds us: "Surely, since Christ promised that he would be present not in all councils whatsoever but laid down a special mark [i.e., Scripture] by which a true and lawful [council] might be distinguished from the rest, it behooves us never to neglect this distinction."[28]

So, again, why hold that the councils are divinely endorsed? Crisp's answer is an important one: "it seems extremely implausible to think that God would allow the vast majority of the Christian Church to be led into error on matters central to the faith by believing the canons of an ecumenical council."[29] That is, we should see the councils as Spirit-guided since it's implausible to suggest that God would permit the church to be misled by conciliar error on matters that are central to the faith.

In thinking about why we should suppose that the councils are theologically binding, we must distinguish between two theological principles. The first is:

P1. God ensures that the majority of the church does not formally err on those doctrines that are central to the Christian faith.

While it is extremely difficult to determine what is doctrinally central, we can agree that it is generally that which is *integrally related to the gospel and absolutely essential for the mission and life of the church*. Understood in this way,

---

28. John Calvin, *Institutes of the Christian Religion* 4.9.1–2 (ed. John T. McNeill; trans. Ford Lewis Battles; Philadelphia: Westminster, 1960), 2:1168.

29. Crisp, *God Incarnate*, 14, n. 9. Also see Thomas Oden, *Classic Christianity: A Systematic Theology* (New York: HarperOne, 2009), 181–83.

P1 states that God would not allow the majority of the church to explicitly embrace doctrines that significantly distort or impoverish the gospel or the church's main function.

P1 is very plausible. The fact that God has revealed himself in Christ and in written form shows that God cares about the beliefs of the church. And it simply seems incredible to suppose that God would take the trouble to reveal himself to humanity, only to later let that which is theologically central be lost and misunderstood by the majority of the church. So, I think both the monothelite and the dyothelite should affirm P1.

The second principle goes right to the heart of the dispute concerning the theological viability of monothelitism. It is:

P2. God has ensured that the teachings of the Third Council of Constantinople are true and binding on the (evangelical) church.

If God has ensured the truth of this council that intended to draw lines between orthodoxy and heterodoxy, it's safe to conclude that monothelitism is off limits. But, of course, the evangelical monothelite objects to P2.

To convince their monothelite friends that they should reject monothelitism because it violates a council, dyothelites must therefore provide sufficient reason to believe that P2 is true. They might do this by claiming that one can just know, directly, that P2 is correct because the Spirit bears witness to this reality. This could come in the form of a kind of expansion of Alvin Plantinga's religious epistemology.[30] Alternatively, one might hold that the Third Council of Constantinople is true and binding on the basis of testimony, the say-so of the universal church or a subset of it.[31] I think both of these paths might very well be fruitful ways of justifying the belief in P2. The problem, however, is that they will do little to nothing to convince monothelites of P2.

Suppose that one feels that the Holy Spirit directly testifies to her that the Third Council of Constantinople is a true and binding rendering of biblical teaching. This may be sufficient to justify her belief, but it won't, by itself, give the monothelite who has not had such an experience sufficient reason to abandon his view. He, after all, thinks that he can discern that dyothelitism is not taught or implied by Scripture.

Say, then, that the dyothelite appeals to the testimony of much of the

---

30. See, Alvin Plantinga, *Warranted Christian Belief* (New York: Oxford University Press, 2000).
31. Resources for this view can be found in Thomas M. Crisp, "On Believing That the Scriptures Are Divinely Inspired," in *Analytic Theology: New Essays in the Philosophy of Theology* (ed. Oliver D. Crisp and Michael C. Rea; New York: Oxford University Press, 2009), 187–213.

church as reason to affirm P2. Although it is certainly true that many of our beliefs are justified via testimony, two reasons suggest that mere testimony won't compel the monothelite in this instance. First, even though most evangelical theologians affirm dyothelitism, they typically only accept the first four ecumenical councils; and many significant Protestant creeds that are often subscribed to by evangelicals explicitly state that God does not ensure the truth of every council. Article XXI of the Anglican Thirty Nine Articles of Religion provides one notable example: "General Councils ... when they be gathered together, (forasmuch as they be an assembly of men, whereof all be not governed with the Spirit and word of God) they may err, and sometimes have erred, even in things pertaining to God." [32] While neither of these considerations constitutes an explicit rejection of P2, together they strongly suggest that many evangelicals are inclined to reject this proposition. If this is right, the evangelical further appears to have significant testimonial evidence from within her tradition against P2, which in turn implies that testimonial evidence alone cannot be used to vindicate it. The philosopher Thomas (not Oliver) Crisp explains:

> Testimony is a source of justification for many of our beliefs. In the ordinary case, though, if one's only evidence for belief that P is testimony that P, then, one thinks, one's evidence for belief that P is *defeated* if one comes across testimony that ~P and has no reason for thinking the one bit of testimony more trustworthy than the other. So suppose you form a belief that it's half-past-four on the basis of testimony from me. (Say too my testimony is your only evidence that it's half-past-four.) You thereupon overhear testimony to the effect that it's half-past-*five* and have no reason for trusting my testimony over this latest bit of testimony. Then, one thinks, your original testimonial evidence has been defeated and you've reason to be agnostic about the time. [33]

Assuming that Thomas Crisp is correct and that the evangelical's relation to the testimonial evidence for P2 is sufficiently similar to the case described here, it would follow that the evangelical testimony that ~P2 is enough to undercut one's testimonial justification in P2.

---

32. The *Book of Common Prayer* (Cambridge: Cambridge University Press, 1968 1662.), 620. Oliver Crisp seems to implicitly acknowledge that many will reject P2 when he states: "Dispute about how the canons of one of the ecumenical councils are theologically binding depends in large part upon one's ecclesiology ... some Protestants will complain that this [understanding of councils as infallible and binding] gives too much weight to ecclesiastical authorities, which might be mistaken in their interpretation of Scripture, as some think was the case respecting the Iconoclastic Controversy." From, *God Incarnate*, 14, n. 9.

33. Crisp, "On Believing That the Scriptures Are Divinely Inspired," 201–2 (Crisp's emphasis).

Second, one doesn't normally exclusively rely on testimony that such-and-such is the case when she believes that she is both well positioned to judge the truth of this matter and finds cause to judge it false. If my wife tells me over the phone that Tim just purchased a brown dog, I reject her testimony if I'm in Tim's living room staring at his new white four-legged friend. While it would be foolish of the monothelite to claim that his epistemic vantage point is quite as clear as that, I assume that most monothelites feel that they are well positioned to discern that dyothelitism is not supported by Scripture, which thereby enables them to reject the testimony on behalf of P2.

So to convince a person of P2, one will need to provide compelling evidence for it. One important kind of evidence for believing such a thing is Oliver Crisp's suggestion that God wouldn't allow the church to promulgate a teaching in an ecumenical council as central to the faith if it is not both central and true. Although I believe Crisp is operating with a broader conception of what is central to the faith than the one I described,[34] this is generally what I take Crisp to be proposing when he states the councils are overseen by the Spirit because "it seems extremely implausible to think that God would allow the vast majority of the Christian Church to be led into error on matters central to the faith by believing the canons of an ecumenical council."[35] The idea here appears to rest on something like the following assumption regarding God's providence:

PA. God would not allow a state of affairs as bad as the erring of an ecumenical council. (Or, more modestly: God *probably* would not allow a state of affairs as bad as the erring of an ecumenical council.)

God would not allow this, so the thought goes, because it would be extraordinarily bad for the life of the church to trust the false information given to her by a council.

It's far from transparent, however, that conciliar error would be detrimental to the life of the church if God were to allow error only on

---

34. I understand Crisp to be using the phrase "central to the faith" more generally to denote that which concerns foundational Christian doctrines (such as the Trinity or the incarnation), whereas I (as explained) understand this notion to concern that which is integrally related to the gospel and absolutely essential for the mission and life of the church. Thus, according to Crisp's usage, Latin and social models of the Trinity might be considered central to the faith. These models would not be central to the faith on my usage, however, since a (reasonable) mistake here would not undermine the gospel or the mission and life of the church.

35. Crisp, *God Incarnate*, 14.

peripheral doctrines—doctrines that don't significantly undermine the gospel or the church's worship and mission. This is presumably how the monothelite who holds to P1 sees the promulgation of dyothelitism at the Third Council of Constantinople: its dyothelitic teaching is mistaken, but the mistake isn't one that threatens to erode the faith. So the monothelite who agrees with P1 can replace PA with:

PA★. God would not allow a state of affairs as bad as the erring of an ecumenical council on matters that are central to the faith, but he would allow conciliar error on peripheral matters (e.g., matters that don't significantly undermine the gospel or the church's worship) if he had sufficient reason for doing so.

The monothelite who postulates PA★ concurs with the defender of PA that insofar as the councils promulgate on issues that are in fact central to the faith, they teach only what is true. But the proponent of PA★ adds that framers of the councils might sometimes overstep their bounds and seek to address issues that are not central to Christianity; insofar as they do this, God would in principle allow them to fall into error.[36] However, if the church formally errs on some peripheral issue—for example, as the monothelite sees it, whether Christ has one or two wills—then this will not substantially hinder the mission and worship of the church, and so God might allow it if he has some greater or equal good to gain.

Based on the distinction between PA and PA★, the monothelite can then highlight reasons for thinking we are not in a good epistemic position to discern whether or not God can always secure the basic teachings of the councils without giving up some greater good. In other words, our monothelite can claim that PA cannot be used to support P2, since we are not sufficiently well positioned to judge that PA rather than PA★ is true. One cause for thinking this can be sketched as follows. God allows all kinds of negative states of affairs that surprise us—misguided theological systems, moral evil, animal and human suffering, and so on—states of affairs that appear as bad as, or nearly so, as conciliar error, at least on peripheral doctrines. But if God allows negative states of affairs to be instantiated that appear nearly as bad as conciliar error, what's to say he will not allow conciliar error as well, provided the error is not central to the faith?

I think the case against confidence in PA is best framed within different

---

36. PA★ is in line with the previously cited Article XXI of the Anglican Thirty Nine Articles of Religion.

understandings of divine providence. I will therefore consider three such views that represent the spectrum of ways evangelicals conceptualize God's governance of the world.

First, suppose that theological determinism is true (and is compatible with human freedom)—that God is the sufficient cause of all events and actions in the world in that he deliberately and without constraint establishes the causal conditions that inevitably lead to these events and actions.[37] If so, then reflection on the world should make us deeply skeptical about our abilities to discern what God might or might not "allow." He, for example, determined from all eternity that there should be a Great Schism between the Eastern and Western portions of the church. God also unconditionally decided that the Western church should fall so far into moral and theological error that, as the Protestant sees things, a Reformation would be required. Furthermore, the theologically motivated sins of the church—such as the long history of anti-Semitism, the Crusades, the subjugation of women, the slaughter of Christians by other Christians, and so on—all come from God's hand if theological determinism is true.[38] But if God frequently determines that the church should theologically err in the ways described, it seems we're barred from claiming he would not determine the same with a council on something that's not theologically essential to Christianity (i.e., we cannot say that PA rather than PA* is true). Reflection on the darker aspects of the church's otherwise glorious theological history should be enough to make us at least agnostic about PA if we affirm theological determinism.

But matters are still more grim. In addition to theological errors, there are horrendous states of affairs that seem at least as bad as conciliar error. Think, for instance, of the earth's long biological evolutionary history, built on the back of innumerable instances of animal suffering. There are also countless moral evils, such as rapes and murders, unjust wars, and genocidical endeavors, to mention only the tip of the iceberg. Yet all of this is part of God's "Plan-A" if he unconditionally determines the events and actions of the world. I submit that this would reveal that God's ways are incredibly different than we can hope to understand, since who among us thinks he can grasp why God might determine the kinds of suffering and evil we see?

---

37. My description of theological determinism is a slight modification of William Hasker's as found in "Does God Take Risks in Governing the Word?" in *Contemporary Debates in Philosophy of Religion* (ed. Michael L. Peterson and Raymond J. Vanarragon; Malden, MA: Blackwell, 2004), 223.

38. Some of these sins are documented in Jeremy M. Bergen, *Ecclesial Repentance: The Churches Confront Their Sinful Pasts* (New York: T&T Clark, 2011).

But if God has good reasons unbeknownst to us for causing these countless instances of suffering and evil, why suppose he does not have such reason to determine conciliar error on some secondary doctrine (i.e., why suppose that PA rather than PA* is correct)? The conclusion: if theological determinism is true, we are in no epistemic position to affirm PA.

To escape these problems with theological determinism, let's suppose that open theism is true. According to the open theist, God has gifted his rational creatures with libertarian freedom and does not know what they will freely do in the future. God therefore has considerably less control over the course of human history than the theological determinist postulates, which leads to much of the evil we observe. But, the open theist says, giving up this control is worth it since moral responsibility, soul making, the ability to love, and a host of other goods all require libertarian freedom. This is not to say that God cannot intervene and ensure that certain events will in fact happen, but given that God wants creatures to exercise their freedom in significant ways, he must be willing to put up with a lot he does not approve of.

The open theist might maintain that God's ways are less mysterious than it seems the theological determinist must hold; nonetheless, on the assumptions that the open theist makes, it is far from clear that conciliar pronouncements reflect the will of God. For were God to systematically intervene in the ways required to secure the rulings of all councils, this might, for all we know, undermine much of the value associated with the exercise of creaturely freedom (to say nothing of other values of which we're unaware). And, importantly, the Great Schism and the Reformation, not to mention large-scale evils inside and outside of the church, all suggest that God might not place enough value on conciliar accuracy to intervene as might be required. In other words, if God allows the kinds of suffering and moral and theological errors that pervade our world—states of affairs that separately and jointly appear as bad as, or in the vicinity of, conciliar error—it seems we are not in a good position to affirm that he would not allow a council to promulgate a false doctrine that will not substantially undermine the life of the church. Certainly one might feel that she has excellent grounds for P1, but absent compelling independent reason for thinking that each council concerns only that which is doctrinally central to the faith, the open theist should not be confident of PA.

The final major position I wish to discuss on divine providence is Molinism, the doctrine that God utilizes his knowledge of the counterfactuals of creaturely freedom to guide the world. As those acquainted with the Molinist literature know, Molinists draw a distinction between *possible worlds* and *feasible worlds*, the latter being a subset of the former that God can actualize. First, let us assume that prior to creating, God has several feasible worlds available to him that contain many of the goods possessed by the actual world to the same degree (a large Christian population, several instances of moral virtue, and the like), but these worlds have no or few instances of suffering, evil, and false theologies. Given this, God could've actualized a world that, from our perspective, seems much more worthwhile; but God instead choose to actualize this world replete with theological errors and shattered by evil and suffering. If this is the case, then difficulties similar to those associated with the joint affirmation of theological determinism and PA arise once again: (1) when he could do otherwise, God intentionally actualizes states of affairs that seem as negative as conciliar inaccuracy, and so there is no good reason to suppose he didn't bring about conciliar error; and (2) by choosing to actualize this world so full of moral evil, suffering, and inaccurate theology, when he could have actualized a world without these ills, God acts in ways that are so different than we would expect that we simply cannot predict the ways of God and so cannot be confident that he will be interested in ensuring that the councils always stay true.

This first scenario assumes that God has several feasible worlds available to him that are similar to the actual world but surpass it in value (at least given our scale of value). God might not be so lucky, however, with the feasible worlds he is presented with when choosing to create. He might instead have no feasible worlds available to him that are both sufficiently high in value and yet maintain conciliar accuracy. This second outcome can be seen as one that faces a problem similar to that which hinders the open theist who wants to affirm PA: while (all other things being equal) God might want to procure conciliar truthfulness, he might not be able to do so without sacrificing something he values more.

Given the Molinist schema, though, it might be that neither of these descriptions of God's feasible worlds apply. For instance, it might be that there are no feasible worlds available to God that are categorically better than *this* world, and that conciliar accuracy is part of some of those worlds that rank among the highest in value. In fact, it might be that our world—the world that God chose to actualize—is such a world: it ranks highly in value among God's feasible worlds, and its ecumenical councils are all accurate. In that case, the Molinist can maintain that God can secure conciliar accuracy without letting go of something he values more (and so avoids the problems facing the open theist who wants to hold to PA), and our Molinist need not hold that God's ways are so mysterious that we cannot affirm PA (as it seems the theological determinist must).

Nevertheless, the Molinist shouldn't rest too comfortably on PA. For we don't know that God has the right kind of feasible worlds available to give us confidence in PA—the feasible worlds that rest in the third group described. We would need God to reveal that to us, or have a good independent argument on its behalf. But unfortunately, it's doubtful that we have either of those. What we have is a world that is filled with significant evil, suffering, and inaccurate theologies, states of affairs that separately and jointly seem as bad as conciliar error on peripheral doctrines. Presumably God allows these other negative states of affairs because he has sufficient reason for so doing. For all we know, however, the same could be true about the negative state of affairs of conciliar error.

I believe this survey of these three major conceptions of divine providence illustrates why we are not epistemically situated to discern whether God can always ensure the basic teachings of councils without giving up some greater good, and why we don't have sufficient reason to affirm PA rather than PA*. What we would need to affirm PA is some reason to suppose that God puts a premium on conciliar accuracy such that he is willing to forego many other goods to achieve it, or reason to think that he need not forgo any countervailing goods to maintain conciliar accuracy. We don't have direct access into the mind of God on this matter, however; and the fact that he allows so many other kinds of heinous states of affairs should greatly temper our confidence in PA.[39] But if we can't be confident of PA, it won't lend much to support P2 (the conviction that God has ensured that the teachings of the Third Council of Constantinople are true and binding on the church).

The defender of P2 can regroup, though, and rely not on PA but PA* to convince one of P2. For if one has good independent grounds to suppose that dyothelitism is central to the faith—crucial for the life of the church and essential for the gospel—then this plus PA* entails that this

---

39. It might be thought that Christians must rely on something close to PA to believe in the (Protestant) biblical canon. The idea here would be that trust in the canon presupposes that God was intimately involved in its formation, and the reason for believing this is the conviction that God would not allow the evil of losing inspired books. But if this is granted, then one should also believe that God would not allow the councils to err. However, all one needs to do, to respond to this kind of worry, is to point out good reason for affirming the canon that does not rest on the assumption that God would not allow an evil as great as canonical error. See Thomas Crisp's "On Believing That the Scriptures Are Divinely Inspired," for a discussion of candidate reasons. Unfortunately, these candidates are unlikely to work to convince one of PA or P2.

teaching of the Third Council of Constantinople is true. And given that this council sought to establish not only what is true, but also what is to be theologically binding on Christendom, then it stands to reason (although does not strictly imply without additional premises) that dyothelitism is doctrinally binding.

Historically, theologians certainly thought that they had excellent grounds to conclude that dyothelitism went right to the heart of the faith, indeed to the very gospel. Following the soteriological maxim of Gregory of Nazianzus, "The unassumed is unhealed,"[40] theologians argued that if the Word did not assume a distinct human will, he could not redeem humanity. If these theologians were correct about the importance of the dispute over the number of wills Christ possesses, then this coupled with PA★ can be used to vindicate P2.

But were these theologians correct to think that Gregory's maxim reveals that dyothelitism is central to the faith? That is far from clear. One can cast doubt on this motive for thinking that dyothelitism is central to the faith by showing that even if we subscribe to Gregory's maxim, we aren't forced to embrace that Christ has two wills. As I understand it, this maxim means that the Word must assume a complete human nature to redeem. It should be clear from what we've discussed, though, that the monothelite can agree with this maxim without surrendering his doctrine. The will, the monothelite submits, is something that is properly predicated to the person, not to the nature. Thus the Logos can assume a complete human nature without assuming a (distinct) will.

If this is deemed inadequate, the monothelite can go further (as we've seen) and maintain that the Logos assumed a human will in the sense that he takes on properties that are, together with his divine will, sufficient for the possession of a human will. If either of these maneuvers is on target, then dyothelites and monothelites can mutually affirm Gregory's slogan; they just part ways in their understandings of human nature, or the way in which that nature is possessed by the Logos. Are these differences central to the faith, such that mistakes here are injurious to the gospel or the church? It's hard to say that they are; which means it's hard to see that PA★ gives us much cause to affirm P2.

On the supposition, then, that we don't have grounds to affirm P2, it seems that CAT is too stringent. For without good reason to affirm that

---

40. Gregory of Nazianzus, "To Cledonius the Priest against Apollinarius," in *Christology of the Later Fathers* (ed. Edward R. Hardy; LCC; Philadelphia: Westminster, 1954), 218.

the sixth ecumenical council is endorsed by God, this council, for all we know, is merely the expression of bright theologians from a previous age. In which case, it might be that we can reject the dyothelitism of this council provided that our theological communities can't, after sufficient labor, find biblical support for it.

THE VIABILITY OF MONOTHELITISM RECONSIDERED

Given that CAT seems too stringent and that both evangelical monothelites and dyothelites are committed to the primacy of Scripture, we should take a second look at CUP. Previously I mentioned that the fear with CUP is that it too easily divorces one from a hermeneutic that has been tested and approved by the church over the ages. The worry is that if an individual adopts a stance toward councils where they can be rejected if they are not seen to be biblically based, then there is nothing in principle that keeps him from dismissing other perhaps more important councils. A prominent example taken from history concerns the doctrine of the Trinity, where a considerably large group of Protestants—notably those in Italy and northern Europe—advocated abandoning the doctrine on the grounds that it's biblically unwarranted.[41] With such examples on hand, one might be understandably anxious about the monothelitic adherence to CUP, concerned that it does not have the resources to stave off the degeneration of classical Christianity.

Now strictly speaking, if this worry were to be pressed into the services of an argument against CUP, it seems this would be an instance of the slippery slope fallacy. Nevertheless, I think it is worthwhile to note that the defender of CUP who subscribes to PA* has a means for taking some of the ecumenical councils with utter seriousness, even as binding on the (evangelical) church. She can argue for this conclusion by appealing to Scripture, to PA*, or a combination of the two. For example, she might appeal to PA* to defend the doctrine of the Trinity against Arians, who object that it's not biblically supported. For she might argue that a corollary of PA* is that God would not allow the vast majority of the church to formally embrace idolatry—a state of affairs that would be the case if God allowed the universal church to formally endorse a doctrine that

---

41. For details, see Massimo Firpo, "The Italian Reformation and Juan de Valdés," *Sixteenth Century Journal* 27 (1996): 353–64.

would have them mistakenly worship Jesus as God. Likewise, if one can show that the Chalcedonian understanding of the incarnation is intimately connected to the gospel and life of the church (perhaps by appealing to principles like "God alone can save" and "what is not assumed is not healed"), then one can utilize PA* to defend that. It is therefore far from clear that the monothelite who subscribes to both CUP and PA* cannot have a historically based Christian faith, yet part with the Third Council of Constantinople.[42]

Even so, many evangelical theologians will remain deeply skeptical about the acceptability of monothelitism. Given the wide reception of the two-wills doctrine by Catholics, the Orthodox, and conservative Protestants, these theologians will think that a tremendous burden of proof is placed on the monothelite.[43] This is significant because no contemporary monothelite has produced a lengthy and detailed work seeking to demonstrate the superiority of his position. Unless and until one does that, I suspect that monothelitism will not generally be considered a live theological option among evangelical theologians. Be that as it may, I hope I've shown that the case against the admissibility of monothelitism should not altogether be closed.[44]

---

42. Perhaps, then, CUP should be modified in a way that gives *tradition* greater epistemic weight in biblical interpretation. One might proffer:

T-CUP. The (evangelical) Christian is free to reject a conciliar pronouncement if this pronouncement is neither central to the Christian faith, nor taught nor implied by Scripture. T-CUP has the benefit of respecting the great Christian tradition. The difficulty would be coming up with a criterion for what is central to the faith (although perhaps one could proceed on a case-by-case basis).

43. The thought might be that God works through theologians to bring his church into communion with himself. This is not to say that dyothelitism cannot be questioned and ultimately abandoned, but that what has been affirmed "everywhere, always, and by all" (*ubique, semper, et ab omnibus*) is an excellent indicator of the Spirit's leading. If one accepts this notion, a significant burden of proof is placed on the monothelite.

44. Work for this project was supported by the Center for Philosophy of Religion at the University of Notre Dame. I am also extremely grateful to Joshua Rasmussen, Mike Rea, and Luke Stamps for discussions regarding the content of this paper, and to Oliver Crisp, Kathryn Pogin, and Amber and Scott Wessling for slogging through an extraordinarily rough draft of this chapter and giving me invaluable feedback. Extra special thanks belong to Tim Pawl for reading two drafts of this chapter and for talking over the ideas contained within.

CHAPTER 9

JESUS' NEW RELATIONSHIP WITH THE HOLY SPIRIT, AND OURS

How Biblical Spirit-Christology Helps Resolve a Chalcedonian Dilemma

TELFORD C. WORK

WHEN I BEGIN TEACHING the doctrine of incarnation in my introductory theology course at Westmont College, I enjoy handing out a "Jesus Quiz" with true-or-false statements such as these:

1. *Mary is God's mother.*
2. *Jesus has 23 human chromosomes and 23 divine chromosomes.*
3. *It's okay to portray Jesus as an African-American man.*
4. *It's okay to portray Jesus as a Jewish woman.*
5. *Like us, Jesus got his power to do miracles from the Holy Spirit.*
6. *Jesus could have taken himself down from the cross if he had wanted.*

The statements goad my students into thinking through implications of incarnation that many had never considered before. I want to suggest an unusual way of interpreting Chalcedonian theology that better guides our interpretation of the Scriptures concerning Jesus, smoothes tensions that can surface between "Word-Christology" and "Spirit-Christology," and better explains the deep connections among doctrines of Trinity, humanity, incarnation, pneumatology, salvation, and ecclesiology.

Against the Nestorian vision of a "communion" or "conjunction" of natures between the divine person and human person of Christ, Cyril of Alexandria insisted upon a *unifying* (*henosis*) of natures in the *one* person of Christ.[1] Against Nestorius's "two sons," Cyril defended Jesus' single personhood by claiming that the divine person of the *logos* had assumed an impersonal human nature. "In all respects," claimed Cyril, "the Word of God the Father *is* with the ensouled flesh he united with himself, in one person [*prosōpon*]."[2] The divine Word and the human Jesus are not two tenuously connected subjects, each with its own set of relationships to God, humanity, and the rest of creation. He is one. Therefore, the truly divine nature of the one growing in Mary's womb made her, properly speaking, the bearer of God, just as his truly human nature made her, properly speaking, mother of David's heir. Had Mary not borne God "after the flesh,"[3] the cross could not have borne it either.[4] At Ephesus in AD 431, the Church broadly followed Cyril over Nestorius, affirming "one divine nature, the Word incarnate."

Chalcedon's later formula retained the logic of Ephesus while better respecting each school's critiques of the other's excesses. Jesus Christ is "in" or "of" two natures, without confusion or change (opposing extreme Cyrillian schools such as Eutychian Monophysitism), and without division or separation (opposing Antiochian movements such as Nestorianism).

A COMMUNICATION OF ATTRIBUTES?

Somehow, then, Jesus is a new nexus of the divine and the human. Cyril (writing shortly before Chalcedon) develops this in terms of something named variously the *idiomatōn koinōnia* (cf. 2 Peter 1:14), *antidosis idiotētōn*, and *communicatio idiomatum*. This is usually translated "communication of attributes," but is better translated "communication of proper qualities."[5] Attributes of one nature are, in Christ, transferred to the other, without violating the integrity of either nature. Cyril illustrates the communication of divine attributes to Jesus' humanity as something like iron's

---

1. Cyril of Alexandria, *On the Unity of Christ* (trans. John Anthony McCuckin; Crestwood, NY: St. Vladimir's Seminary Press, 1995), 72–74.
2. Ibid., 7:109.
3. Ibid., 7:64–65.
4. Cyril too links the birth of the incarnate Word to his suffering (ibid., 127ff).
5. Richard A. Muller, *Dictionary of Latin and Greek Theological Terms* (Grand Rapids: Baker, 1985), 72–74, 142.

transformation in fire.[6] This incarnational revolution takes on a cosmic scope in the Eastern Orthodox doctrine of theosis or divinization.[7]

Luther appropriated Cyril's Alexandrian vision, whereas Calvin was more loyal to the Antiochian tradition that continues to stress the distinction of divine and human even after the incarnation. In the Reformed tradition, the communication of attributes is replaced by a mere reciprocation of names (*antidosis onomatōn*). Calvinism maintains that Mary is theotokos in that we may name the whole incarnate person of Christ by synecdoche, by referring to only a part.[8] The incompatibility of these two approaches thus divided not only Alexandrian and Antiochian Christology in antiquity, but has continued to distinguish and divide Lutheran and Reformed Protestantism since the sixteenth century.

Is the impasse necessary? Perhaps not if there are other ways of approaching the Chalcedonian tradition.

IMPERSONAL HUMANITY?

It was axiomatic in Chalcedonian Christology that there could be no full *impersonal* expression of a nature—no "anhypostatic natures." (One might say, for example, that a book or a love song is a concrete expression of human nature, but one would still not say that it is an irreducibly full one—that a text is a "person.")[9] Cyril had held that a divine person assumed and "personalized" an impersonal human nature. This could be taken, and perhaps had to be taken, as compromising Christ's humanity, in that it held that "the human [nature] of Christ has no human [person]."[10] This sets the stage for the divinization of an *abstracted* humanity rather than of particular persons in fellowship: "The effects of our new first-fruits, that is Christ," says Cyril, "shall again pass into the *entire human race*."[11] As a result, Jesus' membership in Israel, no longer constitutive of his character, but only of his salvation-historical location "according to the flesh," falls

6. Cyril, "Lectures," NPNF2, 7:132–33.

7. As Athanasius had put it much earlier: "He assumed humanity that we might become God," claims Athanasius at the climax of *On the Incarnation of the Word*. Athanasius, *On the Incarnation of the Word* (Crestwood, NY: St. Vladimir's Seminary Press, 1993), paragraph 54.

8. Muller, *Dictionary*, 74; John Calvin, *Institutes of the Christian Religion*, 2.14.1. I confess that this approach troubles me, as Luther's troubles me in other ways.

9. This is the route my doctrine of Scripture takes in affirming the true divinity and humanity of the Bible. See Telford Work, *Living and Active: Scripture in the Economy of Salvation* (Grand Rapids: Eerdmans, 2001), ch. 1.

10. John McIntyre, *The Shape of Christology* (2nd ed.; Edinburgh: T&T Clark, 1998), 95.

11. Cyril, "Lectures," *NPNF2*, 7:106 (emphasis added).

into neglect.[12] Humanity becomes a *thing* assumed ("he took *what* was ours," Cyril says).

Leontius of Byzantium (and later John of Damascus and Karl Barth) took a different route, positing instead that the human nature of Jesus *finds* its personhood in the personhood of the Word, and so is "enhypostatic." Here the relationships of a human life would be those of the divine person. This is a big improvement. However, it repeats some of the problems of anhypostatic Christology. Are Jesus' human relationships truly organic or merely forensic? Are they not just genuine but *constitutive* of him? Is Mary really the mother of *her* son, or just a surrogate?

Furthermore, the enhypostatic case demands a strong "analogy of personhood." Human personhood must be enough like divine personhood for divine personhood to express both natures adequately. The logos then gains anthropomorphic qualities such as consciousness and will (thus both Alexandrian "Monotheletism" and orthodox "Dyotheletism"). One is then faced with the dilemma of whether to call God unipersonal or tripersonal. Among enhypostatic Christologians, John of Damascus follows the Cappadocian tradition, which is friendlier to the idea of multiple subjectivities in the Godhead, while Barth follows the Augustinian, which resists or rejects it.[13]

By contrast, Piet Schoonenberg proposed an enhypostatic Christology that reverses its terms. It is the anhypostatic *divine* nature that finds its personhood in the *human* Jesus. Since we know humanity is necessarily personal, but only know divine personhood insofar as God identifies with the creature Jesus, he says we are on firmer ground in insisting on the priority of Jesus' personhood than on the preexistent Word's.[14] This is insightful—it helps us resist the anthropomorphizing of divine personhood. However, what then would be the distinction between Jesus and the one who sent him, besides the flesh of Jesus himself? The problems of anhypostatic Christology return, now visited upon God rather than humanity. God becomes "persons" only in the Son's incarnation. The Holy Spirit becomes the divinity of Jesus. The relations of these "persons"

---

12. While Cyril affirms Jesus' Jewishness (ibid., 7:82–84, 93, etc.) in the course of appreciating Jesus' full humanity, Jesus' particular ethnicity does hardly any soteriological work in his argument.

13. In fact, Augustine himself is friendlier to social Trinitarianism than usually acknowledged (see, e.g., in Colin Gunton, *The Promise of Trinitarian Theology* [2nd ed.; Edinburgh: T&T Clark, 1997], 30–55). See *On the Trinity* 15.7.11. Furthermore, Augustine is less speculative and more exegetically informed than is commonly acknowledged (especially among readers who have skipped *On the Trinity* books 1–7).

14. Piet Schoonenberg, *The Christ: A Study of the God-Man Relationship in the Whole of Creation and in Jesus Christ* (New York: Herder & Herder, 1971), cited in Ralph del Colle, *Christ and the Spirit: Spirit-Christology in Trinitarian Perspective* (New York: Oxford University Press, 1994), 148–52, 217–19.

(Schoonenberg remains unclear in what sense one should call the Spirit personal) are exclusively a function of their relations with human persons, not their relations with each other.[15] The Mother of God is responsible for God being Father and Holy Spirit as well as Son! Schoonenberg's project, grounded in his claim of a fundamental immanence of God in the world, undermines the historical uniqueness of the incarnate Jesus.

John McIntyre proposes a fully Chalcedonian alternative to these positions, one reportedly advocated by Ephraim of Antioch.[16] Ephraim generally follows Cyril, but explains the hypostatic union as a union *of persons*. In McIntyre's words, "While the two natures as such are not confused or compounded one with the other, the two hypostaseis are. Accordingly, the *hypostasis* of Jesus Christ is a fusion of the human and the divine hypostasis: it is synthetos hē hypostasis."[17]

McIntyre judges that this rarely enunciated articulation of Nicene and Chalcedonian logic solves some of its rivals' problems. The personal subject who is God the Word is also the personal subject who is Jesus of Nazareth. In him, both the divine and the human natures that are expressed in Jesus are fully, concretely, relationally intact. Jesus' unity relies on no necessary analogy of being and requires no stronger analogy of personhood than the constitutive relationalities of mutual otherness in both natures. Yet it avoids the double personhood of Nestorianism that would reopen the chasm between God and humanity. Its symmetry honors the symmetry in biblical Christological formulas such as Romans 1:2 without transplanting them into a metaphysically foreign context. It allows us to say that the one "begotten before all ages of the Father according to the divinity, and ... born of the Virgin Mary, the Mother of God, according to the humanity" is "one and the same Christ, Son, Lord."

A CONCURRENCE OF RELATIONS

For Jesus to be one person in (or of) two natures is for him to be one concrete expression of both. Now a person is a full, indivisible instance of a nature, who is constituted, described, and distinguished from other such

---

15. Del Colle criticizes Schoonenberg's proposal as modalistic not so much with regard to the Father as with regard to the Spirit (*Christ and the Spirit*, 155, 219).

16. Ephraim defended the catholic faith at Chalcedon against the Monophysites, later becoming Patriarch of Antioch. Karl Krumbacher, *Geschichte der Byzantinische Litteratur* (Munich, 1897) ranks Ephraim with Leontius, explaining his obscurity to the fact that so many of his works have been lost. See Adrian Fortescue, "Ephraim of Antioch," in *The Catholic Encyclopedia* (ed. Kevin Knight, online ed.) (www.newadvent.org/cathen/05500a.htm).

17. McIntyre, *Shape of Christianity*, 101–3.

persons by his or her relationships with them. So the *idiomatōn koinōnia* involves a concurrence[18] of relations[19] in the concrete Jesus.

I think "concurrence of relations" is better language than "communication of attributes" for respecting and exploring the biblical material about Jesus. Those related *to* Jesus participate directly in one of his sets of relations and indirectly, through him, in the other. Both sets of relations are truly, fully, and naturally themselves. So, different Scriptures hold, in Christ humanity gains intercession (Heb 2:10–18); in Christ God gains sympathy (4:14–15). Human beings dwell with God (Col 3:1–4); God dwells with human beings (Eph 2:21–22; Rev 21:3). Those made in God's image gain the Father as their own Father (Matt 6:9); the Father gains them as adopted children (Gal 4:5) and coheirs with Jesus (Rom 8:17; Eph 3:6).[20] Humanity gains a knowledge of the Father (John 1:18); the Father gains knowledge of them (Gal 4:9). The Holy Spirit rests on a man (John 1:32–34); a man issues the Holy Spirit (Acts 2:33). Mary gains the Lord as her own son; the Lord gains Mary as his own mother (Luke 1:43). Jacob regains God as King; God gains David's son as an heir who no longer embodies Israel's rejection of God as king (1 Sam 8:7). Jesus is a fitting image of the invisible God whose very name is relational: "I will be with you" (Exod 3:12–15).[21]

The concurrence of relations better respects that salvation is first and finally relational. In Christ the life of God and the life of humanity open up to each other without reserve or qualification. "You will be my people, and I will be your God." "His name shall be called Emmanuel." "I have called you friends." "Hail, O favored one, the Lord is with you." "I am with you always."

The concurrence of relations affirms that the attributes of both natures are made common to the *person* of Christ (idiomatōn koinōnia), while avoiding the speculation of naming attributes *transferred* from one nature *to the other* (such as omnipresence to the body of Jesus). Furthermore, it

---

18. The term "concurrence" seeks to maintain fidelity to the Chalcedonian term syntrechousēs (Latin *concurrente*).

19. Since personhood is not to be reduced to relationality, as if persons were pure relations, communicatio idiomata need not be *reduced* to the communication of relations.

20. Cf. Cyril, "Lectures," *NPNF2*, 7:63: "'I am going to my Father and your Father; to my God, and to your God' (John 20:17). In his case the Heavenly One is his natural Father; in our case he is our God. But insofar as this true and natural Son became as we are, so he speaks of the Father as his God, a language fitting to his self-emptying. Still, he gave his very own Father even to us, for it is written: 'Yet to those who did receive him, those that believed in his name, he gave them authority to become the children of God' (John 1:12)."

21. Francis Schüssler Fiorenza and John P. Galvin, eds., *Systematic Theology: Roman Catholic Perspectives* (Minneapolis: Augsburg Fortress, 1991), 1:156–57.

does not force us to decide whether in God there are three quasi-human subjectivities, or one, or zero. That is, it does not force the category of *personhood* to determine the category of divine *personality*.[22] It draws from the best that both Alexandria and Antioch have to offer, preserving both the continuing distinction between God and humanity and the revolutionary change in the relations among them that recharacterizes the world in Jesus.

The concurrence of relations respects the original and eternal uniqueness of Jesus. The unity of human and divine is both *specific* and *unique* to the person of Jesus. The Father and the Spirit are not incarnate. It is *through the Son* that their connection with the world is made new. It is fully and uniquely *in him* that the relationships constituting humanity and divinity concur and enrich each other.

THE FALSE PROBLEM OF JESUS' BAPTISM

Focusing on concurrence of divine and human relations rather than an abstracted union of natures is both true to Nicea and Chalcedon and is better suited to interpreting biblical representations of Jesus. Let me illustrate by examining an event that has proven thorny to theology: Jesus' baptism.

Before this turning point, Jesus has lived a quiet, even unexceptional life. We only hear of one noteworthy event between his infancy and his baptism: an anecdote of his fondness for his Father's house that is reminiscent of the boy Samuel (Luke 2:41–51). But once he is baptized, Jesus is on fire. He gathers disciples, prophesies powerfully, exorcises, and heals.

The first apostolic preaching acknowledges a great transformation in the Jordan. "You know ... the word which was proclaimed throughout all Judea, beginning from Galilee after the baptism which John preached: how God anointed [echrisen, "christened"] Jesus of Nazareth with the Holy Spirit and with power; how he went about doing good and healing all that were oppressed by the devil, for God was with him" (Acts 10:36–38).

---

22. In his *Disputation with Pyrrhus*, Maximus the Confessor denies that Jesus has what comes to be called a "gnomic will." By this Maximus means "deliberating in a manner like us, having ignorance, doubt and opposition." If we do not collapse these together as he does, we can deny the presence of a sinfully 'divided self' in Jesus without denying deliberation out of ignorance or genuine temptation. However, Maximus cannot follow us, because he also claims that "the humanity of Christ does not simply subsist in a manner similar to us, but divinely." The unity of natures as he understands them communicates omniscience to the human Jesus. (Maximus appeals further to a rather forced reading of Isa 7:16 LXX, which itself somewhat distorts the Hebrew meaning, to support his argument.) By contrast, admitting Jesus' ignorance, as Mark 13:32 clearly does, affirms that Jesus enjoys a truly human relationship of *trust* or *faith* in the Father. For more on Maximus's understanding of the hypostatic union, see Hans Urs von Balthasar, *Cosmic Liturgy: The Universe according to Maximus the Confessor* (San Francisco: Ignatius, 2004), ch. 6.

The Adoptionist explanation for the change in the baptismal Jesus so violated the faith that Chalcedonian churches drew back even from making claims as bold as those in the Gospels and Acts. In January, many of our churches observe remembrances of Jesus' baptism, demonstrating that we have found Jesus' baptism too important to ignore in our worship; but theologically it is still too hot to handle. While Jesus' baptism is prominent in the East's Feast of the Theophany (January 6), and gaining ground over the visit of the Magi as the occasion for western Epiphany on the same date, it is so firmly subordinated to incarnation that Jesus' baptism has long been treated as *merely* a revelation of what has long been the case. As a Russian Orthodox catechism puts it:

> It is at this point that the first disciples believed in him and recognized in him the long-awaited Christ. Not that he became Messiah precisely on this day (as certain heretics have claimed), for the Son is Christ for all eternity. He does not *become* Christ, for the Holy Spirit always rests with him.... It is on the day of his baptism, however, that this eternal reality is manifested to mankind.[23]

Epiphany and Theophany thus conventionally celebrate an *appearing* of the Triune God: his public debut (or "reveal," for us fans of reality television), and nothing more.

THE PLACE OF SPIRIT-CHRISTOLOGY

Yet Jesus' baptism is the focal point of another fruitful approach to Christology: *Spirit-Christology*, a movement that claims, in the words of Ralph del Colle, that "the relationship between Jesus and the Spirit is as important to conveying the truth of the christological mystery with its soteriological consequences as that of Jesus and the Word. The latter without the former leads to a truncated christology and ... one that is seriously lacking in trinitarian perspective."[24]

On this matter Chalcedon fails to guide us, not because it is wrong, but because it is silent—on the role of the Holy Spirit in Jesus' career. Both Eastern and Western theology have so concentrated on Jesus the Word made flesh that the Holy Spirit's relationship to Jesus has suffered neglect. The Church has become so exclusively focused on incarnation that it can no longer hear what the Bible says about Jesus *the Spirit-Anointed*, Jesus *the*

---

23. Olga Dunlop, trans., *The Living God: A Catechism* (Crestwood, NY: St. Vladimir's Seminary Press, 1989), 1:56.

24. Del Colle, *Christ and the Spirit*, 4.

Messiah. Its teaching on Jesus often minimizes, and sometimes elides, the Holy Spirit's role between Annunciation and Pentecost. The prominence of Jesus' baptism in the apostolic preaching of Acts contrasts starkly with its invisibility in the creeds of the early and later Church.

Writers from the eve of the Chalcedonian era illustrate the tendency. Cyril (along with the Fathers generally) *equates* anointing with incarnation: "The title Christ, and that which it signifies (that is, an anointing) ... signifies wonderfully well that he has been anointed in being made man."[25] Even David Coffey's Spirit-Christology holds to Jesus' conception as the occasion for the Spirit's anointing.[26] A Russian Orthodox catechism pushes back the Father's anointing into eternity.[27]

Both of these moves make Jesus' baptismal transformation inexplicable. They cannot honor the literal sense of Luke 4:18, which is Jesus' inaugural sermon, which has so obviously followed up on Jesus' Spirit-baptism: "The Spirit of the Lord is upon me, because he has anointed me to preach good news to the poor."

Among the casualties of reducing anointing to incarnation is the Church's own relationship to the Holy Spirit, which Luke-Acts links to Jesus' baptismal relationship. The Church is named as Christ's body far more often than the Holy Spirit's temple. Its signs and wonders are harder to understand, since Jesus' signs and wonders have been accounted for by his sheer divinity rather than his pneumatic gifts. The believer is charged to be an imitator of Christ (meaning only the Son), without mention of the companionship of the indwelling Paraclete who makes this possible.[28] A similar discrepancy exists with John, where the Spirit is "given" to Jesus without measure (John 3:34) and later made available to his own (7:39).

Adoptionism's legacy has left many worried that Spirit Christology is necessarily a dichotomous alternative to incarnational (or "Word") Christology, and a heretical one at that. We seem to face a dilemma between Word Christology and Adoptionism. If the prebaptismal Jesus is already fully divine, is he not already filled with the Holy Spirit? If he is not filled with the Holy Spirit, how can he be fully divine before his baptism?

---

25. Cyril, "Lectures," *NPNF2*, 7:66.

26. "In the anointing theology of Coffey, the Father anoints Jesus with the Holy Spirit to divine sonship, this being identical with the incarnation." David Coffey, *Grace: The Gift of the Holy Spirit* (Sydney: Catholic Institute of Sydney, 1979), 120, 127, 130, cited in del Colle, *Christ and the Spirit*, 124. Our criticism here is not that the Spirit is not the agent of the Son's incarnation, but that the anointing at the Jordan is not *identical with*, nor merely a manifestation of, incarnation.

27. Catherine Aslanoff, *The Incarnate God* (Crestwood, NY: St. Vladimir's Seminary Press, 1995), 1:164–65.

28. Cf. del Colle, *Christ and the Spirit*, 9.

Spirit-Christologies that either *substitute* or *identify* Word with Spirit as the element of divinity in Jesus do nothing to dispel the worry.[29] More recently, theologians such as Joseph H. P. Wong, Philip Rosato, Yves Congar, Walter Kasper, and Ralph del Colle[30] have persuasively argued that each category says too little by itself, and thus that they are not only potentially compatible, but actually necessary to one another's health. The qualitative difference between the Son's and the Spirit's relationships with the Father distinguishes the Son's incarnate union with holy humanity from the Spirit's inhabitation of it.[31]

Growing in Favor with God: Jesus' New Relationship with the Holy Spirit

How are Word- and Spirit-Christology to be reconciled? It helps to rephrase the question as it applies to our example: What was the relationship between Jesus and the Holy Spirit before his baptism? After his baptism? With respect to his *divinity*, both answers are the same as they were, are, and will be forever: The Son is begotten by the Father before all worlds, and so on. But with respect to his *humanity*, the answers are not. John's baptism changes Jesus' *human* relationships with the Father and the Holy Spirit.[32]

After all, human relationships naturally change. So do Jesus' human relationships with God. Like Samuel, who similarly remained in God's

---

29. Among several examples del Colle offers is James D. G. Dunn's account of New Testament Christology (*Christology in the Making* [Philadelphia: Westminster, 1980]; see del Colle, *Christ and the Spirit*, 141–47) and Piet Schoonenberg (*The Christ*, 148–56, 217–19). However, this and other movements within the common umbrella of "Spirit-Christology" do not cause del Colle to disown the label for his own Trinitarian account (del Colle, *Christ and the Spirit*, 7 n.1), "one that preserves the integrity of hypostatic differentiation within the Trinity" (92). Quite rightly—after all, there are many defective *incarnational* Christologies.

30. Del Colle (ibid., 7) cites Wong as representative of the others: "By a 'Spirit-orientated Christology' I do not intend a Spirit Christology in place of Logos Christology." See Joseph H. P. Wong, *Logos-Symbol in the Christology of Karl Rahner* (Rome: LAS, 1984), as well as Yves Congar, *I Believe in the Holy Spirit* (3 vols.; New York: Seabury, 1983); Walter Kasper, *Jesus the Christ* (New York: Paulist, 1976); Jürgen Moltmann, *The Way of Jesus Christ* (San Francisco: Harper, 1990); and Bruno Forte, *The Trinity as History* (New York: Alba, 1989).

31. Del Colle, *Christ and the Spirit*, 111–12, on the Spirit Christology of David Coffey, which develops the work of Karl Rahner's *The Trinity* (New York: Crossroad, 1997).

32. This is not the direction Spirit-Christology takes in the neo-Scholastic Catholic tradition, where Jesus' relationship with the Holy Spirit is understood in terms of the nature and means of the divine indwelling (del Colle, *Christ and the Spirit*, 79). But it is at home in the Reformed tradition. Commenting on Matthew 3:16, Calvin remarks, "in the fullness of time, to equip him for the fulfillment of the office of Redeemer, he is endowed with a new power of the Spirit.... He comes forth as a divine man, under the royal power of the Holy Spirit. We know that he is God, manifested in the flesh, but his heavenly power is also to be thought upon in his Person as a minister, in his human nature" (quoted in Philip W. Butin, *Revelation, Redemption, and Response: Calvin's Trinitarian Understanding of the Divine-Human Relationship* [New York: Oxford, 1995], 65–66). Butin characterizes Calvin as teaching "perichoretic empowerment of the Son by the Spirit" (ibid.).

presence while his family returned home after a feast (Luke 2:41–49; cf. 1 Sam. 1:21–22), Jesus also "increased in wisdom and in stature, *and in favor with God* and humanity" (Luke 2:52; cf. 1 Sam. 2:26). The chapter divisions of Luke have obscured rather than clarified this extraordinary claim. That Luke 2:52 directly follows Jesus' childhood sojourn to Jerusalem is commonly appreciated. It is less often noted that it also directly precedes the account of Jesus' baptismal anointing, which begins in the next verse and which parallels 1 Samuel 2:35: "I will raise up for myself a faithful priest, who will act in accordance with my wishes and my purposes. I will build for him an enduring house, and he shall walk before my anointed evermore." The verse not only recaps the childhood of Jesus, but also leads the readers into the transformative inaugural moment in Jesus' messianic career.

Jesus' self-sacrifice and the Father's acceptance of it fundamentally alter his human relationships with God and with his people. He gains a *new human* relationship with the Holy Spirit, as one indwelt and empowered.[33] He gains a *new human* relationship with the Father, as a spokesman, an intercessor, and a ruler. He gains new human relationships with humanity, as the appointed representative of a restored Israel (Isa 11:1–5). The one chosen from before the foundation of the world is this day inaugurated to do the purpose God has set forth for him (Eph 1:4–9).

Stress on a communication of attributes often sidelines the transformation displayed here. Treating incarnation as a union of generalized divine and human natures leads us away from a Trinitarian view of Jesus. Theologians then puzzle over Jesus' spiritual growth. We worry over how Hebrews 1 assigns divinity to a glorified human rather than after the fashion of John's Prologue (when we even notice the difference). We debate which divine attributes Jesus did and did not manifest during his Messianic career, assuming that works of power are straightforward exercises of the Word's omnipotence and worrying that they might compromise Jesus' humanity. Can Jesus have known that he was divine? Is it just a show when he has to ask God for divine power, as he does at Lazarus's tomb (John 11:41–42)? Likewise, we wonder if his human limits qualify his true divinity. How can he not heal in his hometown (Mark 6:5)? How can he know the future of the temple but not the time of his future coming (Mark 13)?

---

33. Compare the argument of Maurice de la Taille, S.J., that, in del Colle's words, "there is a distinct and proper mission of the Holy Spirit in the doctrine of the *inhabitation* of the just person" (*Christ and the Spirit*, 71, emphasis added). But here the inhabitation is a function of incarnation, not of baptism.

Was his so-called "kenosis" a hiding of his divinity, a shedding of it, or an expression of it?

These problems gain such force when Word-Christology is isolated from Spirit-Christology. When we honor both together, we will be more alert to the Trinitarian context of Jesus' miracles. As Jesus' signs indicate, the Father's work through and in him (John 14:10; cf. Matt 18:18–20), so some of Jesus' deeds are straightforward indicators of his divinity, for instance his authoritative teaching (7:29) and the wind and sea's obedience to him (8:23–27), while others are "by the Spirit of God" (12:22–32). Nor will we need to qualify Jesus' acts as Calvin does (let alone Zwingli) as "according to his humanity" or "according to his divinity," because Jesus' signs and wonders neither compromise his humanity nor even suggest "human" omniscience or omnipotence.

This is because Jesus' career has forged relationships with God that are *shared* (Acts 8:14–17). In John, the Son's works are those of the indwelling Father—signs of an intrinsically relational gift of Spirit and truth that Jesus passes on to his disciples.[34] In our baptisms, we inherit his gospel story, dying in Christ and sharing in God's vindication of Christ. We are adopted and know it because of the Spirit's crying "Abba! Father!" who now lives in *our* hearts (Gal 4:6). The baptism of Jesus is the beginning of his ministry (Luke 3:23), the sign of Israel's restoration, and the point of departure for the Christian doctrine of the Church.[35]

CONCLUSION: CLOSING OUR THEOLOGICAL DISTANCE FROM THE NEW TESTAMENT CHURCH

I want to conclude with an additional thought. Second Temple Judaism and apostolic Christianity had understood the Spirit as an aspect of God like his arm, hand, finger, face, or word—as "his living impact here and now," Alasdair Heron writes.[36] In first-century Israel, it was the Son who needed witnesses; the Spirit of YHWH needed no introduction. The New Testament does not see Jesus as validating the Spirit's reality, but the

---

34. I owe this observation to Marianne Meye Thompson.

35. Del Colle, *Christ and the Spirit*, 121: "In scholastic language, [the Father's presence to Jesus in divine sonship] is the proper work of the Son in the grace of union at the basis of the incarnation, while [the Father's presence in anointing] in the person of the Holy Spirit is associated only with the created grace of Jesus' humanity, giving a strong pneumatological cast to the consequent grace of headship mediated by Christ to all humanity."

36. Alisdair I. C. Heron, *The Holy Spirit* (Philadelphia: Westminster, 1983), 8.

Spirit's presence to Jesus as the Father's validation of Jesus' lordship (John 3:34–35; Acts 2:33; 10:36–38). By the time Basil of Caesarea wrote *On the Holy Spirit* in the middle of the fourth century, things had changed. Basil could take his audience's incarnational theology basically for granted, at least rhetorically (chs. 6, 10, and 17), yet he needed to reassure them that the Spirit really is the Lord! The Father and the Son were by now firmly fixed in Christian imagination; the Spirit was the mysterious one.

The shift shows the triumph of incarnational theology—a triumph I want to be so clear that I celebrate—but also displays a growing distance from the world of the apostles and prophets. Theological interpretation that honors their focus on an anointed human, a God whose very name is relational, and an eternally royal and priestly "commonwealth of Israel" is a step closer to the heart of their faith and closer to Jesus, the only Word and Wisdom of the Father.

CHAPTER 10

RECLAIMING THE CONTINUING PRIESTHOOD OF CHRIST

Implications and Challenges

ALAN J. TORRANCE[1]

IN 1625, Charles I became king of England. Now Charles had inherited from his father, James VI of Scotland, the convenient conviction that, as king, he had absolute, divine authority. Charles I not only believed in the divine right of kings, but he *enacted* that belief. Anyone who questioned his decisions was deemed to be questioning God and thus guilty of blasphemy. In March 1629 he dissolved parliament and reigned for eleven years free from any such encumbrance.

The leading opponents of Charles I were, of course, the Puritans, who opposed the divine right of kings and also the Erastian belief in the supremacy of the monarch in the church. Like the Covenanters in Scotland, the Puritans followed Calvin by proclaiming that there was only

---

1. I should like to dedicate this essay to my late father and teacher, James B. Torrance, who was an inspiration to me as to so many others. My discussion in this chapter draws on and seeks to develop key themes in his essay, "The Vicarious Humanity of Christ," in *The Incarnation* (ed. T. F. Torrance; Edinburgh: Handsel, 1981), 127–47. Moreover, I am greatly indebted to my two sons, Andrew and David Torrance, and also to William Tooman, Ryan Mullins, Richard Crocker, and Oliver Crisp, for their helpful input and comments.

one King in the church—indeed, only one King with any divine rights, and that was the Lord Jesus Christ! It is no surprise, therefore, that on the enthronement of Charles I Puritans had started leaving English shores and setting sail for New England, driven by a vision for a new, democratic society where their Christian beliefs and worship would be free from the tyranny of a monarch claiming divine rights. The leader of the first large wave of migrants was John Winthrop, who famously articulated that vision on board the *Arbella* in 1630: "For we must consider that we shall be as a City upon a hill. The eyes of all people are upon us."[2] Ever since Alexis de Tocqueville's classic *Democracy in America*, Puritanism has been perceived as providing American democracy with a solid foundation.[3] The Puritans acknowledged one Lord and one King under whom we are all created equal—a theological vision that underpinned America's democratic ideals and its profound vision of human dignity and equal opportunity.

But it wasn't only the divine right of kings that the Puritans rejected as heresy, for many also opposed the Episcopal system of government[4]—a system viewed even less favorably in Scotland. Indeed, when the king attempted to impose an Episcopalian system on the Scottish church, the resulting turmoil gave rise, in 1639–40, to "The Bishops' Wars," which led ultimately to a military alliance between the English Parliament and the Scottish Covenanters against the Royalists and the defeat of the cause of the king in the First Civil War.[5]

So why relate this piece of history in a paper on the continuing priesthood of Christ? Because those events, almost four hundred years ago, have had an unquantifiable impact not only on the shape of our theology, but on the evangelical understanding of worship in Britain and the United States. As I mentioned, the Puritans and the Covenanters opposed the divine right of kings by insisting there was only one King with any divine rights, namely, the Lord Jesus Christ. So when Charles I and Archbishop Laud sought to impose a priestly hierarchy controlled by the king, they responded, "We recognize only one priesthood in the church!" And whose was what? Not Jesus Christ's! The *priesthood of all believers*!

---

2. This is a quotation familiar to millions of American school children and beloved by presidents from both parties—and cited, indeed, by both John F Kennedy and Ronald Reagan.

3. Sheldon Wolin of Princeton (*Tocqueville between Two Worlds* [Princeton, NJ: Princeton University Press, 2001], 234) comments, "Tocqueville was aware of the harshness and bigotry of the early colonists"; nevertheless he saw them as "archaic survivals, not only in their piety and discipline but in their democratic practices."

4. The Puritans were angered by the resistance that the English bishops were putting up to the 1619 conclusions of the Synod of Dort.

5. See www.british-civil-wars.co.uk/index.htm

The democratic concerns that stemmed from repudiating the divine right of kings resulted in a profoundly significant departure from Calvin's key emphasis on the sole priesthood of Christ in worship and the Lord's Supper. The priesthood of Christ was replaced by a quasi-democratic focus on the priesthood of all believers. The impact of this on the shape of evangelical worship in both our countries has been immense. As a result, the focus in the practice of worship and in our understanding of prayer was transferred to the individual, to the self. I become my own priest, the sole mediator of my own worship. My father, James Torrance, describes the resulting interpretation of worship as follows: *"worship is what we do . . . we worship God, Father, Son and Holy Spirit, we pray to Christ as God, we invoke the Holy Spirit, we respond to the preaching of the Word, we intercede for the world, we offer our money, time and service to God, we remember the death of Jesus in the Sacrament."* [6]

Although this view might be defended on the ground of the "priesthood of all believers," "it falls short," he argues "of the New Testament understanding of participation through the Spirit in what Christ has done and in what Christ is doing for us in our humanity." The initiative is no longer with the sole Priest of our confession, the one true worshiper and *leitourgos*.[7] We are, in effect, turned back upon ourselves to generate what is required of us. The result is human-centered, do-it-yourself-in-response-to-Christ worship that all too easily "generates weariness." Jeremy Begbie refers to this as "worship as task," as opposed to worship as "gift."[8] What I will suggest is that a New Testament understanding of worship sees it as the gift of participating by the Spirit in the incarnate Son's union and communion with the Father—in *Jesus Christ's* continuing intercessions, in *his* ongoing worship, in *his* Amen to the Father as our *leitourgos*, in *his* presiding at the Lord's Supper, and in *his* mission to the world. As Douglas Farrow[9] and Gerrit Dawson[10] have argued so convincingly, taking seriously the doctrine of the ascension has a profound impact on every facet of our theology.

So let us now consider, albeit briefly, some of the key elements in the biblical witness to the priesthood of Christ and its significance.

---

6. James B. Torrance, "The Vicarious Humanity of Christ," in *The Incarnation: Ecumenical Studies on the Nicene-Constantinopolitan Creed A.D. 381* (ed. T. F. Torrance; Edinburgh, Handsel, 1981), 129–30.

7. In Hebrews 8:2, *leitourgos* denotes "servant of the people" in the sanctuary.

8. J. B. Torrance describes it as "legal worship" as opposed to "evangelical worship."

9. Douglas Farrow, *Ascension and Ecclesia: On the Significance of the Doctrine of the Ascension for Ecclesiology and Christian Cosmology* (Edinburgh: T&T Clark, 1999).

10. Gerrit Dawson, *Jesus Ascended: The Meaning of Christ's Continuing Incarnation* (London: T&T Clark/Handsel, 2004).

PRIESTLY TRADITION IN SCRIPTURE

The origins of the priestly tradition in the Old Testament can be traced back at least to the action of Noah. When the flood subsides, he built an altar to the Lord. Abraham and the other patriarchs also built altars and offered sacrifices, which gave rise to a priestly tradition whose role was to represent the people before God. In the encounter between Abraham and Melchizedek, however, we find what Gerard O'Collins describes as a "startlingly different" turn in priestly activity. This priest-king blesses Abraham "in the name of 'God Most High [El Elyon]'" (Gen. 14:19–20). Melchizedek represents God to Abraham.[11]

This is significant, of course, for understanding Hebrews' identification of Jesus as a priest in the order of Melchizedek. Melchizedek combined the offices of king and priest and thus represented God to the people and the people to God not only as priest but also as king. As Sigmund Mowinckel famously argued, the leader of the cult in old Israel was the king. The king is "the representative of the Deity, yet in a still higher degree he is the representative of the people in the presence of the Deity: he prays, intercedes, offers up sacrifice, and receives power and blessing." Moreover, "the covenant is concentrated in him; and through him and in his line the promises are mediated. Through him the congregation stands before God and meets God."[12]

During the period of the monarchy, the role of representing Israel to God became increasingly focused on the priest. Indeed, as Horst Preuss argues, "the priests became the only ones who may 'draw near' to God at the altar and serve him" (e.g., Lev 21:17; Num 18:7). At the same time, they would bless people in the Lord's name (Deut 10:8) and, very importantly, instruct them in the *Torah*; indeed, the book of Deuteronomy "places the priest's role with regard to instructing in the divine law above the sacrificial practice."[13] After the return from the exile in Babylon, however, leading worship and offering sacrifices became the primary activities of the priest. Of course, the ultimate failure of the priests to mediate God's calling faithfully led to the emerging significance of the prophets as the faithful servants of the word of the Lord.

---

11. Gerald O'Collins and Michael Keenan Jones, *Jesus our Priest: A Christian Approach to the Priesthood of Christ* (Oxford: Oxford University Press, 2010), 3.

12. Sigmund Mowinckel, *He That Cometh* (Oxford: Blackwell, 1959), 89. That is, the king represents God's covenant commitment to Israel but he also enacts on behalf of the people the response to the covenant. I will return to the significance of this later.

13. J. M. Scholer, *Proleptic Priests: Priesthood in the Epistle to the Hebrews* (Sheffield: Sheffield Academic Press, 1991), 18.

By way of a brief aside, this led to some uncertainty in Reformation times as to whether we should conceive of Christ as having the twofold office of Priest and King (*duplex munus*) or a threefold office of Prophet, Priest, and King (*munus triplex*). If Christ fulfilled the priesthood as it ought to be, then there was no need for an additional prophetic office. It wasn't until the 1545 edition of his *Institutio* that Calvin opted for a threefold office over a twofold office. Until then and throughout his commentaries, Calvin (appears to have) considered Christ's prophetic role as included within his priesthood—and there was biblical justification for that. Jesus Christ faithfully communicated God's word in his person as the true priest—a separate prophetic office was superfluous.[14]

To return, however, to our fundamental point, the priesthood represented a twofold movement. As Werner Dommershausen argues, "in oracles and instruction, the priest represents God to the people; in sacrifice and intercession, he represents the people to God."[15] And, as O'Collins argues, "priestly mediation runs in two directions: from God to the people and from the people to God."

In summary, God was represented to Israel and Israel to God in the person both of the high priest and also of the king. Moreover, each served as a kind of covenantal hinge between God and Israel representing God's covenant commitment to the people and also the people's response to the covenant.

THE ONE AND THE MANY

This brings us to the fundamental importance of the concept of the "one and the many" so deeply engrained in the consciousness of Israel. Israel was chosen from among the nations to be a kingdom of priests, a holy nation (Exod 19:6). Theologically, her election and calling out of Egypt as God's beloved child (Hos 11:1) was in order to be the recipient of God's grace for humanity as a royal priesthood. As the one called on behalf of the many, she was also chosen to be a light to the nations, to communicate God's covenant righteousness to the Gentiles in a manner that so echoed God's gracious covenant faithfulness that a bruised reed would not be broken or a smoldering wick extinguished.

Moreover, the whole concept of the one for the many was "written deeply in the liturgical practices and sacrificial life of old Israel.... The firstborn son symbolized this vicarious role and in turn the tribe of Levi was elected as the one tribe to act for the many (for all the sons of

---

14. J. F. Jansen, *Calvin's Doctrine of the Work of Christ* (London: James Clark, 1956), 39–59.

15. W. Dommershausen, "*kohen*, priest," in *TDNT*, 8:70 (cited in O'Collins and Jones, *Jesus Our Priest*, 3).

188

Israel)."[16] On the day of atonement the worship of the people was led by the high priest, who "stood before the people as their divinely appointed representative, bone of their bone, flesh of their flesh, their brother, in solidarity with the people he represented. All that he did he did *in their name*. This was symbolized by the fact that he bore their names engraved on his breastplate and shoulders 'as a memorial' (Exod 28:12) before God."[17] Following the liturgical acts of cleansing and sacrifice, he takes a goat, lays his hands on it, and vicariously confesses the sins of all Israel in an act of vicarious penitence acknowledging the just judgments of God. The life of the *one* goat is accepted by the Lord in place of the lives of the *many*. As a further symbol of God's forgiveness of sin, the priest (Lev 16:21) lays both hands on the head of the second goat, the goat for Azazel, and confesses over it all the wickedness and rebellion of the Israelites. At the high point of the cult, the people would then watch as the goat runs off into the wilderness, carrying away the sin of the many once and for all. (Indeed, the goat was traditionally pushed off the cliffs of Mount Azazel so that it could never return—so that there was no risk of the goat returning from the wilderness and reminding the people of their past failings, as if God had not swept them away in an unconditional act of forgiveness grounded in his *ḥesed*.) The priest then "takes the blood in a vessel, ascends into the Holy of Holies, and there vicariously intercedes for all Israel that God will remember his covenant promises and graciously forgive. He then returns to the waiting people with the Aaronic blessing of peace."[18]

This whole conceptuality of the "one on behalf of the many" in all these forms can be argued, theologically, to have been a remarkable provision of God's grace within the covenant whereby the one is given to represent the *many* and the *many* are included, forgiven, and accepted by means of the *one*.

CHRIST'S PRIESTHOOD IN THE NEW TESTAMENT

An enormous amount requires to be said about how this rich conceptuality was utilized by the New Testament writers. Priestly elements in traditions of the Feast of the Passover as also Yom Kippur are evident throughout the writings of Paul, as also in 1 Peter and Revelation. Suffice it to say, in the eyes of the New Testament writers, God was perceived as sending his own beloved Son to be the elect Servant-King and the sole Priest representing the true

---

16. J. B. Torrance, "The Vicarious Humanity of Christ," 138.
17. Ibid.
18. Ibid.

Israel—the One on behalf of the many, the One whose identity is understood through the appropriation of this rich cultic tapestry of Old Testament concepts and in whom the relevant insights are recapitulated and fulfilled.

So what can be said more precisely about the role of Christ's priesthood in this other than that it integrates the entire conceptuality of old Israel? Clearly, the high priest offers himself as an *ephapax* sacrifice—the priest becomes the victim, the paschal lamb. As Augustine put it, he was "the truest Priest" and "the truest sacrifice." It is imperative, however, that in emphasising the sacrificial element we don't lose sight of the risen, ascended Priest, who never ceases to represent God to humanity and humanity to God, who, clothed with his earthly humanity, remains the one Mediator between God and humankind.

It is at precisely this point that the evangelical tradition has tended to focus exclusively (rather than inclusively) on the paschal event of the cross, which suggests that, to all intents and purposes, the true Priest sacrificed himself for our sins, bringing to an end *his* representative role, which was then replaced by the continuing priesthood of believers. In short, Christ's mediation is usurped by us—by our own self-mediation in worship and prayer such that *I* become the sole priest of *my* confession! It is ironical that Reformed evangelicals have in practice made a move that parallels the worst form of Pelagian liberalism!

The whole thrust of the gospel, however, is surely that the One who is the true Priest, Mediator, and Representative of humanity is *raised from the dead* and is not only raised but *ascends* to the Father such that he remains, as Hebrews makes so clear, the sole Priest of our confession. As John has it, he is the One in whom we abide or, as Paul puts it, the One in whom the many participate (*koinōnein, metechein*). So important is this to Paul that he uses the phrase *en Christō* or its close equivalent at least 163 times in his writings[19]! In short, Christ is the risen, ascended, and living Head of his body, the One in whom we abide, the One in whom the many participate, the true Priest of our confession.

Just think how many evangelical hymns and choruses refer to Christ as the risen and ascended King. But how many refer to him as the ascended Priest?[20]

---

19. Professor Douglas Campbell provided me with this figure.

20. Even then, our interpretation of Christ as King too easily misses the human-Godward element of the kingship as it is fulfilled in Christ. As we have seen, the divinely appointed kings of Israel did not simply represent God to the people, they represented the people to God—Jesus is fulfilling his kingly office in his role as Servant-King representing the people before God. (If space allowed, we would discuss the remarkable theological insights to be found in Deutero- and Trito-Isaiah on this theme.)

CHRIST'S PRIESTHOOD IN THE BOOK OF HEBREWS

So let us now look at the argument of Hebrews. As Gerald O'Collins and Keenan Jones argue at some length, Hebrews does not stand alone in reflecting on Christ's priesthood. Rather, it develops a theme that is at least implicitly touched on by all four Evangelists, Paul, and the other New Testament writers.[21] Clearly, of course, it would have been highly problematic for the New Testament writers to use the term "priest" of Jesus, given that he belonged to the tribe of Judah. Some explanation was required as to why he could be described as priest when he wasn't from the tribe of Levi. The author of Hebrews seeks to provide just that. So what is his justification for describing Christ as *hiereus* (6 times) and *archiereus* (10 times)? First, citing Psalm 110:4, he argues that Christ is "a priest forever after the order of Melchizedek." As the Messiah, a convincing argument could be offered that he was prefigured by Melchizedek and consequently belonged to a priesthood that predated the Aaronic priesthood (Heb 5:5–6). By fulfilling the role prefigured in Melchizedek, the "king of righteousness," Jesus integrated in his person the roles of both priest and king and, importantly, the bidirectional representation evident in *both* of these offices.

So what were the key qualifications that he needed to meet to fulfill the role of priest? This is addressed in Hebrews 5:

1. Every high priest must be chosen from among human beings.
2. The priest is called by God to represent the people—that is, he cannot be self-appointed.
3. The priest is appointed in order to offer gifts and sacrifices before God for sin.

All three criteria are, of course, supremely and uniquely fulfilled in Jesus Christ. The first criterion is met by means of the incarnation. The eternal Son of God, "through whom he made the universe" (Heb 1:2), meets the criterion of solidarity with humanity by becoming incarnate.[22] The one who is exalted at the right hand of Majesty in heaven (1:3) is truly one of us—flesh of our flesh, bone of our bone. He can represent us to the Father as one who has not only shared our human condition, notably, growth, suffering, and death (5:7–9), but, still further, has been tested or tempted in every way (4:15) such that he is a high priest who can sympathize with

---

21. O'Collins and Jones, *Jesus Our Priest*, 45.
22. Ibid.

our weaknesses. The book of Hebrews reminds us how he prayed, and did so in painful and threatening situations (5:7); how he grew, was tested, and made perfect through suffering (2:10–18); and, above all, how he endured death (2:9, 14; 5:7), a death by crucifixion (6:6).[23]

All of this, moreover, was characterised by "obedient fidelity" to God the Father. He is a faithful High Priest who has identified with us in the most radical way and is to be viewed as the pioneer and perfecter of our faith; but he is now risen, ascended, and "seated at the right hand of the throne of God" (Heb 12:2) as one who is able to offer himself without blemish to the Father (9:14). (This high priest did not require the sacrifice of a bull!)

Two further significant points should be made about the argument in Hebrews. First, the language of Father, Son, and Holy Spirit suggests an incipient Trinitarian or, at the very least, "diffusely Trinitarian"[24] theology.[25] Its trajectory is clearly in the direction of a Trinitarian theology of participation by the Spirit in the incarnate Son's communion with the Father as our priest.

Second, Hebrews refuses to allow us to identify Christ's priesthood exclusively with his sacrificial death. Indeed, Christ's divine Sonship and his human priesthood, made possible through the incarnation, are intrinsically bound up together. The whole history of Jesus' life constitutes an account of his priestly role. His *life* is a priestly self-offering, fulfilling the will of the Father (Heb 10:7).[26] Given that the incarnation did not cease with his death, his ascended life is characterised by his priestly role—a life of ongoing mediation. Just as Paul argued, in the context of a discussion of prayer, that there is one Mediator between God and man, the man Christ Jesus (1 Tim 2:5), Hebrews develops the significance of this for prayer and worship.

But it is between Hebrews 9 and Romans 8 that the most remarkable parallel is found. Paul's argument is that all that the Torah requires of us (*dikaiōma tou nomou*) is fulfilled in Jesus Christ. Now, of course, the Torah includes extensive obligations vis-à-vis worship, so what do we find in Hebrews? The identical argument is applied to worship. The righteous requirements vis-à-vis worship (*dikaiōmata tēs latreias*) are fulfilled in Jesus Christ, our true representative and priest.

---

23. Ibid., 48.

24. Ibid.

25. C. R. Koester's recent work (*Hebrews* [AB; New York: Doubleday, 2001], 410; cited by O'Collins and Jones, *Jesus Our Priest*, 49) has challenged effectively Harry Attridge's attempt to play down the pneumatological language. Cf. Attridge, *The Epistle to the Hebrews* (Hermeneia; Philadelphia: Fortress, 1989), 250 (cited by O'Collins and Jones, *Jesus Our Priest*, 48).

26. O'Collins and Jones, *Jesus Our Priest*, 50.

Back now to Paul. All that God requires of us is provided by God in our place and on our behalf; *therefore,* there is now no condemnation for those who are *in Christ Jesus.* Moreover, for Paul, this doesn't simply refer to the past reality of Jesus' life; rather, this denotes an ongoing dynamic on God's part. Consequently, the Spirit provides what we in our weakness struggle to provide: "we do not know how to pray as we ought, but that very Spirit intercedes with sighs too deep for words"(Rom 8:26). Then, reminding us yet again that God makes us righteous and we are set free from condemnation, he writes, "It is Christ Jesus, who died, yes, who was raised, who is at the right hand of God, who indeed intercedes for us" (8:34)

Now back to Hebrews. Precisely the same argument features again there. How can we sinners possibly offer prayer and worship that is appropriate? See Hebrews 10:21–22: "since we have a great priest over the house of God, let us approach with a true heart in full assurance of faith, with our hearts sprinkled clean from an evil conscience and our bodies washed with pure water." This alludes explicitly, of course, to the priestly liturgy. In short, we can pray and worship joyfully and free from condemnation because our prayer and worship is sanctified and participates in the true, ongoing worship of our *leitourgos,* the sole Priest of our confession.

In sum, the whole of worship and prayer requires that it be interpreted in the light of what Calvin referred to as the wondrous exchange (the *mirifica commutatio*). The Son has taken what is ours (our confused, tempted struggling humanity that is unable to pray and worship in truth) and has sanctified it in himself so that we might have what is his (healed, cleansed, perfected humanity). So now we are given to share, by the Spirit, in *his* worship, in *his* prayer, in *his* intercessions for us and for the world and, of course, in *his* ongoing mission from the Father to the world.

PRIESTHOOD AND PARTICIPATION

What emerges is a profoundly inclusive, Trinitarian vision of sharing (Hebrews), participating (Paul), abiding (John) by the Spirit, in Christ—not in a dead Christ, but in a living, risen, and ascended Christ, who is our ongoing mediator, representative, intercessor—the sole Priest of our confession. As Athanasius was to write, with Hebrews in mind, "He [Christ] became Mediator between God and human beings in order that he might minister the things of God to us and our things to God" (*Orations against the Arians* 4.6).

In short, the incarnation does not denote a single movement from God to humanity but a twofold movement: it denotes the God-humanward movement (the *anhypostasia*),[27] Jesus Christ is God come *as* God. But intrinsic to the doctrine is the affirmation that God was *truly human*, representing humanity to the Father as our fellow human. It also denotes, therefore, a human-Godward movement—the *enhypostatic*[28] movement.

To take this latter movement seriously has profound implications for the way we think about Trinitarian theology. Traditionally, the West has tended to assume two related principles:

1. The ontological or immanent Trinity (the *deus ad intra*) must not be confused with God's dealings with the contingent order, the economic Trinity (the *deus ad extra*).
2. All works of the Trinity toward the outside are indivisible (*omnia opera Trinitatis ad extra indivisa sunt*). Now, as Stephen Davis has pointed out, this principle is everywhere attributed to Augustine but "is not locatable in his extant writings."[29]

The problem is, that when these two principles are combined, the totality of God's dealings with the world is presented as the *indivisible* activity of the Trinity *ad extra*. This weakens the recognition that it is the Triune communion between the Son and the Father in the Spirit that is opened up to us in Jesus Christ and in which we are given to share—that same communion that has existed from before the foundation of the world.

What I am suggesting is that a biblical understanding of participation requires us to conceive of the Triune economy not only in terms of the *Deus ad extra* but also in terms of the *Deus ad intra*. There cannot, therefore, be any dichotomy between the economic functions and the relations within the divine life. The economy of God's dealings with the contingent order requires to be conceived in the light of the communion *ad intra* between the Son and the Father in the Spirit that existed, as John and Hebrews and, indeed, Paul imply, from before the foundation of the world—a communion that the utilization of the term *indivisa* interpreted in the light of philosophical notions of divine simplicity do not accurately represent. Unless we interpret the divine economy in terms of the Trinitarian relations *ad intra*, we end up imposing a dualism between the Son

---

27. The *anhypostasia* affirms that, were it not for the incarnation, there would be no human Jesus. Consequently, it denotes the coming of God to humanity.

28. The *enhypostasis* complements the *anhypostasia* by emphasizing that in the person of Jesus Christ God is truly *human*. As human, we find Jesus Christ relating to the Father as a fellow human being. Consequently, the incarnation represents not simply a God-humanward movement but a human-Godward movement.

29. Stephen T. Davis, *Christian Philosophical Theology* (Oxford: Oxford University Press, 2006), 71.

and his human nature that seriously undermines the collective biblical witness. The relationship that underpins salvation, reconciliation, and participation in Christ becomes a relationship between Jesus' human nature and the Father, rather than between the incarnate *Son* and the Father.

What I am suggesting is no less apparent in John's Gospel than it is in Paul and Hebrews. After his excursus on abiding in Christ (John 14–15)—which, of course, parallels Paul's participation in Christ—we come to Jesus' high priestly prayer: "For their sakes I sanctify myself, that they also may be sanctified through the truth" (17:19). Then two verses later, "As you, Father, are in me and I am in you, may they also be in us, so that the world may believe that you have sent me" (17:21).[30] Precisely the same emphasis underlies Hebrews 2:11–12: "For the one who sanctifies and those who are sanctified have one Father. For this reason Jesus is not ashamed to call them brothers and sisters."

THE THEOLOGICAL IMPLICATIONS OF THE PRIESTHOOD OF CHRIST

So what are the implications of the argument so far? Quite simply, the priesthood of Christ points to three fundamental affirmations that constitute the ground and grammar of a biblical understanding of the grace of God:

- the eternal communion between the Son and the Father in the Spirit
- the vicarious or representative humanity of the incarnate Son (conceived as the servant King, the Priest, the Head, the firstborn of creation)—the One on behalf of the Many
- union with Christ by the Spirit—the participation of the Many in the One[31]

---

30. And then, "I made your name known to them, and I will make it known, so that the love with which you have loved me may be in them, and I in them" (17:26).

31. What we have seen is that there is a twofold ministry of the Spirit. There is a humanward movement in creating, revealing, and renewing us in worship, but there is also, however, a "Godward ministry of the Spirit of leading us to the Father through Christ, where the Spirit intercedes for us" (J. B. Torrance, "The Vicarious Humanity of Christ," 145). The Son of God came to humanity in a transforming and reconciling event in order to take that lost humanity to participate in the unique love, knowledge, and communion that characterise his relationship to the Father. Jesus' whole life was an act of the redemption and sanctification of our humanity creating a new and redeemed humanity in himself for reconciled communion with the Father in him. This characterised his entire ministry from its very beginnings in the Jordan when he submitted to the baptism of repentance for the remission of sin and the Father pronounced, "This is my beloved Son in whom I am well pleased," and the Spirit descended on him right through to his *baptisma* on the cross. In short, "Christ is presented as uniting us with himself in his twofold ministry of bringing God to humanity and humanity to God" (ibid., slightly altered).

What should be clear from this is that such an approach recognises no dichotomy between worship and worthship, that is, between prayer, intercession, praise, and ethics. All require to be interpreted as participation "in Christ"—that is, our participation (in every facet of our lives) by the Spirit in the incarnate Son's communion with the Father as our ascended Priest, Mediator, and Representative.

What this means is that there is no condemnation and thus no grounds for fear. We are set free. And it is precisely in and through recognising this that our minds are reschematised by the Spirit so that we might become subjectively in ourselves what we already are objectively in Christ. To that extent the Lord's Supper constitutes a reconciling *habitus* by means of which we are liberated from all that would enslave and oppress us and, thereby, created anew. For the one who presides by his Spirit is the one who, in the deeply symbolic words of institution, *took bread* (took our humanity), *gave thanks* (lived that life of gratitude which fulfills the law), *broke it* (offered up his life for us on the cross), and *gave* (gave us his sanctified life) such that as we receive his life, he unites us with himself by the Spirit.[32] In this way, we are lifted up by his Spirit to participate in his praise, in his thanksgiving, and in his intercessions as he makes our meagre, confused worship and intercessions his own, thus sanctifying them.

There is a popular "awareness test" that invites participants to count the number of passes between a group of basketball players.[33] It then asks if you noticed the moonwalking bear? As the video is replayed, one notices that a moonwalking bear was moving through the middle of the players from right to left across the centre of the screen, and of which one was likely to have been completely oblivious by virtue of being distracted by watching the passes between the basketball players. In Protestant worship, obligations (both tacit and explicit) are placed on worshipers to confess, to repent, to sing, to pray earnestly, to listen intently to the sermon, which, too often, amounts to a series of exhortations and condemnations that further focus worshipers on themselves. Consequently, it is easy to fail to recognise the defining reality at the very heart of the whole business—namely, the one who is standing with us as Immanuel, presenting us with his life as a free gift, praying and interceding on our behalf, and making our worship his and his worship (and worthship) ours.

---

32. See Calvin's profound exposition of this in his *Institutio* 4.17.2, where he articulates the relationship between the sacrament and the "wonderful exchange" (*mirifica commutatio*).

33. www.youtube.com/watch?v=Ahg6qcgoay4 (accessed 10 Feb., 2013).

THREE DETRIMENTAL THEOLOGICAL INFLUENCES

So why have we so failed to see the "moonwalking bear"? This paper opened by pointing to a theological move made for socio-political reasons that had a dramatic impact on the significance attached to the continuing priesthood of Christ in Protestant thought since Puritan times. I could also, of course, discuss the impact of various facets of the human psyche—the desire to take responsibility and also the credit for our response to God that has displaced due appreciation of the significance of Christ's vicarious role. Other complementing factors include a jaundiced distrust of the concept of priesthood per se within much of the Protestant tradition—something that reading the Gospels and their portrayal of a dysfunctional (high) priesthood can too easily serve to enforce subliminally.

I will conclude, however, by considering three key theological factors that have been highly pertinent here throughout the history of Christian thought.

A MISPLACED FEAR OF ARIANISM

In his 1925 classic *The Place of Jesus Christ in Liturgical Prayer*, Josef Jungmann showed that during the first three centuries, prayer was to the Father and through Christ the High Priest. After the Arian debates, however, fear of misunderstanding meant that believers no longer prayed, "Glory to the Father, through the Son and in the Holy Spirit" (*Gloria Patri* per *Filium* in *Spiritu Sancto*), but "Glory to the Father and the Son and the Holy Spirit" (*Gloria Patri* et *Filio* et *Spiritui Sancto*).[34] Catherine Mowry LaCugna endorses this, arguing that almost all the extant texts of the pre-Nicene Church were characterised by a mediatory pattern of prayer whereby "doxological prayer is offered up to God through Christ."[35] By the end of the fourth century, however, the situation had changed. As Graham Redding argues, drawing on Jungmann, "Liturgical prayers, which once had been addressed to the Father through Christ, were just as likely now to be addressed to the Son alone, or to the Father *and* the Son, or to the Father *and* the Son *and* the Holy Spirit."[36] In response to the condemnation of Arianism, a fear of subordinationism meant people

---

34. Josef Jungmann, *The Early Liturgy to the Time of Gregory the Great* (trans. F. A. Brunner; Notre Dame, IN: University of Notre Dame Press, 1959), 123 (cited in Graham Redding, *Prayer and the Priesthood of Christ in the Reformed Tradition* [Edinburgh: T&T Clark, 2003], 18).

35. C. LaCugna, *God for Us: The Trinity and the Christian Life* (San Francisco: Harper, 1991), 114 (cited in Redding, *Prayer*, 14).

36. Redding, *Prayer*, 15

were concerned exclusively with "emphasising the deity of Christ and highlighting his grandeur within the triune Godhead."[37] The impact, LaCugna argues, was dramatic: "The praise of God through the only-begotten Son has become the praise of God the Son. Likewise, the Spirit who makes possible the praise of God becomes an object of praise, worshipped and glorified together with the Father and the Son."[38]

In sum, fear of Arianism meant that the church played down the priesthood of Christ, making him the object of worship rather than the mediator of prayer and worship.

INCIPIENT APOLLINARIANISM

Another response to Arianism was, of course, Apollinarianism, which sought to uphold the Greek disjunction (*chorismos*) between the divine and creaturely realms, between the *kosmos noētos* and the *kosmos aisthētos*, but by different means. Whereas the Arians repudiated the divinity of Christ, the Apollinarians rejected the full humanity of Christ and sought to defend Greek dualism by interpreting Christ as a fusion of a divine Logos or mind and a creaturely body. Christ was not held to be fully human in that he did not have a human mind. He was a divine mind veiled by human flesh. The theological equivalent of a Stepford wife, he resembled humanity but was not *homoousios* with it.

As Athanasius saw so clearly, if we accept an Apollinarian account, then the soteriological work of Christ was no longer "in our place" and was ultimately, therefore, neither "on our behalf" nor "for our sakes."[39]

Incipient Apollinarian tendencies in the church undermine a biblical emphasis on the continuing priesthood of Christ and his mediatorial, representative role in worship.[40]

Such tendencies stem from a failure to take seriously that in Christ the Son assumes full humanity in order to redeem it. As not only Athanasius but Irenaeus, Gregory of Nazianzus, and, further, Cyril of Alexandria saw so clearly, he takes what is ours so that we might participate in his redeemed humanity. What this means is that Jesus' humanity is not to be considered a

---

37. Ibid.

38. LaCugna, *God for Us*, 127 (cited Redding, *Prayer*, 22).

39. T. F. Torrance, *The Trinitarian Faith* (Edinburgh: T&T Clark, 1988), 165. Cf. Redding, *Prayer*, 25–26.

40. In many ways, modern debates about Athanasius have exemplified the confused assumption that to hold to the incarnation is to emphasise the divinity of Christ and play down his real and, indeed, continuing humanity. Graham Redding's invaluable monograph articulates this in analysing the arguments between T. F. Torrance, Charles Twombly, and Trevor Hart, on the one hand, and Aloys Grillmeier, R. P. C. Hanson, and Maurice Wiles, on the other (*Prayer*, ch. 1).

charade; it is real humanity. To the extent that the church fails to take this seriously, she can only play down the human priesthood and saving mediatorship of Jesus Christ, thereby undermining the real human kinship with us that was "one of the major emphases of Athanasius in the *Contra Arianos*, as well as in other writings where he expounds the doctrine of the saving humanity of Christ in terms of his obedient life and self-sanctification on our behalf, and yet it is so often completely omitted by patristic scholars."[41]

LATENT ANTI-TRINITARIAN TENDENCIES

I have mentioned two Christological tendencies that have undermined a proper appreciation and appropriation of this fundamental doctrine. The third tendency relates to the doctrine of God. An incipient anti-Trinitarian or functionally Unitarian orientation has further weakened an appreciation of the dynamics of participation. This results in large measure from a failure to hold together the doctrine of the incarnation with the doctrine of the Trinity such that the Trinity takes on a mere formulaic status, becoming a piece of practically irrelevant orthodoxy.

A major influence here is allegiance to confused forms of divine simplicity. It is widely accepted that the simple is the seal of the true (*simplex sigillum veri*).[42] For this reason, a god who is simple, singular, and unipersonal possesses greater initial plausibility than one who is tripersonal and apparently, therefore, complex.[43]

Still more significantly, there are some seductive philosophical arguments for divine simplicity that stem from "perfect being theology." If we suggest that God is distinguishable from his defining properties, then that appears to make him contingent on them in some sense. Divine aseity seems to imply, therefore, that we should not say that God *possesses* his defining attributes but rather that he is *identical* with them — that is, he

---

41. T. F. Torrance, *Theology in Reconciliation* (Grand Rapids: Eerdmans, 1975), 229. Cf. Redding's perceptive discussion and analysis of Torrance's argument in *Prayer*, 42–44.

42. As Richard Swinburne argues, not to mention the majority of philosophers of science, if we are to choose between two theories, the one that is simplest is the one that, other things being equal, we ought to endorse (cf. Swinburne, *The Existence of God* [Oxford: Oxford University Press, 1979], 58–59).

43. As the history of Arianism through the ages has shown, a god who is transcendent and untainted by the complexities of involvement in the spatio-temporal order has greater inherent intellectual appeal than one who is identified with a particular piece of human history on Planet Earth! Now preconceptions of this kind have a subliminally diluting and filtering influence on our interpretation of God's actual self-disclosure in the spatio-temporal order. One impact of submitting the gospel to the Procrustean beds of these foreign philosophies has been a tendency to play down Christ's continuing priesthood. Suffice it to say, theology requires the redemption of our minds from subliminal affiliations of this kind. We are not to be schematised by the secular order to use Paul's terminology — or taken captive through philosophy!

is them. God and all his properties are mutually identical, which makes God simple.

This, of course, is immediately problematic given that properties are abstract entities and, thus, causally inert, whereas God is a person. Indeed, it makes no sense whatsoever to identify a person with an abstract entity.[44]

I should add that attempts have been made, for example, by Bergmann and Brower, to defend divine simplicity against this conclusion by utilising a "truthmaker defense" that makes God the truthmaker of the essential predications.[45] As Brower makes clear in a later article, the validity of such a truthmaker defense is *necessary* to a defense of divine simplicity.[46] Given recent critiques of the truthmaker defense, this simply raises the question as to the justification for submitting Christian doctrine to such a doctrinally (and, indeed, philosophically) problematic Procrustean bed!

There are also arguments for divine simplicity from divine necessity. A maximally perfect being must be a metaphysically perfect being without contingent modal status. This suggests that there must be a tight connection between the divine nature and the divine existence. Nothing is more essential to a thing than that with which it is identical. Hence, a maximally perfect God must be simple.[47] Again, it is not possible to explore this further. Suffice it to say, powerful counterarguments are offered by Alvin Plantinga and others.

Most significant for our purposes, however, are the theological implications of arguments for divine simplicity. As Duns Scotus realised 700 years ago, to suggest that God is Creator, Redeemer, and Lord is "repugnant to divine simplicity."[48] Moreover, as Eleonore Stump argues, Aquinas was unable to be consistent in holding to divine simplicity and the

---

44. As William Vallicella puts it, "Given that properties are abstract entities, and abstracta are causally inert, then God is abstract and causally inert—which is of course inconsistent with the core tenet of classical theism according to which God is the personal creator and sustainer of every contingent being. No abstract object is a person or a causal agent. No abstract object can be omniscient, or indeed know anything at all." See "Divine Simplicity," in *Stanford Encyclopedia of Philosophy* (http://plato.stanford.edu/entries/divine-simplicity/).

45. M. Bergmann and J. Brower, "A Theistic Argument against Platonism (and in Support of Truthmakers and Divine Simplicity)," in *Oxford Studies in Metaphysics*, Volume 2 (ed. Dean W. Zimmermann; Oxford: Oxford University Press, 2006), 357–86.

46. In "Making Sense of Divine Simplicity," he argues, that "the truthmaker interpretation is not only sufficient for making sense of divine simplicity, but also necessary" (*Faith and Philosophy* 25/1 (2008): 23. He reiterates this in his conclusion: "I have argued that the doctrine of divine simplicity makes sense if—and apparently only if—we are prepared to interpret it in terms of a truthmaker account of predication" (ibid.).

47. These formulations are drawn from http://plato.stanford.edu/entries/divine-simplicity/ (accessed 10 Feb. 2013).

48. Cited in Ryan Mullins, "Something Much Too Radical to Believe: Towards a Refutation of Divine Simplicity," www.academia.edu/572124/Something_Much_Too_Radical_To_Believe_Towards_a_Refutation_of_Divine_Simplicity, 13 (accessed 13 Feb, 2013). Forthcoming in *Reformed Theological Journal*.

incarnation.[49] Still further, Ryan Mullins shows how divine simplicity and the attendant view that God is pure act lead to modal collapse whereby "everything is absolutely necessary" and necessarily "everything must occur exactly as it in fact does"—a position that is clearly odious to Christian theology.

What we can conclude from these brief discussions is that it is imperative that the Christian theologian not submit the reality of God's self-disclosure to the Procrustean bed of philosophical affiliations. To do so can all too easily constitute not only disobedience (that is, a refusal to interpret God in the light of God's Self-revelation) but a de facto denial of God's Self-disclosure per se.

So where does this leave us? In order to make sense of the gospel, we are obliged to affirm that who God is toward us in Christ, he is eternally and antecedently in himself. There is thus an integrity that unites the being and act of God. There is, therefore, "simplicity" in the sense that there is no "duplicity" in God. That is not to suggest, however, that there is any theological ground for endorsing simplicity of the kind that leads to modal collapse or that submits the doctrines of the Trinity and the incarnation together with the grammar of participation to a foreign and radically reductionistic, Procrustean bed! At the same time, it remains entirely appropriate to affirm a singularity of will within the Trinity. That is, the Son and the Spirit *will* that the Father's will be done.

Furthermore, it is clearly appropriate, in affirming God's Lordship to affirm aseity and, in asserting his covenant faithfulness, to affirm divine constancy. What should be clear, however, is that to interpret the divine perfections with reconciled minds is to ensure that the direction of the pressure of interpretation in our interpretation of God is always *from* God's Self-disclosure and not *to* God's Self-disclosure and *from* a prior, controlling philosophical allegiance. The danger of the doctrine of divine simplicity, as it has conditioned our interpretation of God in Western thought, is that it has fallen foul of the latter temptation.

In an article that emphasises the necessity of affirming Trinitarian relations for interpreting participation, Gijsbert van den Brink writes, "If indeed we need a participation-oriented account of salvation in order to do justice to the heart of the gospel, it seems that we need a social model

---

49. Eleonore Stump, "Aquinas' Metaphysics of the Incarnation," in *The Incarnation: An Interdisciplinary Symposium on the Incarnation of the Son of God* (ed. Stephen Davis, Daniel Kendall, and Gerald O'Collins; Oxford: Oxford University Press, 2002), 203. (Cited in Mullins, "Something Much Too Radical," 13.)

of the Trinity for that very same reason. For communion and participation with God is only realized in the double movement of incarnation and ascent of the Son, with whom we are united by the Spirit." [50]

In short, the gospel bears witness to a *koinōnia* between the Father and the Son in the Spirit that defines God as love and, indeed, as mutual love in his innermost being.[51] It is that same *koinōnia* that constitutes the ground and grammar of the inconceivably good news that by sheer grace we fallen creatures are given to participate, by the Spirit, in that very divine *koinōnia* in and through the continuing priesthood of Christ. This *koinōnia* is ontologically primitive and not an affirmation that should be regarded as subject to arguments grounded in philosophical assumptions vis-à-vis divine simplicity.

The argument of George Hunsinger's admirable paper in this present volume is that a proper Christology should underpin revelation, reconciliation, ethics, and, finally, worship and spirituality. It is interesting to consider the extent to which a proper emphasis on the continuing priesthood of Christ serves to highlight precisely these foci.

1. The priesthood of Christ is the priesthood of the Logos, to use Athanasius's expression. As we have seen, Christ as Priest includes the prophetic, properly conceived, in and through his "exegeting" the Father. Participation in the sole priesthood of Christ is participation in Christ's epistemic, noetic, and semantic communion with the Father—the Priest discloses God to humanity in and through commandeering, reconciling, and sanctifying our language and thought forms. In this way, the words are filled with new meaning such that they might become a faithful and truthful means of God's self-presentation to the body.

2. As we have already seen, central to the significance of Christ's priesthood is his redemption of our humanity by taking what is ours that we might have what is his. The Priest becomes the offering and thereby gives up his life as a ransom for many, but is then raised and now comes to

---

50. Gijsbert van den Brink, "Social Trinitarianism: A Defence against Some Recent Criticisms," *IJST* (forthcoming). Unfortunately, the phrase "social model of the Trinity" has become ambiguous, and certain recent forms of "social trinitarianism" have been too influenced, one suspects, by a socialist and egalitarian model of human relationships whereby the latter, rather than the biblical witness, becomes the driving force in formulating the doctrine of God. There are hints of this in the approaches of Jürgen Moltmann, Leonardo Boff, and Geervarghese Mar Osthathios. Moreover, other advocates of social Trinitarianism, such as John Zizioulas and Colin Gunton, have come too close to displacing the *homoousion* with a personalist ontology.

51. This is to reject Karl Rahner's statement that "within the Trinity there is no reciprocal 'Thou,'" and again, "there is properly no mutual love between Father and Son, for this would presuppose two acts" (*The Trinity* [trans. Joseph Donceel; London: Burns and Oates, 1970], 76 and 106.

us, by the Spirit, as our ascended Priest and representative to unite us with himself, and invites us to share in *his* life and to participate in *his* mission to the world.

3. The extent to which this underwrites ethics should be clear. Participation in the priesthood of Christ is participation in the ongoing work of reconciliation of the one who stands as the representative and mediator not least of the oppressed, the poor, the sick, the marginalized victim, the sexually abused, the despised ethnic minority and, indeed, the enemy. To recognize and to affirm the ongoing priesthood of Christ is to participate in his mediation of the concerns of the totality of humanity and in his plea to the Father on their behalf. In sum, the whole of Christian ethics/worthship unfolds as the gift of participation by the Spirit in the continuing priesthood of Christ.

4. Worship and prayer. I have already discussed worship and the Eucharist, but let me end with an anecdote as an illustration of the fact that I do not regard the continuing priesthood of Christ as merely a piece of abstract, Christological dogma or orthodoxy.

In January 2008, my wife, Jane, died of cancer. She was the most wonderful Christian woman, wife, and mother. Watching her die in pain as the cancer spread throughout her body was hard, and seeing our children witness her gradual disintegration not only physically but mentally as the cancer spread through her brain was extremely hard. There were times when, in my grief, I really struggled to find the wherewithal to pray and, indeed, to know how to pray and what to pray for. In sum, I did not know how to pray as I ought. In the depth of that valley the continuing priesthood of Christ became more relevant than I can begin to articulate—the fact that as I held Jane in my arms, the risen, ascended Priest of our confession was present by the Spirit interceding on our behalf meant that we could repose in his presence and know that communion that is the beginning and *telos* of everything.

The prayer I held on to during that time and, indeed, later when I succumbed to clinical depression, was the Lord's Prayer, recognizing that this was indeed the *Lord's* prayer. I was not left to pray on my own, "My Father, who art in heaven far removed from where I am." The sole Priest of our confession was present by his Spirit praying, '*Our* Father, which art in heaven, hallowed be thy name, thy Kingdom come, thy will be done."

To discover the significance of the continuing priesthood of Christ is to discover the gospel in a manner that stands to transform every facet of our lives and, indeed, of our worship. It is to discover what it means to live *en Christō*, by the Spirit and, thereby, what it means to be set free to live *excurvatus ex se*!

Does our Lord's continuing vicarious priesthood undermine our human response? Does it weaken the law? No, it strengthens the law by presenting us with the height and depth of the love of God as a concrete and dynamic reality—and in a way that liberates, motivates, and upholds human agency by affirming who we are and establishing that life of participation through which we were created to glorify God and enjoy him forever.

The constructive concern of this paper is to challenge and, indeed, to redefine the affirmation of our forefathers. We recognize only one King with divine rights, namely, the one Lord Jesus Christ, who as King represents God to humanity and humanity to God. And we recognize only one Priest, in whose sole priesthood we are given to participate by grace as a royal priesthood of believers.

SUBJECT INDEX

205

AUTHOR INDEX